natural  English

upper-intermediate student's book
Ruth Gairns & Stuart Redman

OXFORD
UNIVERSITY PRESS

contents

in **unit four** ...

joke doggy humour

natural English
connecting ideas
frequency phrases
'sitting on the fence'
Internet language
making and responding to requests

grammar & vocabulary
nouns in groups
future simple and continuous
adjectives describing reactions
synonyms
the language of editing
wordbooster
words of similar meaning
making the most of your dictionary

speaking
talk about your cinema-going habits
discuss mobile phone use
talk about websites
make and comment on predictions

listening
joke: *doggy humour*
vox pops: people describe their cinema-
    going habits
overhearing mobile phone conversations:
    tune in, listen carefully, listening challenge
listening booklet listening and
    pronunciation exercises

reading & writing
The van that drove through 'Braveheart'
e-mail netiquette and e-mails
how to ... write and edit e-mails
small screen survey
write an e-mail to a teacher

extended speaking
small screen survey
Discuss different types of questionnaire.
Then correct mistakes in a survey, add your
own ideas, and discuss the survey. Analyse
and present the results.

test yourself! on unit four

in **unit five** ...

cartoon oops!

natural English
talking about test/exam results
so, anyway, so anyway
expectation and surprise
spoken v. written English
introducing and focusing
not that + adjective

grammar & vocabulary
narrative tenses
modifying and intensifying adverbs
anxiety
adding emphasis

wordbooster
taking exams
phrasal verbs

speaking
invent / tell a driving story
talk about the driving test
discuss difficult challenges and how you
    would react
devise challenges for a TV show
how to ... emphasize what you feel

listening
people tell driving anecdotes:
    tune in, listen carefully, listening challenge
people describe TV challenges
a woman describes her experience of exams
listening booklet listening and
    pronunciation exercises

reading & writing
Excuse me, is it day or night?
write a driving story
write your opinion about exams

extended speaking
taking exams
Describe your own experience of exams. Then
discuss the pros and cons of exams, and write
a summary of your opinion.

test yourself! on unit five

in **unit six** ...

joke good news, bad news

natural English
worth / value
talking about needs
you get ...
apparently, it appears / seems that
getting attention
passives in news reporting

grammar & vocabulary
past simple and present perfect passive
indirect questions
feelings and emotions
collocation
expressing opinions and interest
wordbooster
dangers and disasters
knowing your prepositions

speaking
discuss the pros and cons of being a
    news reporter
talk about TV news in your country
give opinions about topical issues
carry out vox pop interviews
how to ... be an ace reporter

listening
joke: *good news, bad news*
people describe TV news in different countries:
    tune in, listen carefully, listening challenge
vox pops: street interviews
radio news
listening booklet listening and
    pronunciation exercises

reading & writing
Training and understanding the territory
write a radio news report

extended speaking
radio news report
Listen to a radio news report, collect ideas,
update the stories, prepare a bulletin, and
read the news. Then conduct vox pop
interviews about the news.

test yourself! on unit six

contents

in **unit ten** ...

joke absent-minded

natural English
things like that / that sort of thing
expressions with *tell* (recognize)
buying time to think
adding ideas
clarifying your position

grammar & vocabulary
definite or zero article
definite or indefinite article
relative clauses
memory
making judgements

wordbooster
animals
word building

speaking
talk about the elderly
discuss topical issues
talk about cosmetic surgery
develop a human interest story

listening
joke: *absent-minded*
interviews in a TV discussion programme:
   tune in, listen carefully, listening challenge
people talk about pets for children
listening booklet listening and
   pronunciation exercises

reading & writing
My day as a 75-year-old
Surgeon's knife threatens marriage
how to ... write a human interest story
write a summary of your opinions

extended speaking
animals in society
Listen to people talking about pets. Then
discuss statements about animals in society,
and write a summary.

test yourself! on unit ten

---

in **unit eleven** ...

cartoon saying the right thing

natural English
exaggerating
imagining someone else's situation
letter writing clichés
reacting to ideas
informal and formal language

grammar & vocabulary
past conditionals
mixed conditionals
reporting what people say
describing character

wordbooster
phrases and phrasal verbs
use your dictionary

speaking
say what you would do in hypothetical
   situations
reactions to the reading text
give your verdict on law and order issues
role play a phone conversation and a
   conversation with the boss

listening
anecdotes about making the right decision:
   tune in, listen carefully, listening challenge
phone conversation: an apology and
   explanation
listening booklet listening and
   pronunciation exercises

reading & writing
Prison letters
how to ... write an apology
e-mail apology
formal letter of apology
case study

extended speaking
crimes and misdemeanors
Read and discuss a case study. Then describe your
case study, and give your reactions to a different
one. Evaluate your performance in this activity.

test yourself! on unit eleven

---

in **unit twelve** ...

joke Sherlock Holmes

natural English
phrases with *mean*
phrases with *go*
rephrasing an idea
saying how easy something is
fronting

grammar & vocabulary
reported questions
like, as, such as
sleep and times of day
games

wordbooster
collective nouns
attitude adverbs

speaking
role play game show telephone interview
discuss how to keep the brain active
explain the rules of a game
play different games
how to ... explain the rules of a game

listening
joke: *Sherlock Holmes*
description of the rules of a game
a medical expert talks about keeping your
   brain active: *tune in, listen carefully,
   listening challenge*
people play a word game
listening booklet listening and
   pronunciation exercises

reading & writing
Milllionaire hopefuls – go for it!
Be a brain gymnast!
descriptions of TV game shows
write notes on an interview

extended speaking
game shows
Read about and discuss TV game shows. Then
develop your own game and present your ideas
to the class. Play one of the games.

test yourself! on unit twelve

---

pairwork *p.148 to p.150*   **language reference** with cover & check exercises *p.151 to p.175*

welcome

lead-in

1 **Think!** When you meet new people, what do you notice first about them?

eyes / face	hair	hands	height
build	clothes	voice	*other*

natural English
noticing

The first thing I notice about people is ...
Actually, I'm not very observant.
I tend to notice people's eyes.
To be honest, I don't notice people's clothes / what people are wearing.

Practise saying the phrases with a partner.

2 Compare your ideas with a partner using the **natural English** phrases.

3 Put the phrases below under the correct heading. (Some phrases could go under both.) Add your own phrases.

meeting people for the first time	greeting people you already know

Hi!
You're looking well.
Sorry, I didn't catch your name.
How are things?
Do you live locally?
What've you been up to?
I'm Joao.
It's nice to see you.
Nice / Pleased to meet you.
How's it going?
Is this the first course you've done here?

4 Practise saying and responding to the phrases with your partner.

5 Get up. Greet as many people as you can in two minutes.

grammar *would, should, could*

1 **Think!** Read situations 1 and 2. Which would you find more difficult? Why? Compare your ideas with a partner.

SITUATION 1

Imagine a famous English-speaking film director (known to be outgoing and friendly) is currently making a film in your town, and some scenes are being filmed in your school. He's agreed to come and give a talk to the students about the film industry and his work. You've been chosen to greet him when he arrives and look after him for 20 minutes before the talk.

a How should you greet him? What would be the best way to get the conversation going?

b How would you spend the 20 minutes?

c What could you do to make him feel relaxed?

d Would anything worry you about meeting him?

SITUATION 2

Imagine you're going out on your first date with someone you met at a party a few days ago. You don't know much about him / her, but you seemed to get on well when you first met. You've arranged to meet for a drink at 7.00 in a café that you know well, but which the other person has never been to.

a How would you dress / prepare for this date?

b How would you greet the person? How would you begin the conversation?

c What topics could you talk about? Are there any you should avoid?

d Are there any other important *do*s or *don't*s?

listen to this

1 Listen to a German student greeting the film director. Choose the correct word / phrase in each sentence.
  1   She sounds friendly / polite but distant.
  2   She tries / doesn't try to relax him.
  3   He wants to be called Mr Solomons / Dan.
  4   They start talking about his career / his lecture.

2 Did she behave in the same way that you would? Tell a partner.

go to **listening booklet** *p.2 for the tapescript*

2 Find the words *would*, *should*, and *could* in the questions in **exercise 1**.
  1   Why do we use *would*, and not *will*?
  2   What's the difference between *How should you greet him?* and *How would you greet him?*
  3   What's the difference between *What could you do?* and *What would you do?*

3 **Think!** Choose <u>one</u> of the situations and prepare to answer questions a to d.

language reminder

You need to use *would* when you are imagining a specific situation.

You can use the present tense to describe real or general experiences:
  A I'd ask her what she's interested in.
  B Would you?
  A Yes, because you need to find things in common to talk about.

4 Compare ideas with somebody who chose the same situation.

5 Find somebody who discussed the other situation. Do you agree with their answers?

it's your turn!

1 **Think!** Prepare to answer these questions.
  1   When was the last time you met someone new? Will you meet again?
  2   How often do you meet new people, and in what situations?
  3   When is it easy to meet people?
  4   How would you react if you were invited to a party where you didn't know anyone?
  5   How do you feel about making contact with new people over the phone, by e-mail, or on the Internet?

2 Compare your answers in small groups.

sport

Yesterday, I was babysitting for this rich woman who lives on the ninth floor of a **posh** apartment block ...

... and when I got back from the playground with her **kid**, NONE of the lifts were working.

So I called **Her Ladyship** and told her the lifts were out of order, and do you know what she said?

'Oh, honestly, Agrippine! Use the stairs!'

'The stairs? But I haven't got my Reeboks on'.

So she says, 'For goodness' sake! It won't kill you!'

Not much! In those shoes with a **three-ton brat**. That woman's unbelievable!

Anyway, I went up – nine floors, believe me, it's no joke.

'BUT WHERE'S CAROLINE?'.   'Downstairs, why?'

'Calm down! I'll go and get her when they've fixed the lift.'

Anyway, she **went berserk** and fetched the child herself.

And then on top of everything, she refused to pay me. Do you know a good lawyer?

life with Agrippine

in groups ...

Have you ever done any babysitting?
Who for, and what was it like? What kind of problems do you think babysitters have?

cartoon time

Read the cartoon. Think of three words / phrases to describe Agrippine.

What would you do if you were Caroline's mother?

1.1 Listen and follow the cartoon. Look at the phrases in the **natural English** box. Underline the phrases you hear. How do you say them?

natural English
showing impatience

Oh, honestly!	Oh, really!	Not again!
For goodness sake!	You're hopeless!	

Tell a partner three silly things you've done recently.

example A I was late for ... / I forgot to ... / I've lost my ...
B React impatiently!

in unit one ...
tick ✓ when you know this

natural English
showing impatience ☐
talking about activities ☐
describing difficulty ☐
describing your language ability ☐
asking follow-up questions ☐
sharing experiences ☐

grammar
-*ing* form and infinitive ☐
wishes and regrets ☐

vocabulary
learning ☐

wordbooster
sporting collocations ☐
collocation in dictionaries ☐

glossary

posh ⓖ expensive and elegant

kid ⓖ child

Her Ladyship ⓖ a woman who thinks she's very important

three-ton ⓖ very heavy

brat ⓖ badly-behaved child

go berserk /bəˈzɜːk/ ⓖ get very angry

ⓖ this symbol means that the word / phrase is informal

reading

would you pass the fitness test?

lead-in

1 **Think!** In your family:

  1 Who's the strongest and fittest?

  2 Who does the most sport and what do they do?

  3 Who never does any exercise?

  4 How fit are you?

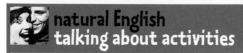

natural English
talking about activities

My husband **plays a lot of** tennis.
My brother **doesn't get much exercise.**
My sister **does a bit of** judo at the weekends.
My father **doesn't do any sport at all.**

Practise saying the phrases with a partner.

2 With a partner, ask and answer the questions using the **natural English** phrases.

read on

1 Work in two groups, A and B. A read the text opposite and B read the text on *p.149*. Complete the glossary.

2 In A / B pairs, give and follow instructions for each physical test. Make a note of how well you do.

natural English **(1.2)**
describing difficulty

I found it hard / easy to jump from a standing position.
I found the balance test **quite tricky / challenging.**
Catching the ruler **was quite / very difficult.**
  NOT ~~I had difficulties to catch ...~~
I was good / hopeless at the leg strength test.

Listen and circle the words you hear.
Practise saying the sentences.

3 Were you above / below average in the tests? Were they difficult? Tell the class, using the phrases in the **natural English** box.

HOW DO **YOU** MEASURE UP?

DO YOU WANT TO BE A TOP FOOTBALLER? AN OLYMPIC GYMNAST? Or would the simple act of being able to catch a ball fill you with joy? We offer tips and exercises to increase your physical confidence. And we've enlisted the help of ex-Chelsea and England
05 footballer, **GRAEME LE SAUX.**

BALANCE

How long can you stand on one leg with your eyes closed before you lose your balance? Try doing this exercise and time yourself; your time is up when you open your eyes or lose your balance. For
10 a person in their 20s, 60 seconds would be excellent (Graeme Le Saux managed 65 seconds). For someone in their 60s, 15 seconds would be good.

Shutting your eyes can make your balance **go to pieces.** If you did this test with your eyes open, for example, you could probably do it

glossary

Fill the gaps.

_____ (para 1) advice

go to pieces (para 3) stop operating normally

_____ (para 5) the finger next to your thumb

¹⁵ four or five times as long; try it and see. The important thing is to concentrate on the feel of the right movement, and gymnastics is the best sport for developing overall ability. Practising also makes a big ²⁰ difference: if you test yourself over a period, your times will improve considerably.

REACTION TIME

Reaction time involves using many skills: you see something, decide what to do ²⁵ about it, then respond with an effective movement. You can test this ability with a simple experiment.

Hold your hand out with your thumb and index finger parallel with each other, ³⁰ about 3 cm apart. Ask a friend to hold a 30cm ruler vertically 2 or 3 cm above your fingers. When your friend drops the ruler, see how quickly you can catch it between your thumb and finger.

³⁵ Most people catch the ruler after letting it fall 15 to 20 cm; faster than that is excellent. The test can be developed by trying it first with one hand, then the other; you should be quicker with your ⁴⁰ dominant hand.

Children have much faster reaction times these days, largely as a result of playing video games, says sports scientist, Mark Abberley.

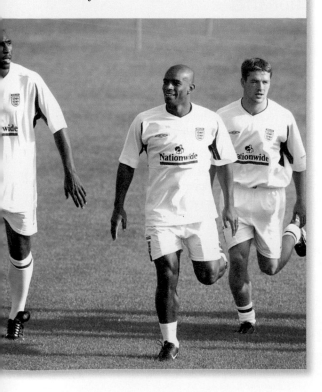

grammar -ing form and infinitive

1 Read the information below and complete with examples from the article.

-ing forms can be used as nouns in different ways:	examples
– after certain verbs e.g. enjoy + -ing, imagine + -ing	_____ _____
– after prepositions e.g. about + -ing before + -ing	_____ _____
– as a subject (or object) e.g. reading is fun, reading poetry is hard	_____ _____

2 Which sentence in each pair sounds more natural?

a Jogging keeps me in good shape.
b It keeps me in good shape to jog.

a Working on your own can be lonely.
b To work on your own can be lonely.

go to **language reference** *p.151*

3 **Think!** Use *-ing* forms to make true sentences about yourself.

example <u>Cycling to work</u>_____ helps to keep me fit.

_____ helps to keep me fit.

_____ helps me to relax.

_____ cheers me up when I'm depressed.

I'd love to try _____ .

I've never been interested in _____ .

I've always been good at _____ .

4 Compare your sentences with a partner's. Are they similar?

5 Put these verbs / phrases in the correct place in the table below.

keep	give up	be willing to	get used to
used to	practise	finish	mind
try	be prepared to	remember	regret
start	look forward to	take up	tend

verb + -ing form	verb + infinitive	verb + either -ing form or infinitive

test your partner

– *Practise.*

– *Practise doing.*

– *That's right.*

go to **language reference** *p.151 and p.152*

6 Fill the gaps with a suitable verb.

1 I can remember _____ picture stories when I was a child.

2 I must remember _____ my books back to the library.

3 I tried _____ her latest novel, but the bookshops have sold out.

4 Have you tried _____ the Internet? It's great.

5 I really regret not _____ to ski when I was younger.

6 We regret _____ you that your application has been unsuccessful.

7 Work in groups of three or four. Make sentences using the verbs / phrases in **exercise 5** on *p.11*. Take it in turns to say one word each.

example

A I **B** gave **C** up **D** skiing

A after **B** I **C** broke **D** my

A leg

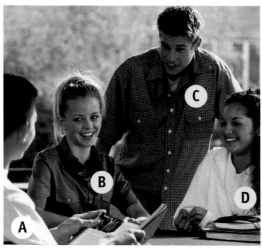

wordbooster

sporting collocations

1 Cross out the noun in each line which does not collocate with the verb.

GO	rollerblading	for a run	ski
TAKE PART IN	a race	a team	the Olympics
JOIN	a club	a team	a sport
LOSE	a match	an award	the final
WIN	a match	a prize	the opposing team
PRACTISE	your tennis serve	sport	your technique
DO	table tennis	aerobics	weightlifting

2 Replace each incorrect noun with a correct one from this list.

a cup	karate
heading the ball	a competition
an aerobics class	a race
windsurfing	

test your partner
– You can win a competition.
– That's right.
– You can take part in a team.
– That's wrong.

collocation in dictionaries

1 Look at the dictionary entries and answer the questions.

1 What nouns are used with *latest*? Think of two more.

2 What kinds of things could you *flick through*?

lat·est /'leɪtɪst/
■ *adj.* [only before noun] the most recent or newest: *the latest unemployment figures* ◊ *the latest craze / fashion / trend* ◊ *her latest novel* ◊ *Have you heard the latest news?*

PHRV ˌflick ˈthrough /ˌflɪk ˈθruː/ to turn the pages of a book, etc. quickly and look at them without reading everything.

entries from *Oxford Advanced Learner's Dictionary* ISBN 019431510-X

2 Use your own dictionary. What collocates with these in the context of learning or reading?

1 to dip into _____

2 _____ by heart

3 to skip _____

4 to look up _____

5 _____ the gist

listening
learning

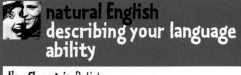

lead-in

1 Think! Prepare to ask and answer.

1 How many languages can you speak, and how well?

2 Which other languages would you like to learn, and why?

natural English
describing your language ability

I'm **fluent in** Polish.

I **speak** Spanish **reasonably well.**

I **can get by in** Portuguese.

I **speak** French, **but it's a bit rusty** /ˈrʌsti/.

I **know a few words of** Japanese.

I wish I could speak Italian.

2 Ask and answer the questions in small groups. Use the **natural English** phrases.

grammar wishes and regrets

1 Look at sentences 1 to 8. Which refer to past events or situations? Which refer to the present / future?

1 **I wish I was / were** better at maths.

2 **I wish I hadn't done** Greek at school.

3 I wish I knew how to cook better.

4 **I regret not** working harder at school.

5 I'm glad I can speak English.

6 **I wish I'd** done more sport at school.

7 I'm glad I didn't give up learning the guitar.

8 **I wish I could** read faster.

2 Write the phrases in **bold** from **exercise 1** next to each paraphrase.

1 I can't do it, but I'd like to. ___I wish I could___

2 I'm not, but I'd like to be. _____

3 I didn't do it, and now I'm sorry. _____ ; _____

4 I did it, and now I'm sorry. _____

3 Work with a partner. Say the sentences in **exercise 1** which are true for you. Change the others to make them true.

example   I wish I was better at maths. That's true.

Latin
I wish I hadn't done ~~Greek~~ at school.

dance salsa
I wish I knew how to ~~cook well~~.

4 Ask your partner questions using the prompts below.

examples   Don't you wish you were incredibly rich?
Aren't you glad you're not famous?

Don't you wish …?

Aren't you glad …?

Do you ever wish …?

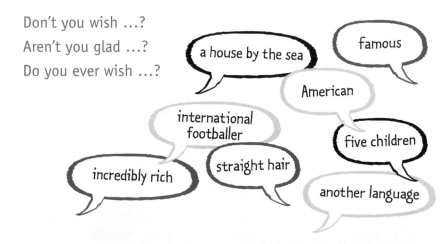

a house by the sea

famous

American

international footballer

five children

incredibly rich

straight hair

another language

go to **language reference** *p.152*

listen to this

tune in

1 What do you think the people in the photos are learning to do?

2  1.3 Listen to Trude and Julia describing something they decided to learn. What subjects did they choose?

Trude   Julia

3 What do you think they might say about their experiences? Tell a partner.

listen carefully

4 Look at the table. Listen to the complete descriptions and tick ✓ who said what.

		Trude	Julia
1	The teacher was great.		
2	It was very challenging.		
3	The other students affected my progress.		
4	It was very satisfying.		
5	I regretted not doing it earlier.		
6	I regretted not working harder.		

listening challenge

5 1.4 Listen to Eric. What did he learn to do, and did he enjoy it? Tell a partner.

Eric

listening booklet *p.2 to p.5 for tapescripts and exercises*

Are **you** prepared to persevere?

1 If you had to speak in English all the time in class (and never use a word of your own language), how long could you _____ **it up**?

2 When you're watching a film in English, do you find it hard to **get** _____ **to** the speed of natural conversation? Is your normal reaction to _____ **with it**, or stop listening and just read the subtitles?

3 When you're learning something, do you _____ **discouraged** easily if you're _____ **slow progress**? Or does it make you more determined to **get** _____ **at it**?

4 If you want to improve your pronunciation, do you have to practise a lot? Or can you just _____ **it up** by listening to people?

5 If you were studying in an English-speaking country with a friend, would you speak in your own language? Or would you _____ **a go** at speaking to each other in English?

6 A friend tells you that listening to English cassettes in your sleep will help you to learn. Would you say, 'That's a load of rubbish'? Or be prepared to _____ **it a try**?

vocabulary learning

1 Complete the phrases in the questions above with these words.

give	keep	persevere /pɜːsɪˈvɪə/
get	making	pick
used	have	better

2 Write the phrases in your notebook.

3 Ask and answer the questions in small groups, giving reasons for your answers.

it's your turn!

1 **Think!** Decide on a skill that you learnt recently.
   1 What did you learn, and why did you decide to give it a try?
   2 How did you learn it, and what kind of progress did you make?
   3 What helped you most, and what didn't help at all?
   4 Do you have any regrets?
   5 How well can you do it now?

2 Ask and answer with a partner.

3 In your own time, write about the experience you chose in **exercise 1** in about 100 words. Use questions 1 to 5 as a framework to help you.

extended speaking
Learn these phrases for later
I made good / slow progress.
Unfortunately, I didn't keep it up.

I wish I'd read more.
I wish I hadn't given it up.

have a great conversation

keep going

1 With a partner, choose a topic and talk about it. Keep going for three minutes!

food we like or dislike

things we like / dislike about our town

our pets

things we find funny

2 Read 'Six ways to have a successful conversation'. Answer the questions.

   1 What do you agree / disagree with?
   2 Which happened in your conversations?
   3 Are there other things that make a successful conversation?

SIX WAYS TO HAVE A SUCCESSFUL CONVERSATION
BY WALTER ANDERSON

(1) Do more than just listen. Show a real interest by nodding, smiling, saying 'Really?', or 'That's interesting!', etc.

(2) **Ask open-ended questions and do your best to avoid questions that are easily answered with a 'yes' or 'no'.**

(3) Say the other person's name. Each of us responds to the sound of our name, so use the other person's name frequently in the conversation.

(4) **Agree enthusiastically; disagree gently. If you must disagree, be polite. 'I'm sorry, but I can't agree,' can stop a conversation cold.**

(5) Don't monopolize the conversation: let the other person talk too. Even if you know a lot about a subject, the other person is probably more interested in what they have to say.

(6) **Don't change the subject. It's rude to ask a question, wait for the answer, then respond by bringing up another topic.**

develop the conversation

1 How do you mean (exactly)?
2 What does that involve?
3 How come?
4 What for?
5 What's it like?
6 What sort of thing?

Match questions 1 to 6 with paraphrases
a to f.

a What do you have to do?
b Can you describe it to me?
c Can you give me some examples?
d Why? (What's the reason?)
e Why or how did that happen? I don't understand.
f Could you explain that more clearly?

1 With a partner, decide on follow-up questions for these conversations.

1 A I'm going to Finland next week.
   B Really? _____ ?

2 A I bought a new outfit for the wedding yesterday.
   B Oh, yeah? _____ ?

3 A Our sports club organizes lots of social events.
   B That's nice. _____ ?

4 A My sister's got a new job working for a charity.
   B Sounds interesting. _____ ?

5 A Maria ended up in Scotland.
   B Eh? _____ ?

6 A What's your domestic situation?
   B Er, _____ ?

2 Practise the conversations with your partner.

3 Choose two topics from the prompts below and have a short conversation. Try to use follow-up questions.

something you bought recently
somewhere you're planning to go
a job you're going to apply for
your own topic

talk about your childhood

1 (1.5) You're going to hear people comparing childhood experiences. Listen to **conversation 1** and answer the questions.

1 Which topic do they talk about?
2 Was their experience similar or different?

2 Listen to **conversation 2** and answer the same questions.

3 Listen to both conversations again. Tick ✓ the phrases you hear from the **natural English** box below.

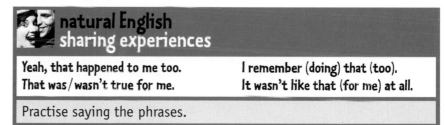

Yeah, that happened to me too.	I remember (doing) that (too).
That was/wasn't true for me.	It wasn't like that (for me) at all.

Practise saying the phrases.

it's your turn!

Work in groups. Talk about your schooldays. Use these prompts.

friends at school	your classmates and teachers
special days at school	what you learnt
feelings about school	clothes you wore

⊙ extended speaking

Learn these phrases for later

What does that involve?	How do you mean, exactly?
The same thing happened to me.	It wasn't like that for me at all.

extended speaking

are you a runner or a reader?

you're going to:

collect ideas
listen to some people talking about reading in their lives

share experiences
talk to a partner about either sport or reading at different stages in your life

write a summary
write a short summary about your partner

but first ...
look back at the **extended speaking** boxes in this unit. You can use this language in the activity.

 collect ideas

1 **Think!** Are you a sporty person, or do you prefer to read? Find a partner who gave the same answer.

2 *(1.6)* Look at 'reading' below. Then listen to Michael and Trude's conversation. Tick ✓ the points they talk about.

3 Listen again. Are these statements true or false?

1 Michael talks more than Trude.

2 Trude contributes her own experiences.

3 Trude doesn't show much interest in what Michael says.

4 Michael shows he's listening to Trude.

5 Michael disagrees gently with Trude.

4 **Think!** With your partner from **exercise 1**, look at your chosen topic, 'reading' or 'sport'. Prepare what you're going to say.

READING

A TALK ABOUT ALL OF THESE

- your earliest memory of reading
- reading in your childhood (at school and outside)
- what you had to read at college/university
- particular likes and dislikes in reading (e.g. fiction or non-fiction, science fiction, biographies)
- what you're reading at the moment
- things you wish you'd read earlier

B CHOOSE ANY TWO OF THESE

- your all-time favourite book
- reading in different languages
- reading books more than once
- collecting/keeping books and magazines
- the best place to read and why
  your own ideas _____

SPORT

A TALK ABOUT ALL OF THESE

- your earliest memory of sport
- sport at college/university
- current sporting activities that you do
- sporting injuries you've had
- your own sporting achievements
- any regrets or missed opportunities in sport

B CHOOSE ANY TWO OF THESE

- sports you enjoy watching
- the cost of sport
- making friends through sport
- dangerous sports
- how competitive you are
  your own ideas

_____

 share experiences

5 You have fifteen minutes to talk about reading or sport.

checklist

– Use the prompts for each topic to find out about each other.
– Use follow-up questions to learn as much as possible.
– If your partner runs out of things to say, help them with some questions.

6 Think! When you have finished, note down some similarities and differences between what you and your partner said.

examples   We're both very competitive.
              Neither of us read much in English, but we both want to!

language reminder

We both Both of us	love football. (plural verb)
We've both had Both of us have had	sporting injuries.
Neither of us	reads poetry. (singular verb)

7 Tell the class about the things you have in common.

 write a summary

8 You have five to ten minutes. Write a summary of what your partner told you. Work alone.

9 Show your partner what you wrote. Do they think it is accurate?

---

test yourself!

How well do you think you did the extended speaking? Mark the line.

0   **10**

From this unit, write down:

1 a different verb which collocates with each of these nouns:
_____ *rollerblading*, _____ *a club*, _____ *aerobics*, _____ *your tennis serve*, _____ *the final*, _____ *a competition*.

2 the missing preposition / particle:
be good __ sth, flick __ a book, take part __ a race, persevere __ sth, have a go __ sth.

3 three verbs / phrases from this list which are followed by *-ing*:
used to, be prepared to, get used to, look forward to, be willing to, keep.

Complete the sentences. The meaning must stay the same.

1 I regret leaving the company.
  I wish _____ .

2 I decided to have a go.
  I decided to give _____ .

3 I made good progress.
  I got _____ .

4 I lose motivation easily.
  I get _____ .

Correct the errors.

1 I wish I can speak French.

2 I can't remember to meeting him before.

3 To read is the best way to relax.

4 I'm fluent in Dutch, and I can go by in German.

Look back at the unit contents on *p.9*. Tick ✓ the language you can use confidently.

two

flying high

parrot the bird in the story

lean across position your body across sb or sth (the parrot in picture 2)

(pretty) fed up 🌀 (quite / very) annoyed, angry

grab hold of take hold of sb or sth suddenly or violently (picture 6)

burly /ˈbɜːli/ big and strong

how to ... react to a joke

That's a terrible joke.

That's a good one.

That's quite funny!

I don't get it.

do you get it?

with a partner ...

When was the last time you went by plane?
What do you remember about the flight?

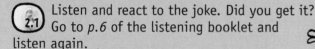

| service | food | other passengers | the weather |

joke time

Look at the pictures. What's happening in each one?
What's going to happen next?

 2.1 Listen and react to the joke. Did you get it?
Go to *p.6* of the listening booklet and
listen again.

natural English

That was ... of you!

If someone tells you about something they did, you can reply:

That	was wasn't	very brave / nice / kind / clever of you!
That was (a bit)		silly / careless / stupid of you!

A Tell your partner something nice / kind / clever / careless you
did recently.
B Reply with one of the phrases above.

physical actions

Why might you do the following in a passenger plane?

| bend down | reach up | grab hold of sth / sb |
| lose your balance | lean against sth / sb | get down on your knees |

example lean across sb
You might do this if you're sitting by the window,
and the stewardess passes you your meal.

listening
airport experiences

lead-in

1 Think! How would you describe people who work on planes, trains, or buses in your country? Think of examples / reasons.

> polite / rude   friendly / unfriendly   patient / impatient   cheerful / miserable

> *example* Ticket inspectors are sometimes really unfriendly; probably because they work long hours and have to deal with difficult members of the public.

2 Compare your ideas with a partner.

saying how things sound

That sounds	right / OK / fine / better.
That doesn't sound	right / polite / (very) appropriate / natural.
That isn't	
That's	wrong / odd / rude / unnatural.

Use *should* to correct something that is wrong or inappropriate.

No, that sounds wrong. It should be ... / I think he should say ...

3 Look at the phrases in the **natural English** box. Correct the sentences in the speech bubbles below (some are correct).

> *example* **A** 'Give me a window seat.' That sounds a bit rude.
> **B** Yes, it doesn't sound very polite. I think it should be 'Could I have a window seat?'

passenger

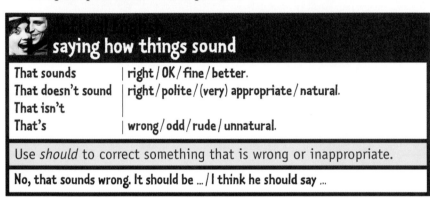

1 Give me a window seat.

2 Why have I to pay for excess baggage?

3 Is it OK if I take this as hand luggage?

4 What time lands the plane?

5 Do we get a meal on this flight, madam?

check-in staff

6 Would you prefer an aisle seat or a window seat?

7 Move your suitcase; it's in the way.

8 I'm afraid your flight is delay.

9 OK, now you must show me your ticket.

10 Have a good flight!

4 Think! Imagine situations A to E took place in an airport in your country.

1 What would you do / say?

2 If the situation didn't improve, would you become less polite?

3 Would it be different if you had to deal with these situations in English?

You're queueing in a self-service restaurant. The people working behind the counter are talking to each other and not working very hard.

You're sitting in the departure lounge and the people next to you are making a lot of noise. You have to wait another hour, and the lounge is full.

You arrive at check-in two minutes late. The staff say the flight is closed.

Your suitcase is two kilos over the weight limit. The airline charges you for excess baggage.

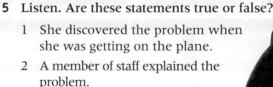

Your flight is delayed, but no one will tell you the reason for the delay or how long it will be. An hour passes, and you still know nothing.

5 Compare your ideas in small groups.

listen to this

tune in

1 (2.2) You're going to hear people describing airport experiences. Listen to the beginning of Michael's story and answer the questions.

  1 Which part of the airport was he in?
  2 What's the animal in the photo called?
  3 What's happened so far?

2 What do you think happens next? Tell a partner.

3 Listen. Were you right?

Michael

listen carefully

4 Lynne had a problem with her ticket. What do you think it could be? Tell a partner.

5 Listen. Are these statements true or false?

  1 She discovered the problem when she was getting on the plane.
  2 A member of staff explained the problem.
  3 The date on the ticket was 28th December.
  4 She didn't check the ticket before going to the airport.
  5 In the end, she didn't go anywhere.

Lynne

listening challenge

6 **(2.3)** Ralph was passing through an airport where the security was very tight. Listen and decide where he was and what happened. Tell a partner.

7 Has anything interesting or unusual ever happened to you or anyone you know at an airport? Tell the class.

Ralph

go to **listening booklet** *p.6 and p.7 for tapescripts and exercises*

it's your turn!

1 **Think!** Remember a situation where you did something and then realized you shouldn't have done it. (Or something you didn't do, but should have done.) Use these prompts to help you.

a holiday
a journey
a relationship
something you spent money on
your own topic _____

example
a beach holiday in spring: 'I should have waited until later in the year.'

2 Move round the class, tell your story and listen to other people's. Has anybody had a similar experience to you?

grammar *should have* + past participle

1 Read the examples based on the tapescript in **tune in**. Complete the explanations with *did* or *didn't do*.

	examples	explanations
1	The Greek man should have checked it was OK to take the hamster on the plane.	He _____ it and he was wrong.
2	He shouldn't have taken the hamster to the airport.	He _____ it and he was wrong.

2 Practise saying the sentences. Use the contracted forms *should've* /ˈʃʊdəv/ *checked* and *shouldn't've* /ˈʃʊdəntəv/ *taken*.

3 Think back to the stories and the joke in this unit. With a partner, make sentences with *should / shouldn't have* + past participle.

1 Lynne _____ .
2 Ralph _____ .
3 The customs official _____ .
4 The parrot _____ .
5 The passenger _____ .
6 The stewardess _____ .
7 The steward _____ .

go to **language reference** *p.153*

ⓔ extended speaking
Learn these phrases for later
That doesn't sound very natural.
I think it should be ...
We should have included ...
We shouldn't have put ...

wordbooster

health and medicine

1 Label the pictures with a partner. Use these phrases if necessary.

How do you say this in English?

What's the English word for 'pastillas'?

1 _____

2 _____

3 _____

4 _____

5 _____

6 _____

7 _____

8 _____

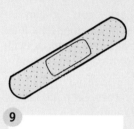

9 _____

10 _____

11 _____

12 _____

2 Practise saying the words / phrases.

3 Ask and answer these questions in groups.

1 Which of the problems in **exercise 1** have you had / do you never get?

2 Which medical products have you used?

3 Have you ever been ill on holiday? What happened?

tourist information

There are some ways of asking questions in English which sound particularly natural, and you can learn them as lexical phrases.

1 Order the words to make questions.

1 best from to **the river** way getting here what's the of?

2 advance book in do **train tickets** to I have?

3 any of **tickets for the concert** is chance there getting?

4 cost in much to **the exhibition** it how does get?

5 here **to eat** can something get we round?

6 best to the get what's **souvenirs** place?

2 Work with a partner. Take turns to ask and answer the questions in exercise 1, but change the word / phrase in bold.

example

A What's the best way of getting to the **castle** from here?

B Go up the hill and turn left. It's straight in front of you.

reading
lost for words

Words fail me

lead-in

1   With a partner, use the prompts below to decide how you would communicate these sentences in a country where you don't speak the language.

   1   I need some batteries for my personal stereo.

   2   I've got a sore throat.

   3   I'll give you fifty dollars for that painting.

   4   Where's the toilet?

   5   There's a dog barking outside at night and it's keeping me awake.

> point at things   use mime or gestures
> make noises   draw things
> write things down, e.g. numbers

2   Think of two more situations and communicate them to the class without words.

read on

1   Read the article with the glossary.

2   Work with a partner.

   A   You're an interviewer; make questions using the key words.

   B   You're Dieter Graf; use the information in the text to answer the questions.

   1   Where / from?

   2   What / living?

   3   done / lot / travelling?

   4   Why / decide / produce / book?

   5   Why / book / unusual?

   6   What kind / people / use?

   7   problems producing it?

   8   been successful?

Forgotten the Spanish for *shower*? Can't tell '**broccoli**' from '**cauliflower**' in Cantonese? Help is at hand, says Justine Picardie, thanks to a visual dictionary.

05 Pointing has always been the traditional way to make oneself understood in a foreign country. What if there is nothing to point at, though – if you're in a hotel reception, and you want to report a problem with your shower, for example? Well, here's an answer.

10 *Point it* is a small visual dictionary that provides pictures of 1,200 useful items for travellers. 'If you don't know the Italian or Japanese word for '**tap**' or '**loo** paper', you just point at the picture,' explains Dieter Graf, the architect from Munich who designed the book after finding himself helpless in various situations around the world.

Furthermore, Graf is clearly not alone. His book has sold over half a million 15 copies since it was first published in 1992, and it's been used by, among others, Swiss UN workers, and the Dutch Olympic team in Japan. Despite its simplicity, it took Graf 16 years to research. 'During my travels, I photographed many things,' he says, 'such as squatting toilets, bus stations, Chinese policemen, and Indian taxi passengers. It can be 20 dangerous, though. In Nigeria I was arrested when I photographed a jeep that belonged to the Chief of Police. At Munich railway station, a well-dressed lady asked me why I had photographed her train compartment – she thought I was a detective sent by her husband!'

You can see why the book has become such a big success. Even the laziest 25 armchair traveller could have hours of fun **flicking through** the pictures. The book opens with seven pages of food, then a double page on animals. But the following page reveals the same animals cut up into steaks and chops before moving on to fruit, vegetables, and drink. And so on.

I introduced it to a well-travelled group of friends, who were generally very 30 positive about it, although several women were worried about the picture of a baby and a doll next to a **syringe**, and one man felt there was not enough help for tourists in search of romance. 'Well, you could always point to this,' said his wife, pointing to a photo of a girl in a swimming costume.

Sunday Telegraph Magazine

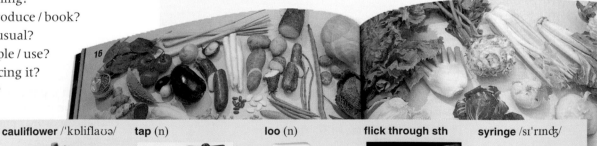

| glossary | broccoli /ˈbrɒkəli/ | cauliflower /ˈkɒliflaʊə/ | tap (n) | loo (n) | flick through sth | syringe /sɪˈrɪndʒ/ |

grammar possibility and probability

1 Fill the gaps below with these words.

might	likely /'laɪkli/	won't	bound /baʊnd/
definitely /'defɪnətli/	unlikely	highly unlikely	doubt /daʊt/

100%	It'll _____ happen.	it's sure to happen
	It's _____ to happen.	it's almost sure to happen
	It'll probably happen.	it's probable
	It's _____ to happen.	it's probable
	It may / _____ happen.	it's possible
	It's _____ to happen.	I don't think it'll happen
	I _____ (if) it'll happen.	I don't think it'll happen
	It's _____ to happen.	I'm fairly certain it won't happen
0%	It definitely _____ happen.	it's sure not to happen

test your partner

– It's sure to happen.

– It'll definitely happen.

– That's right.

go to **language reference** *p.154*

2 Which items do you think would be in Dieter Graf's 'Point it'? Use the language from **exercise 1**, giving your reasons.

example I think it'll definitely have pictures of jewellery. Tourists might want to buy things like that.

jewellery	furniture	clothes	types of accommodation
toys	buildings	tools	types of transport
wild animals	weather conditions	colours	camping equipment
illnesses	feelings	crimes	*your own idea*

it's your turn!

Are these likely to happen to you in the next year? Why / why not?

have a holiday	have more than two holidays	go on safari
go abroad for a holiday	go on a sightseeing holiday	go skiing
have a holiday romance	meet tourists in my home town	

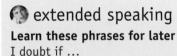 **extended speaking**

Learn these phrases for later

I doubt if ...	We're bound to ...
We definitely won't need ...	We're (un)likely to ...

---

though and although

Though /ðəʊ/ and *although* /ɔːl'ðəʊ/ show a contrast between two clauses.

I enjoyed it, **though** not everyone did.
Although we need to carry out more tests, the results are promising.

Though is commonly used in spoken English at the end of a statement to add a different or surprising fact / opinion.

I enjoyed it. Not everyone did, **though**.
He was always very charming to me. I didn't trust him, **though**.

3 Find the examples of *though* and *although* in the text. Complete the sentences in your own words. Compare with a partner.

1 _____ . It rained all the time, though.

2 _____ . The journey back was terrible, though.

3 Travelling can be fun. _____ , though.

4 Dieter Graf's book looks interesting. _____ , though.

go to **language reference** *p.153*

4 Ask and answer with a partner.

1 What do you think about the book?

2 Are there any problems with it?

3 Would you use it?

how to ...
get the information you want

vocabulary tourists' phrases

1 You're going to read about tourist information centres in Britain. First, complete the phrases with a suitable word.

   1 _youth_ hostel
   2 _____ and breakfast accommodation
   3 _____ attractions
   4 _____ monuments
   5 _____ times
   6 _____ charges
   7 _____ of interest
   8 _____ timetable
   9 _____ resorts
   10 _____ tours
   11 _____ walks
   12 _____ trips

2 Read the text. Are your phrases above the same as the ones in the text?

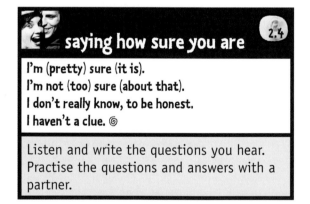

saying how sure you are 2.4

I'm (pretty) sure (it is).
I'm not (too) sure (about that).
I don't really know, to be honest.
I haven't a clue. ☺

Listen and write the questions you hear. Practise the questions and answers with a partner.

3 Do tourist information centres in your country have services like the ones in the text? Talk about them in groups using phrases from the **natural English** box.

tourist information centres

- provide information about tourist accommodation in the area: bed and breakfast accommodation, youth hostels, campsites, hotels, etc. They can book it for you locally or in other parts of the country

- have information and leaflets about local events, entertainments, and tourist attractions including bars and restaurants

- can tell you about museums, historic monuments, art galleries and exhibitions, giving you details of opening times and admission charges

- can recommend particular places of interest

- can give you directions and bus/train timetables

- provide brochures of holiday resorts in other parts of the country

- sell local maps, guidebooks, and postcards

- can tell you about sightseeing tours, guided walks, day trips, etc.

make enquiries

1 Look at the map. What do you think the tourist information advisor will talk about? What questions will the tourist ask?

2 Listen to **part 1**. Tune in to how the tourist information advisor and the tourist sound. Are they friendly / interested or not?

3 Listen to the whole conversation. Put a tick ✓ on the map if the woman is interested in the place, and a cross ✗ if not.

make recommendations

Look at the phrases in the **natural English** box. Compare them with the phrases in the tapescript on *p.8* of the **listening booklet**.

natural English

asking for and making recommendations

Can you recommend any places to see?
Is there anything else you can recommend?

It's worth /wɜːθ/ going to the Butterfly House.
The Theatre museum's well worth a visit.
You should go and see the Modern Art and Photography Museum.
I'd (really) recommend the river trips.

Practise the questions and answers with a partner. Use different places from the map.

it's your turn!

1 Work with a partner. You are tourist information advisors.

1 Invent two exciting attractions.

2 Choose two new locations on the map. Give (opening) times, admission charges, and special features.

example

DOLPHINARIUM
(next to the bridge)

See the dolphins in the pool, with spectacular acrobatic displays every two hours (10.00, 12.00, 2.00, etc); swim in the pool with the dolphins. Open daily until sunset; admission charge £10.00; 20% reduction for students and children under 16.

2 With your partner, think of two questions to ask the tourist information advisor. (Look back at the **wordbooster** on *p.25*).

3 Find a new partner. One of you is a tourist information advisor, the other is a tourist. Ask and answer your questions. Which attractions interest you most?

🔵 extended speaking
Learn these phrases for later
Can you recommend ...?
I'd really recommend ...
I don't really know, to be honest.
I'm sorry, but I haven't a clue.

extended speaking
produce a page from a phrasebook

you're going to:

collect ideas
correct and discuss a sample page from a phrasebook

produce a phrasebook page
think of useful phrases for the chemist's

role play
use the language from your phrasebook in a role play

write a postcard
tell a friend about a medical problem you had on holiday

but first ...
look back at the **extended speaking** boxes in this unit. You can use this language in the activity.

 ### collect ideas

1 Read this page from a phrasebook. Find six examples of incorrect or inappropriate English.

2 Which phrases in section 1 could you use or adapt for a train journey?

ON BOARD A PLANE

SECTION 1 Phrases you may need to say

Excuse me (when you want to get past someone)

Excuse me, why is there a delay?

How much longer we have to wait?

Can I put my bag under the seat?

I'm afraid but my light isn't / my earphones aren't **working**.

When do we land   at Cairo Airport?
                    in Cairo?

Give me another blanket.

Do you have any English / Russian / Spanish **newspapers**?

SECTION 2 Phrases you may hear

Please ensure that your seat belt is fasten and extinguish all cigarettes.

Please put your seat in the upright position.

We're now cruising at an altitude of (9,000) metres.

Can I get you anything for drink?

Do you need to fill a landing card?

Please remain seated until the plane has come to a standstill.

SECTION 3 Useful vocabulary

cabin crew	jet lag
turbulence /ˈtɜːbjʊləns/	steward / stewardess
an aisle /aɪl/ / window seat	runway
overhead locker	terminal building
scheduled /ˈʃeduːld/ / charter flight	

 ### produce a phrasebook page

3 You're going to produce a phrasebook page, 'At the chemist's'. Read the checklist, then produce your page in pairs or threes.

4 Find someone from a different group. Compare your phrasebook pages. Exchange useful words or phrases.

checklist

– Use 'On board a plane' as a model. Use the same three sections. Your phrasebook page shouldn't be any longer than the model.

– Discuss the contents of your page. Think about problems you may have or products you may need to buy as a tourist. Write down all the phrases and words you can think of.

– Agree together on the most useful phrases.

– Don't include words and phrases that are too easy or very obscure. Include words and phrases that others in your class are likely to find useful.

 ## role play

5   **Listen to a conversation at the chemist's.**
   2.6
   1 What's the man's problem?
   2 What does the chemist recommend?

6 **Work with a partner.**

   A You work in the chemist's.

   B You're a customer. Think of a medical problem, and ask the chemist for advice.

7 **Change roles. Practise with a different problem.**

 ## write a postcard

8 **Read the postcard and write a similar one describing a medical problem you've had on holiday.**

PLAZA DE LA MERCED, MÁLAGA, COSTA DEL SOL

> It's fantastic weather down here in Malaga, but I'm afraid I haven't seen very much of it. Unfortunately I rushed out to the beach on the first day and spent three hours in the sun.
> By the evening, I looked like a lobster and I had to go and find a chemist's the next morning for some cream to cool me down.
> I should have been more careful. From now on, I'll be using Factor 30 suntan lotion. See you soon,
>
> love Danny

Photograph: Matilda B. Nottingham
Distribution: MS SUPPLIERS

300
072

PRINTED IN SPAIN

POPPYS CARDS © 2003

Kym Taylor

10 Shakespeare

Newton

Cambs

INGLATERRA

ESPAÑA

9 **Show a partner your postcard and ask each other questions about your experiences.**

---

test yourself!

How well do you think you did the extended speaking? Mark the line.

0	10

From this unit, write down:

1 four minor illnesses, and four things to treat illnesses and injuries.
2 three frequently asked questions in a tourist information centre.
3 three things you might ask or be asked at an airport check-in desk.

Complete the sentences. The meaning must stay the same.

1 I don't know.
   I haven't _____ .
2 You should go and see the castle.
   The castle's _____ .
3 You were very brave.
   That was _____ .
4 That's a bit rude.
   That doesn't _____ .

Correct the errors.

1 It was bound happen.
2 You shouldn't have went there.
3 He's hardly unlikely to come.
4 Sightseeing's fun. It's expensive, although.

Look back at the unit contents on *p.21*. Tick ✓ the language you can use confidently.

free time

life with Agrippine

in groups ...

When you were younger, did you have a regular group of friends? Who was in your group? What did you do together?

Have you got different friends now? Do you do the same things?

cartoon time

Read the cartoon. Is it true to life?

3.1 Listen and follow the cartoon. Then test your partner on the glossary words.

---

natural English
fancy (v)

Fancy is common in informal English to mean *would like* or *want*.

Do you fancy a drink?	**I don't fancy** (the idea of) camp**ing**.
Do you fancy go**ing** out this evening?	**I don't fancy** that **much**.

Practise saying the sentences. Find three other ways of asking or suggesting in the cartoon. Rephrase them using *fancy*.

---

glossary

wanna Ⓖ want to

telly Ⓖ television

There's ... on showing, on the television

stuff Ⓖ things, a general word, e.g. What kind of stuff do you like reading?

the pictures cinema

broke Ⓖ having no money

pathetic Ⓖ useless, no good

put sb on pass the phone to sb

too much on Ⓖ too many things to do

reading family ties

lead-in

1 Make a similar diagram for your family. Write in people's names.

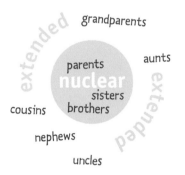

extended
grandparents
parents aunts
nuclear
sisters
brothers
cousins
extended
nephews
uncles

natural English
describing group size

There are **five of us** in my family. NOT We are five.
There are **eight of us in all.**
There are **ten of us altogether** /ɔːltə'geðə/, including my grandparents.

2 Tell a partner about your family, using phrases from the **natural English** box.

　1 Do you get on with everyone in your immediate family?

　2 Describe the closest relationship.

vocabulary good and bad relationships

1 Match the verbs in **bold** in 1 to 8 with definitions a to h.

　1 Parents and children should **consult** each other about everything.

　2 Parents shouldn't **quarrel with** each other in front of their children.

　3 Brothers **compete with** each other much more than sisters do.

　4 Fathers and sons generally **relate to** one another better than mothers and sons.

　5 Children usually **get on with** each other better as they get older.

　6 Parents and children should **hug** each other a lot.

　7 Brothers and sisters should always **stick up for** one another.

　8 Parents and children often **clash with** each other about clothes and appearance.

　a have a good relationship with someone

　b disagree strongly with someone

　c have an angry argument with someone

　d put your arms round someone affectionately

　e support and protect someone

　f try to be better than someone else

　g ask someone for their opinion or advice

　h understand how someone feels so that you can communicate easily with them

2 **Think!** Do you agree with the sentences in **exercise 1**? Why / why not?

3 Compare your ideas with a partner.

DISCO WITH DAD ... WHY NOT?

It's generally understood that most teenagers **wouldn't be seen dead** socializing with their parents, so how come the latest idea of a fun night out
05 involves whole families going clubbing together? And yes, actually enjoying themselves and getting on well with each other ... So instead of parents dropping their kids off outside a club, they all go in
10 together. And apart from the fact that there's no alcohol and no smoking, these clubs are just the same as any other.

The *Groove club* in Manchester is one of the most recent ones to open and provides
15 the perfect environment for parents and teenagers to let their hair down with one another. The music appeals to everyone, there's a great atmosphere, and if you're 15 or over you can go with or without your
20 parents. A regular customer is 16-year-old Dan Cooper, who goes on Friday nights with his dad Martin, 40. Dan doesn't see much of Martin since his parents divorced three years ago so he looks forward to
25 these evenings together.

'It was pretty weird to start with,' says Dan, 'and my friends thought I was mad to want to go clubbing with my dad. But once we'd been a couple of times, it felt just as natural
30 as going to a football match or whatever. Two of my friends have even asked if they can come along with us, just because I keep going on about how brilliant it is. The best thing about it is that me and my
35 dad really have something in common now and we can relate to each other.'

And it's not just the kids who have a good time. Parents really seem to get a lot out of it and clubs like this are a great
40 opportunity for them to make friends as well. They can also relax in the knowledge that their evening won't be ruined by people who've had too much to drink. Having kids around seems to bring out
45 the best in adult behaviour.

As a teenager though, the whole idea would have filled me with horror. If my parents even said 'Hello' to my friends, I would die of embarrassment. I remember
50 going to my cousin's wedding party when I was 15, and several of my school friends were there as well as my whole family. When the disco started in the evening, my family were up there on the dance floor
55 and I remember sitting with my head in my hands. I knew it would be round the whole school the next day. But maybe parent-teenage
60 relationships have moved on since then?

However, not all teenagers are as
65 enthusiastic about mixed-generation clubbing as Dan Cooper. Kelly Simmons, 21, organizes parties for the 13 to 16s and is convinced that most teenagers would much rather go out without their parents.
70 'At my parties', she says, 'I try to create a safe environment that parents would approve of without them actually having to be there. So there's no **booze**, some rules about acceptable and unacceptable
75 behaviour, and I even have 'kiss police' to keep an eye on things!'

read on

1 Read the article and complete the glossary.

2 What do these people think of parents and children going out together? Who do you agree with?

  a Dan Cooper   b the author of the article   c Kelly Simmons

3 **Think!** Would you go to a disco with your parents / children? Why / why not? Can you think of other situations where parents and teenagers go out together?

4 Compare your ideas in small groups.

glossary

(I) wouldn't be seen dead ◎ (I) would never do something because it is too embarrassing

_____ ◎ (para 1) child / children

_____ ◎ (para 2) relax completely / have a good time

_____ (para 3) talk about sb / sth for a long time

_____ (para 4) destroy or spoil completely

booze ◎ alcoholic drinks

different opinions

1  Listen to five people giving their views. Tune in to the speakers. Which ones are teenagers?

2 Read the summaries of each speaker's opinion. Listen again and choose the correct speaker.

a It may work well with one parent but not the other.

b It's a terrible idea; teenagers feel uncomfortable with their parents.

c It's good for family relationships.

d It gives you a chance to see your parents, which is good.

e Teenagers need separate interests from their parents.

speaker 1

speaker 2

speaker 3

speaker 4

speaker 5

grammar *each other / one another, -self / -selves*

1 Look at the article on *p.35* again. Find the words *each other, one another*, and *themselves* in paragraphs 1 and 2.

2 Compare these pairs of sentences. What's the difference in meaning, if any?

1 a The children are good at looking after themselves.
  b The children are good at looking after each other.

2 a The kids hurt each other playing in the garden.
  b The kids hurt one another playing in the garden.

3 a Did you do your homework yourselves?
  b Did you do your homework with each other?

4 a He brushed his teeth and got dressed.
  b He brushed his teeth and dressed himself.

5 a People often talk to themselves when they're worried.
  b People often talk to each other when they're worried.

3 Look at the sentences again. How do you express these ideas in your language?

go to **language reference** *p.155 and p.156*

4 Complete the sentences with a pronoun and your own words.

each other	one another	myself	yourself	himself
herself	ourselves	yourselves	themselves	

1 People who laugh at _____ .

2 My _____ and I talk to _____ every _____ .

3 My _____ and I had to look after _____ when _____ .

4 When I was young, my _____ and I used to _____ .

5 I never _____ when I hurt _____ .

6 My mother enjoyed _____ when _____ .

5 Compare your ideas in groups.

listening

creating a community

lead-in

1 **Think!** Look at the advert below.

   1 Would you apply? Why / why not?

   2 Think of three things you could contribute to the community.

2 Tell a partner.

COME TO THE GARDEN OF EDEN

Looking for **adventure** or a **challenge**? You will find it in the **GARDEN OF EDEN** – and you could win a $30,000 prize!

As part of a TV adventure survival show, we're looking for **12** people to compete against each other over three months in a remote tropical rainforest in Australia.

Contact us at *RDF Media* and tell us ...
– why you'd like to apply
– what you could contribute to the community.

---

grammar obligation, necessity, and prohibition

1 The television company produced guidelines for the project before selecting people. Read 'Laws of Eden' and look at the words in **bold**.

2 In the sentences in 'Laws of Eden', would there be any difference in meaning or use if you changed the words in **bold**, as below? If so, what?

   1 *have got to* instead of *have to*

   2 *are permitted to* instead of *are allowed to*; *mustn't* instead of *shouldn't*

   3 *mustn't* instead of *aren't permitted to*

   4 *ought to* instead of *should*

   5 *are allowed to* instead of *ought to*; *mustn't* instead of *don't have to*

   6 *don't have to* instead of *mustn't*

   7 *can't* instead of *aren't allowed to*

go to **language reference** *p.156 and p.157*

LAWS OF EDEN

1 The group **have to** complete a trek through the rainforest for a day and a night before reaching Eden.

2 They**'re allowed to** take only the possessions that they can carry. They **shouldn't** take anything valuable.

3 Edenites **aren't permitted to** go beyond the boundaries of Eden, or explore the area on their own.

4 They **should** have the right to create their own laws, as long as they don't conflict with existing laws.

5 They **ought to** find some of their food from the surroundings. However, many items will be provided, so they **don't have to** be totally self-sufficent.

6 They **mustn't** kill any animals without the permission of the programme producers.

7 They**'re not allowed to** have access to TV or the Internet, but they can make a call to a friend or loved one once a month.

3 With a partner, imagine you are the producers. Complete the laws below, using the words / phrases in **bold** in 'Laws of Eden'. Add one law of your own.

   1 They _____ medical supplies.

   2 They _____ tools.

   3 They _____ alcohol.

   4 They _____ a leader.

   5 They _____ a whistle round their necks for emergencies.

   6 They _____ .

4 Compare your ideas with another pair.

listen to this

1 **Think!** Imagine you're selecting 12 Edenites for the survival show. Make notes in the table under 'your opinion'.

factors	your opinion
number of men and women	
age range of the participants	
mix of professions and skills	
level of fitness	
selection process, e.g. interviews, tests	

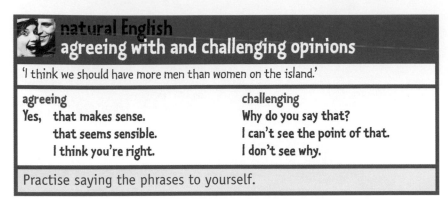

natural English

agreeing with and challenging opinions

'I think we should have more men than women on the island.'

agreeing	challenging
Yes, that makes sense.	Why do you say that?
that seems sensible.	I can't see the point of that.
I think you're right.	I don't see why.

Practise saying the phrases to yourself.

2 With a partner, give your opinions from **exercise 1**. Use language from the **natural English** box.

tune in

3   **3.3** You're going to hear a radio interview. Who's the interviewer talking to? What does he ask about?

listen carefully

4 Listen to the second part of the conversation. Answer the questions.
   1 How many men and women did they choose?
   2 What was the age range?
   3 How did they decide on the range?
   4 Did they choose people with particular skills? Why / why not?
   5 What does she say about levels of fitness?

listening challenge

5 **3.4** Listen to the last part of the interview about the selection process. Note down at least three things participants had to do, then compare with a partner.

6 Listen again with the tapescript if you need to.

listening booklet *p.10 to p.12 for tapescripts and exercises*

it's your turn!

1 **Think!** Imagine you're part of the Eden group in Australia. How can your group entertain themselves for three months? Add three more ideas to the list.
   – competitions where people make or produce things
   – teaching things to the group (e.g. a language, art)
   – *your own ideas*

   _____
   _____
   _____

2 Compare your ideas in small groups. Choose the best three, and tell the class.

extended speaking

Learn these phrases for later
That seems sensible.
I can't see the point of that.
They've got to be …
We ought to choose …

wordbooster

personality phrases

1 Complete each phrase with one of these words.

life	eccentric /ɪkˈsentrɪk/	ego /ˈiːgəʊ/	supportive
neck	control	laugh	articulate /ɑːˈtɪkjələt/

1 A She expresses herself very well.

   B Yes, she's very _____ .

2 A Don't you think he's funny?

   B Yes, he's **a good** _____ .

3 A She's a bit _____ .

   B Yes, she does have some strange ideas.

4 A I think he's **a real pain in the** _____ .

   B I agree. A very annoying guy.

5 A She's rather wild, isn't she?

   B Yeah, a bit **out of** _____ .

6 A He's got a high opinion of himself.

   B Yes, he's got **a big** _____ .

7 A Do you find her ambitious?

   B Well, she wants to **get on in** _____ .

8 A She's always there to help.

   B Yes, she's very _____ .

test your partner

– He's got a very high opinion of himself.

– Yes, he's got a big ego.

– That's right.

2 Look at each dialogue in exercise 1. Are the people's comments positive, negative, or neutral?

3 Put the ⓖ symbol next to the more informal words / phrases.

paraphrasing

Paraphrasing is an important communication strategy if you don't know the word / phrase you want, or the listener doesn't understand. It's also common to paraphrase other people's words to show you're listening and involved.

1 What word / phrase is being paraphrased?

She can be a bit, er, _____ ; she finds it difficult to talk to people she doesn't know well.

He's got a very good, er, you know _____ ; he can see the funny side of life and enjoys laughing at things.

2 In A / B pairs, A turn to *p.148* and B to *p.150*.

how to ... write a website profile

choose personal information

1 **Think!** If there were a 100-word profile of you on a website, what information would it include?

  1 Choose some information about your past and present.

  2 What kind of photo would you like to represent yourself?

2 Compare your ideas in groups.

express information in writing

1 **3.5** Katie is one of the Edenites. Read her website profile, then listen and complete the gaps.

CATEGORIES	TV	RADIO	INDEX	LINKS	SEARCH	

EDEN

KATIE JESSOP (23)

Originally I'm from Glasgow, but I was brought up in Manchester. I went into banking soon after leaving school, but decided
¹ _____ – **I've** always **had itchy feet**. I got a job ² _____ and travelled the world for eighteen months. Since I got back, I've been working as a fitness instructor; ³ _____ gymnast. My proudest moment was
⁴ _____ in the long jump.

If I won the $30,000 on Eden, I'd probably buy a yacht and ⁵ _____ .

My **motto** is ... never run after ⁶ _____ , because ⁷ _____ !

---

glossary

have itchy feet Ⓢ want to travel, do different things

motto sentence/phrase which summarizes your beliefs

natural English
talking about your background

Originally /əˈrɪdʒɪnəliː/ **I'm from** ...
I was (born and) brought up in ...
I come from a (sporty / musical) **family.**
My proudest /ˈpraʊdɪst/ **moment was** ... -ing
I've always dreamt /dremt/ **of** -ing / **wanted to** + verb

Tell a partner at least three things about yourself, using the phrases.

2 Here's a profile of another Edenite. Put the rest of the profile in the correct order.

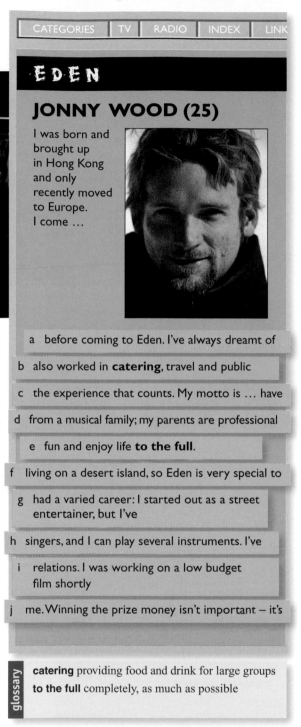

CATEGORIES | TV | RADIO | INDEX | LINK

EDEN

JONNY WOOD (25)

I was born and brought up in Hong Kong and only recently moved to Europe. I come ...

a   before coming to Eden. I've always dreamt of

b   also worked in **catering**, travel and public

c   the experience that counts. My motto is ... have

d   from a musical family; my parents are professional

e   fun and enjoy life **to the full**.

f   living on a desert island, so Eden is very special to

g   had a varied career: I started out as a street entertainer, but I've

h   singers, and I can play several instruments. I've

i   relations. I was working on a low budget film shortly

j   me. Winning the prize money isn't important – it's

glossary
catering providing food and drink for large groups
to the full completely, as much as possible

3 Find three phrases in the profile which also appear in the **natural English** box.

4 Work with a partner. You have two minutes.

   A   Memorize Katie's profile.
   B   Memorize Jonny's profile.

5 Shut your books. Tell your partner as much as you can remember.

grammar sequencing information in a text

1 Look at the time connectors in **bold** in sentences 1 to 6. Answer questions a to d.

  1   Julie took her final exams **shortly before** _____ .

  2   David was interested in archaeology **long before** _____ .

  3   **Soon after** _____ , Lucy got a job in a health club.

  4   **Since** _____ , Claire's been unemployed.

  5   **While** _____ , Don learnt to drive a heavy goods vehicle.

  6   **Prior to** _____ , Geri spent two years in South East Asia.

  a   Which words / phrases in **bold** express 'time before', 'time after', or 'same time'?

  b   Which can be followed by *-ing*?

  c   Which can be followed by a noun?

  d   Which can be followed by a clause?

2 Complete the sentences in an appropriate way.

go to **language reference** *p.157 and p.158*

plan your website profile

1 Work with a partner. Look again at Katie and Jonny's profiles. Make brief notes on the information they include. Is it organized in the same way in both profiles?

2 Make notes on the information you want to include in <u>your</u> 100-word profile. Decide in what order you'll tell it. Compare with a partner.

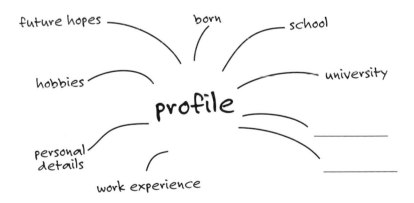

future hopes   born   school
hobbies
profile   university
personal details
work experience

3 Write your own website profile. Use one or two time connectors, and phrases from the **natural English** box.

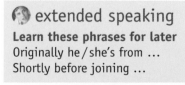

extended speaking

Learn these phrases for later

Originally he / she's from ...
Shortly before joining ...

He / She's always dreamt of ...
While studying at ..., he / she ...

extended speaking

create a band

you're going to:

collect ideas
choose the members of your band, decide on their musical style and image, and how you will promote them

present your ideas
describe your band to the rest of the class

write a profile
create a website profile of one of the band members

but first ...
look back at the **extended speaking** boxes in this unit. You can use this language in the activity.

 collect ideas

1 Read the scenario, then shut your book. Tell a partner what you remember, and what you have to do next.

the story so far ...

Last weekend, you **auditioned** over 100 young performers to form a new band. You were left with the eight people in the photos who you were really impressed with. Although they don't have the right 'image' yet, each performer is very **versatile**: they can sing different styles of music well, they can dance, and they are all enthusiastic and hard-working. Now, you have to decide which of them will be in your final band.

glossary

audition (v) give sb a practical test to see if they are good enough to act, sing, or dance
versatile /ˈvɜːsətaɪl/ having different skills

2 **Think!** Prepare to talk about these notes.

GROUP MEMBERS
- Do you want 3, 4, or 5 group members?
- What are the pros and cons of a small/larger group?
- Who do you think will work well together?
- Do you want boys, girls, or a mixture?

AUDIENCE
Are you aiming at:
  teenagers or adults?
  a sophisticated/trendy audience?

MUSICAL STYLE
What style of music do you want?

3 Compare your ideas with a partner.

4 Read the agenda. In groups of four, compare your ideas and choose your band from the photos. Use the phrases in the **natural English** box. Make clear notes on your decisions.

Isabel
lively, creative, never stops talking!

Sachi
quiet, nervous, very organized, great dancer

Ryan
ambitious, big ego, brilliant performer

Tarsha
very articulate, confident, has sung in group before

agenda

band profile
description of band
- Group members
- Style of music
- Likely audience
- Name of band

promoting the band
image
- Safe? Sexy?
- Political?
- Conventional?
- Other?

appearance
- Clothes/hairstyles?
- Dressed the same or differently?

publicity
Plan the first month's publicity events:
- Where do you want them to perform?
- How can you advertise the band?
- How about interviews?

Tango

fun-loving, good voice,
a bit bossy

Alison

great sense of humour, gets on
well with most people, bit wild!

Polly

quite shy, talented musician
(plays piano), good team player

Justin

good head for business, serious,
supportive of others at audition

natural English
reaching a decision / moving on

When you've agreed a point, you can say:

So that's decided, then. Shall we go on to the next point?
So we agree on that, then. Let's go on to the next one.

present your ideas

5 Prepare to present your ideas to the class. Read the checklist.

checklist

– Your presentation should not take more than five minutes.
– Divide the presentation into sections so that each of you can speak.
– Decide in what order you are going to speak.
– When you speak, look at the audience. Use notes. Don't read from a script.
– When you listen to other groups, note down questions to ask at the end.

6 Practise what you're going to say within your group.

7 Listen to the presentations. Which band do you prefer? Why?

write a profile

8 Choose one member of your band, and create a website profile for them. Look at the profile on *p.40* for guidance.

doggy humour

glossary

weird /ˈwɪəd/ Ⓢ strange
(be) taken aback /əˈbæk/ be surprised by

how ... to react to a joke

I've heard that one before.

That's pathetic!

I don't get it.

That's nice.

do you get it?

with a partner ...

At the cinema, what annoys you most?

- People talking during the film.
- People eating or drinking noisily.
- Mobile phones ringing.

What do you do if somebody near you is annoying you?

joke time

Look at the pictures. What's happening in each one? What's going to happen next?

4.1 Listen and react to the joke. Did you get it? Go to *p.14* of the listening booklet and listen again.

natural English
connecting ideas

I was surprised (**that**) my boss was at the party ...
... **but what was even more amazing was that** he was in a gorilla suit.
I was annoyed that I'd missed the train ...
... **but what was even more infuriating was that** it was the last one.

Look at the tapescript of the joke on *p.14* of the **listening booklet** and find a similar structure.

adjectives describing reactions

Organize the adjectives into three groups of similar meaning.

surprising	strange	weird	annoying	astonishing
odd	irritating	amazing	peculiar	infuriating

Mark the stress and practise saying the words.

---

in unit four ...
tick ✓ when you know this

natural English
connecting ideas ☐
frequency phrases ☐
'sitting on the fence' ☐
Internet language ☐
making and responding to requests ☐

grammar
nouns in groups ☐
future simple and continuous ☐

vocabulary
adjectives describing reactions ☐
synonyms ☐
the language of editing ☐

wordbooster
words of similar meaning ☐
making the most of your dictionary ☐

reading
don't believe everything you see in films

lead-in

1 **Think!** How often do you:

- go to the cinema on your own?
- go to the cinema with friends?
- watch films on TV?
- rent videos?

2 Tell a partner. Use the phrases in the **natural English** box.

3 (4.2) You're going to listen to people talking about their cinema-going habits. Listen to Juliet, the first speaker. Are her habits similar to yours? Tell a partner.

4 Listen to all the speakers. Complete the table.

	How often do they go?	What's unusual about their cinema habits?
1 Juliet		
2 Julia		
3 Michael		
4 Eric		

read on

1 Sometimes mistakes occur in films. With a partner, predict the possible mistakes in these scenes.

1 In one scene, a blue car's chasing a taxi; in the next shot, _____ .

2 In a film set in the thirteenth century, you see that an actor's wearing _____ _____ .

3 In one scene, an actor dies; in the next shot you see _____ _____ .

2 Read the article opposite and answer the questions with a partner.

1 Why did Jon Sandys create this list?

2 Find two examples of mistakes:
   a to do with time / chronology.
   b to do with clothing.
   c made by the actors themselves.

3 Discuss these questions in small groups.

1 Which mistakes are the worst / most embarrassing?

2 Which aren't important?

3 Would you visit this website?

vocabulary synonyms

We often use synonyms to avoid repeating the same language.

example Researchers found that a number of drivers fall asleep at the wheel of the car, although in most cases they only nod off for a couple of seconds.

4 Read the first three paragraphs of the article again. Find synonyms for these words.

film	fans	mistakes (2)
compiled	ruin	

The **van** that drove through **Braveheart**

It's the list that will keep all film-makers awake at night: the guide compiled by movie fans, which gives details of the mistakes appearing in many Hollywood movies. Errors such as clothing that changes colour during car chases, and dead bodies that keep blinking…

05 **T**he Big List of Movie Mistakes has been assembled by Jon Sandys, with the help of thousands of pedantic film buffs who've sent him their howlers. He 10 now has a collection of more than 2,400 mistakes from 700 films displayed on his website www.movie-mistakes.co.uk. 'I started this because I'm a big film fan, and I thought it would be 15 interesting. People accuse me of wanting to ruin films, but it's not my intention to spoil people's enjoyment. It's just a bit of fun, and a lot of people have written to me saying that they 20 are now hiring videos just to find the mistakes.'

According to the list, *Braveheart*, Mel Gibson's film of the Scottish freedom fighter William Wallace (13th 25 century), must be one of the worst examples in film history. During one battle scene a white van can be seen driving by in the background. Elsewhere Gibson (who plays Wallace) jumps 30 over a roof, revealing a pair of modern black **briefs** under his **kilt**. One of Wallace's men speaks his only line in a southern Californian accent. Battle axes flop around because they're 35 made of rubber, and Wallace's executioner has shoes with red rubber soles. An elderly man who gets his arm chopped off, reappears before the end of the film with it back again. 40 Enemies in battle can be seen chatting … and so the list continues.

To spot such mistakes does require a certain mentality. In *Apollo 13*, the story of the ill-fated Moon mission, a 45 character picks up the Beatles album *Let It Be*, which was not released until a month after the launch. Another entry points out that in *Titanic* (which has more than 50 mistakes) there are 50 shots of Pacific ocean dolphins, despite the fact that the ship is actually crossing the Atlantic ocean. Other errors are more obvious. There are African warriors wearing 55 wristwatches in *Zulu*, and at one point in *Pretty Woman*, Richard Gere calls Julia Roberts 'Julia' (her character in the film is called Vivien).

Even Hitchcock isn't immune. Cary 60 Grant's suit changes colour three times as he's being chased in *North by Northwest*; and according to one fan, James Stewart switches from one broken leg to another in *Rear* 65 *Window*.

The Times

glossary	**blink** shut and open both eyes quickly **briefs** /briːfs/ men's underpants **kilt** skirt traditionally worn by Scottish men

grammar nouns in groups

There are three common ways to make noun phrases:

noun + noun
used to express a single idea (compound nouns)
e.g. *a film star; a video camera*

noun's + noun
belonging to people, animals, groups, and institutions
e.g. *the child's scene; the actor's role*

noun + preposition + noun
belonging to an object or thing
e.g. *the back of the cinema; the title of the film*

1 Choose the correct phrase. Then check in the article on *p.47*.

1 a maker of films / a film maker
2 the suit of Cary Grant / Cary Grant's suit
3 a list of mistakes / a mistakes list
4 people's enjoyment / the enjoyment of people
5 the film's end / the end of the film
6 the Atlantic's ocean / the Atlantic ocean

go to **language reference** *p.158*

2 Form eight noun phrases by combining words from groups A and B. Add apostrophes, prepositions, and articles where necessary.

example weather forecast

A	B
wildlife	decision
weather	Internet
quality	show
danger	documentary
chat	responsibility
use	TV programmes
government	forecast
parents	mobile phones

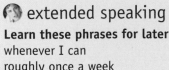 extended speaking

Learn these phrases for later
whenever I can
roughly once a week
the quality of TV programmes
a wildlife documentary

listening
the mobile

lead-in

1 Mobile phones – do you love them, or hate them? Why? Would you use them in the situations in the photos above? Tell a partner.

'sitting on the fence'

This expression means we can't, or don't, want to say which side of an argument we support. These phrases are common in conversation.

It's a difficult issue.	**It's hard to say.**
Well, it depends, doesn't it?	**I can see both sides** (of that argument).

2 **Think!** Which restrictions below do you agree / disagree with, and why?

– Ban <u>all</u> mobile phones in cars.
– Ban all hand-held sets, but allow hands-free sets in cars.
– Allow mobile phones to be used, but only while the car is stationary.
– Ban all use of mobile phones on public transport.
– Limit the use of mobile phones to certain tables in restaurants and bars.
– Ban mobile phone ownership for children under ten.

3 Compare your ideas in small groups. Use phrases from the **natural English** box.

phone police

listen to this

tune in

1 **(4.3)** You're on a train and the man next to you is on the phone. Listen to part of his side of the conversation. Who's he speaking to, and why's he calling?

listen carefully

2 Listen to the whole conversation.

1 Has the woman had a good day?

2 How does he react?

3 What news does he have?

4 How does she react?

5 What's she doing at the moment?

6 What does she want him to do, and why?

3 Is this a typical conversation?

listening challenge

4 **(4.4)** Listen to another conversation. Where's the woman, why's she calling, and what does she arrange?

> **listening booklet** *p.14 to p.16 for tapescripts and exercises*

grammar future simple and continuous

1 What do you think of the Internet? Do you have any favourite websites? Tell a partner.

2 Read about the website called 'Your Cyberfuture'. What do you think of the answers to the questions? What answers would <u>you</u> give?

WEIRD WEBSITES

At last, you can get straightforward answers to all those tricky questions about the future by visiting the new age 'your cyberfuture' website. All you have to do is ask a question, click on ASK, and you will get a confident reply. As the following examples indicate, however, the website doesn't always seem to be listening. Could these answers just possibly be random ones?

I Do you think videophones will catch on?
perhaps not

2 Will everybody own a laptop computer by the middle of the century?
the superficial answer is 'yes'

3 Will my computer crash this afternoon?
this question doesn't have a simple answer

4 Will you still be answering these questions this time next year?
try again later

5 Will I be having dinner at 8.00 tonight?
be careful what you ask, in case you get an answer

6 Will everyone be using mobile phones in ten years' time?
yes yes yes

7 Will people be spending more time on the phone in the future?
no way!

8 Are you telling the truth?
`error_312: cannot connect to the server`

3 Answer the questions with a partner.

1 Questions 1, 2, and 3 use *will* + verb. Can you also use *will be* + -*ing* form (future continuous) in these questions?

2 Questions 4, 5, 6, and 7 use *will be* + -*ing* form. Can you also use *will* + verb in these questions?

go to **language reference** *p.159*

4 Complete the sentences. Use *will* + verb or *will be -ing*.

1 A Shall I ring you at about 4.00?

   B No, don't, I _____ (work) then, but I _____ (be) free at 7.00.

2 A Could I use your computer tomorrow?

   B Sorry, I _____ (use) it all day.

3 In five years' time, everyone in our office _____ (have) their own computer and printer.

4 This time next week, I _____ (revise) for my final exams.

5 Jack doesn't know about the conference yet, but I _____ (see) him tomorrow anyway, so I _____ (tell) him.

6 I don't think our team _____ (win) the match tomorrow.

it's your turn!

1 Work with a partner. Invent five questions about the future, using *will* + verb or *will be -ing*. Then invent five random 'yes' or 'no' answers.

2 Find a new partner. Ask them your questions; they give their random answers. Are any answers correct, do you think?

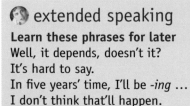

extended speaking

Learn these phrases for later
Well, it depends, doesn't it?
It's hard to say.
In five years' time, I'll be -ing ...
I don't think that'll happen.

wordbooster

words of similar meaning

1 Replace the words in bold in 1 to 8 with the correct form of an appropriate verb from the box. The meaning of each sentence should not change.

check	restrict	ban	boost	allow	censor
decline	reduce	lack	expand	regulate	raise

1 Internet material needs to be **controlled**. However, it isn't really possible to **examine** every website.

2 If you **prohibit** the use of mobile phones on public transport, you'll be **limiting** people's freedom too much.

3 Customers aren't **permitted** to use the internal shop phones.

4 With so many channels, I think the quality of TV programmes is **deteriorating**.

5 They've **cut** the number of programmes in an effort to **improve** standards.

6 We need to **increase** our profits, but at the moment our managers **don't have enough** experience or knowledge to improve things.

7 Mobile phone companies are **growing** very quickly.

8 Sex scenes in films are often **removed** when they're shown on TV.

Words which are similar in meaning in one context may not be synonymous in another.

2 Which noun in each row doesn't collocate with the verb in CAPITALS?

1 you can BOOST ·········· prices ·· sales ·· morale

2 you can INCREASE ··········· prices ·· sales ·· morale

3 you can RAISE ·········· your English ·· efficency ·· taxes

4 you can IMPROVE ····· your English ·· efficency ·· taxes

5 the weather ·· health ·· population figures ·········· can DETERIORATE

6 the weather ·· health ·· population figures ········· can DECLINE

7 the economy ·· trees ·· metal ··········· can EXPAND

8 the economy ·· trees ·· metal ··········· can GROW

test your partner
– What can you boost?
– Sales and morale.
– That's right

making the most of your dictionary

Learners' dictionaries can help you when groups of words have a similar meaning, or are often confused.

1 Look at the dictionary entry, then fill the gaps with an appropriate word.

1 I've got the _____ to go to the States in the autumn.

2 There's a strong _____ that it'll rain tonight.

3 Their anniversary was a very happy _____ for the family.

4 He was given the _____ to take the exam again.

WHICH WORD? (?)
possibility / occasion / opportunity / chance

Occasion, **opportunity**, and **chance** all mean a time when it's possible to do something. **Possibility** and **chance** are used to suggest that something might happen.

Occasion suggests a time that is right or suitable for an activity: *A wedding is an occasion for celebration.*

Opportunity and **chance** suggest that it's possible for you to do something because the circumstances are right at the time: *I had the opportunity to spend a year in Paris while I was a student. I hope you get the chance to relax this weekend.*

Possibility: note that you can't say **a/the possibility to do sth**: ~~I had the possibility to spend a year in Paris while I was a student~~. **Possibility** means the fact that sth might happen or be true and is used with **of** or **that**: *There is a possibility that I might go to Paris to study for a year.* **Chance** can also be used in this way: *I have a good chance of being promoted.*

---

entry from *Oxford Advanced Learner's Dictionary* ISBN 019431510-X

2 Does your dictionary have a similar feature?

how to... write and edit e-mails

read aloud

1 Work with a partner. Say these e-mail and website addresses. Use the **natural English** box to help you.

www.oup.com/elt/naturalenglish

CNN.COM/WEATHER

ros.edwards@hotmail.com

julio@ctv.es

www.bath.co.uk/leisure

your own e-mail address / website

natural English
Internet language

When you say e-mail and website addresses, use the following:

. = **dot**	/ = **forward slash**	CAMERON is written in **upper case / capital letters**.
@ = **at**	**co** /kəʊ/	johnbrown (**all one word**) is written in **lower case**.

2 Listen and check your answers.

vocabulary the language of editing

1 Read the text. Complete sentences 1 to 10 using these words.

double	spelt	hyphen /ˈhaɪfən/	comma
full stop	paragraph	italics /ɪˈtælɪks/	missing
tense	brackets	apostrophe /əˈpɒstrəfi/	

2 Read the text again. Do you agree with the ideas? Tell a partner.

e-mail netiquette

Sending an e-mail isn't the same as writing a letter. When you will e-mail someone, you dont need to start with 'Dear Mr So-and-so', or end it with 'Yours sincerly'. Starting 'Hi Jenny' or Hello Bill' is fine, and you just end it with your own name. However, it's also perfectly acceptable to start the mesage with no greeting.

Do you reply promptly. You should. As e-mail is such a quick and easy way to get in touch with people, they usually expect a reply within a day or so, even if it's just to confirm you've received their message.

Very few things are unacceptable in an e-mail, but one of them is writing in capitals.

It doesn't look friendly, and it's regarded as shouting (you can get some angry responses.

It's also important to *remember* that e-mail isn't very private. Don't say anything that is confidential that someone might forward to other people on the Net. Sometimes a phone-call is safer.

1 That's in the wrong _____ .

2 They've forgotten the _____ .

3 This isn't _____ correctly.

4 It should be _____ s.

5 There's a question mark _____ .

6 That should be a _____ , not a _____ .

7 You don't need to start a new _____ here.

8 You have to close the _____ .

9 It shouldn't be in _____ .

10 This doesn't need a _____ .

edit an e-mail

1 Read the e-mails. Do the writers follow the advice in 'E-mail netiquette'?

2 Work with a partner. Find three typing or punctuation mistakes in each e-mail.

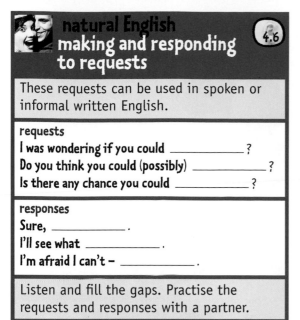

natural English 4.6
making and responding to requests

These requests can be used in spoken or informal written English.

requests
I was wondering if you could _____ ?
Do you think you could (possibly) _____ ?
Is there any chance you could _____ ?

responses
Sure, _____ .
I'll see what _____ .
I'm afraid I can't – _____ .

Listen and fill the gaps. Practise the requests and responses with a partner.

3 In A/B pairs, make requests and respond with a partner.

A You need to borrow a car.
  You want your partner to show you the way to somewhere.

B You're having problems writing an essay in English.
  You need help moving to a new flat next week.

write an e-mail

1 Write Caroline an e-mail with one of these requests. Use Stefan's e-mail and the **natural English** phrases to help you.

– You'd like information about getting temporary jobs in Britain.

– You want addresses of language schools suitable for a ten-year-old relative.

– You want her to find you a pen pal.

– *your own request* _____

2 Give your e-mail to someone in your class. They should write you a very short reply.

From:	Stefan Enquist <lenquist@langschool.se>
To:	Caroline Wilson <langint@BTinternet.com>
Date:	6 January 2003, 16.45
Subject:	penpals

Hello Caroline

How are you? Do you remember me

We were in the same group last summer at the language teachers' conference in Cambridge. I was the guy with long hair and a beard who was always asking questions about the meaning of words. Yes, now you remember, don't you? You used to call me 'Stefan the Talking Dictionary'.

Anyway, now Im back in Sweden, and I'm teaching adult students at upper-intermediate level. They would like to find some e-mail pen pals to write to once a week to practise their english. I was wondering if you could ask your students if any of them would like to become pen pals with Swedish students?

Sorry to bother you with this, but I hope you can help.

Cheers, Lars

From:	**Caroline Wilson <langint@BTinternet.com>**
To:	Stefan Enquist <lenquist@langschool.se>
Date:	20 January 2003, 20.25
Subject:	**RE:** penpals

Hi Stefan

It's nice to hear from you. (how could I forget you? I remember all the teachers in our group; they were great fun, weren't they?

I've got an upper-intermediate class at the moment, so I'll ask if anyone is looking for a pen pal.

If so, I'll give them your e-mail address, and they can get in touch with you directly. I'll suggest that they say a little bit about themselves, why they are learning English and what they'll need it for in the future. Then you can match them with an apropriate Swedish learner.

Hope to see you again sometime.

All the best, Caroline

extended speaking

Learn these phrases for later
There should be an apostrophe here.
You don't need a hyphen here.
There's a question mark missing.
That's in the wrong tense.

extended speaking

you're going to:

collect ideas
think about different types of questionnaires

edit a survey
correct mistakes in a survey about the use of computers, the Internet, and TV, and add two more questions

do the survey
find out your group's opinions

present your summary
analyse the results and plan your presentation

but first ...
look back at the **extended speaking** boxes in this unit. You can use this language in the activity.

 ## collect ideas

1   **Think!** Tick ✓ the questionnaire types below that you've done and prepare to answer the questions.

   1   What was the last one you filled in?
   2   How long did it take?
   3   Do you like doing questionnaires? Why / not?

---

questionnaire types

health or fitness questionnaires	☐
questionnaires about your hobbies or interests	☐
questionnaires about personal finance	☐
feedback questionnaires, e.g. *at the end of a course / holiday / hotel accommodation*	☐
market research questionnaires on products	☐
public transport questionnaires	☐
other types?	☐

2   Compare your ideas in small groups.

 ## edit a survey

3   Read the memo. Shut your book and tell a partner what two things you have to do.

4   In small groups, read the survey opposite and correct the eight mistakes (grammar, vocabulary, spelling, or punctuation).

5   In your group, decide on questions 5 and 10.

6   **Think!** What are your answers to the ten questions?

UNIVERSITY OF LANGTON

From: Jane Hargreaves,
      Head of Media Studies Dept.
To: Class Students

One of my overseas students has handed me a draft of a questionnaire he's prepared. He's made some mistakes in it, and I was wondering if you could proof-read it?

He also told me he would appreciate any ideas for further questions he could ask, (for example, something about the physical effects of these media on people), so please add your own questions for numbers 5 and 10.

 ## do the survey

7   Discuss your answers in your group. Take turns to write notes of your group's answers to each question.

SURVEY

I'm a first-year student in Studies of Media, and I want to find out how people's lives are affected by computers, the Internet, and TV. I intend to include the results of the survey in an article I have to write for the department magazine.

I wondering if you could discuss and complete the questionnaire? When you've finished it, please leave it with the secretary in the department office.

PERSONAL HABITS

1 Please indicate how much time you spend on the following in a typical week:

   - [ ] watching terrestrial TV
   - [ ] using computers (e.g. word processing
   - [ ] watching satellite or cable TV
   - [ ] using the Internett
   - [ ] playing computer games

2 Which TV programmes do you watch? Which computer games do you play?

3 What do you use computers and the Internet for?

4 By 5 years' time, do you think you are using computers more or less?

5 _____ ?

OPINIONS

6 Do you feel that the quality of TV programmes in your country is improving or deteriorating? Why?

7 Do you believe there should be more / less censorship:

a on TV?   b on the Internet?   c with computer-games?

   If so, in what areas? And how should they be regulated?

8 In your opinion, do television and the Internet help to increase interaction between people, or do they reduce it?

9 How do you think TV or the Internet are developing in the future?

10 _____ ?

present your summary

8 Choose the question which created the most discussion in your group. You're each going to present a summary to a new partner. Together, plan what you'll say.

9 Find a partner from a different group. Tell them your summary. Did their group have a similar discussion on the question?

five

oops!
OK, class, here are your tests back.
Go over them carefully and see me if you've got any questions.
Hang on! What the hell's this?
Hey! Let me have a look at your paper.
Right!
Miss, you've given Matthew 8 out of 10, but I've only got 1 out of 10.
That's just not fair, I mean, I copied it all from him.
Yes, but Matthew chose the first question: 'The natural resources of Central Asia' ...
... and you did the second one: 'The evolution of the Amazon rainforest'.
BRETECHER

life with Agrippine

in groups ...

Do people often **cheat** in exams in your country? If so, what kinds of things do they do? Do they usually **get away with it** or do they **get caught**?

Have you got a story about somebody you know?

cartoon time

Read the cartoon. What's your opinion of:

| Agrippine | Matthew | the teacher? |

5.1 Listen and follow the cartoon. Then test your partner on the glossary words.

natural English
talking about test / exam results

I **got eight out of** ten / **80%** / **a B** in the test.
I **only just passed** / **failed** the test / exam.
I **did** (**very**) **well** / **badly** in my exam.
I **got good marks** (NOT ~~good notes~~) in my last exam.

Tell a partner how you did in three tests or exams you've done.

in unit five ...
tick ✓ when you know this

natural English
talking about test / exam results ☐
so, anyway, so anyway ☐
expectation and surprise ☐
spoken v. written English ☐
introducing and focusing ☐
not that + adjective ☐

grammar
narrative tenses ☐
modifying and intensifying adverbs ☐

vocabulary
anxiety ☐
adding emphasis ☐

wordbooster
taking exams ☐
phrasal verbs ☐

listening

what an experience!

lead-in

1 **Think!** Can you drive? If so, look at box A; if not, look at box B.

A DRIVERS

1 How much do you drive, and where to?
2 What do you enjoy / dislike about driving?
3 What kind of driving do you find most challenging?

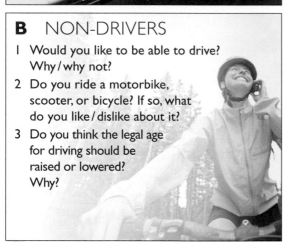

B NON-DRIVERS

1 Would you like to be able to drive? Why / why not?
2 Do you ride a motorbike, scooter, or bicycle? If so, what do you like / dislike about it?
3 Do you think the legal age for driving should be raised or lowered? Why?

2 Compare your ideas with a partner who chose the same questions.

listen to this

tune in

1 Look at the picture below. What parts of the car can you identify?

2 Listen to **part 1** of the story. What do you learn about the man and his journey? What might happen next?

listen carefully

3 Read the sentences, then listen to the whole story. Tick ✓ the ones which are true.

Someone stole ...

the battery. ☐

the car. ☐

some wheels. ☐

the gas/petrol. ☐

He bought ...

a new battery. ☐

a new car. ☐

some new wheels. ☐

some gas/petrol. ☐

A policeman ...

thought it was a stolen car. ☐

thought the car belonged to nobody. ☐

took the car away. ☐

told someone else to take it away. ☐

natural English
so, anyway, so anyway

Use these words/phrases in narrative to change the subject or move the story on.

... and the train was late. **So anyway**, we had a burger and decided to ...

Anyway, it was very hot and we were tired, **so** we left at eight.

listening booklet *p.18 and p.19 for tapescripts and exercises*

grammar narrative tenses

1 Read this short story and answer the questions below.

> A horrible thing happened to me earlier this year when I was living in New York. I'd been working for a TV company for six months and I then went away on holiday for two weeks. When I got back, they'd given my job to someone else, so I moved back to Los Angeles. What a nightmare!

1 Underline the examples of the past continuous, past perfect simple, and past perfect continuous. How are they formed?

2 Match the three underlined phrases with the two dotted lines --- and the cross **x** on the timeline below.

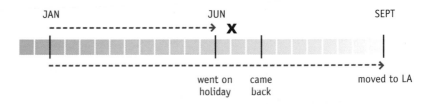

2 Think back to the driving story. Put these events in the correct order.

a someone stole the battery and gas/petrol

b someone stole the wheels

c he went into a restaurant

d someone took the car away

e he came out and couldn't start the car

f he came back, then went to buy some wheels

g he went to buy a battery and the gas/petrol

h he went to the police

i he drove for two hours

3 Reconstruct the story using the past continuous, past perfect, or past perfect continuous. Don't use the past simple.

1 The man _____ when he decided to stop at a restaurant.

2 When he came out of the restaurant, he found he couldn't start the car because _____ .

3 When he got back from the garage, he discovered that _____ .

4 He returned later, and thought that _____ .

5 It turned out that a police officer _____ .

4 The verbs in the text below are in the past simple. Compare with sentences 1 and 2 in **exercise 3**. Which version is more natural?

On one particular day, the man drove for a couple of hours, then decided to stop for a meal. While he was in the restaurant, someone stole his battery and drained the gas tank, so when he came out, his car wouldn't start, and he had to go and buy a battery and some gas.

go to **language reference** *p.159 and p.160*

listening challenge

5  You're going to listen to a story about somebody's driving test. What's happening in the picture, and where's the *barrier*? Listen and tell a partner what happened. Listen again with the tapescript on *p.18* of the **listening booklet** if you need to.

it's your turn!

1 **Think!** With a partner, create a story about driving. Use a range of narrative tenses and an expression from the **natural English** box.

IDEAS

A driving lesson with a couple of near-misses.

A story in which you lose your car or get lost.

A story about transporting either a large animal or a large object.

A story in which you are stopped by the police.

STORY FRAMEWORK

Where were you going, and who was there?

How long had you been going before the main incident happened?

What happened?

What happened in the end?

---

natural English
expectation and surprise

Use these words and phrases for something that was <u>expected to happen</u>:

She passed her test, **as you might expect**.
He kept going and **inevitably** /ɪnˈevɪtəbli/ he ran out of petrol.

Use these phrases for something that was <u>not expected</u>:

He ran across the road and, **to my surprise/amazement**, he threw flowers at me.
It was almost dark but, **for some reason**, he didn't have his lights on.

---

2 Practise telling your story with your partner.

3 Find a new partner. Tell each other your stories. Does your partner think your story is true or invented?

4 Write your story in your own time.

extended speaking

Learn these phrases for later
This happened when I was doing ...
I'd been studying for a couple of hours, when ...
I was sure I'd failed.
So anyway, as you might expect, I ...

wordbooster

taking exams

1 **Fill the gaps in the text below with an appropriate verb. Sometimes more than one is possible.**

cheat	fail	take	get through	do
prepare	sit	come up	turn up	bluff
go on	retake	pass	take place	make a mess of

2 **With a partner, ask and answer the questions.**

the driving test
in your country

the practical test

1 Where does the practical test usually _____ ?

2 If you _____ for the test a few minutes late, are you still allowed to _____ it?

3 If (unfortunately) you _____ the test, how long do you have to wait before you can _____ it? Do you think that's about right?

4 Do people ever _____ in the test?

the written exam

5 Do you have to _____ a written exam as well as a practical one?

6 Is there a specific book you have to use to _____ for the written exam? Do you think that's a good idea?

7 What kinds of questions are likely to _____ in the exam? Do you think the questions are sensible?

8 If you manage to _____ the written, can you _____ to the practical straight afterwards? Or does the practical exam come first?

9 Is it possible to _____ your way through it if you don't know the answers?

phrasal verbs

Many phrasal verbs have more than one meaning. Sometimes they can be intransitive,

> e.g. *The plane **took off**.*
> *He tripped and **fell over**.*

or transitive (needing an object),

> e.g. *He **took off** his coat. / He **took** his coat **off**.*
> *He **fell over** the cat.*

Dictionaries show if verbs are separable / inseparable like this:

> ***take** sth **off*** but ***fall over** sth*

1 **Paraphrase the different meanings of the verbs in bold.**

1 a I'd better **go on** to the next question.
= __continue__

b The exam room's very noisy. What**'s going on** in there?
= _____

c As time **goes on**, you'll get better at parking.
= _____

2 a She didn't **turn up** for her exam.
= _____

b I can't find my driving licence. Oh, well, it**'ll turn up**.
= _____

c Could you **turn up** the radio? I want to hear the traffic news.
= _____

3 a I tried to phone my instructor, but I couldn't **get through**.
= _____

b She **got through** a packet of cigarettes before she took the test.
= _____

4 a I've got my test **coming up** soon.
= _____

b The examiner **came up** behind me and looked at my paper.
= _____

2 **In which two sentences are the phrasal verbs transitive? Are they separable?**

3 **Look up these phrasal verbs in a dictionary. How many of the definitions are new to you?**

pick up or pick sth / sb up	take sth up
make up or make sth up	go over sth

grammar modifying and intensifying adverbs

1 As a challenge, you have to stay awake continuously for 48 hours. What's your reaction to this? Use some of these adjectives.

A		B	
easy	stressful	impossible	exhausting/exhausted
difficult	challenging	terrifying/terrified	ridiculous /rɪˈdɪkjələs/
unpleasant		appalling /əˈpɔːlɪŋ// appalled	

2 **Think!** Add these adjectives to A or B above.

nice   fantastic   awful   frightening

3 Compare your ideas with a partner. Explain your reasons.

4 Which adverbs below can you use with:
- the adjectives in A?
- the adjectives in B?
- both?

extremely   really   absolutely

test your partner

Ridiculous.

– *Absolutely ridiculous.*

– *Yes, or ...?*

5 Complete the diagram using these words.

fairly   extremely   really (x2)   rather   pretty ☺

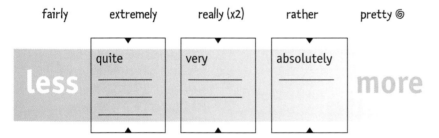

less

quite	very	absolutely
———	———	———
———	———	———
———	———	———

more

go to **language reference** *p.161 and p.162*

6 **Think!** Write your reaction to the challenges below using adverbs and adjectives from **exercises 1** to **5**.

1 You have to spend a month living underground on your own.

2 You have to swim one kilometre to the shore when your boat sinks.

3 You have to make a speech at your best friend's wedding in front of 100 people.

4 You have to spend a weekend alone in a haunted house in the middle of nowhere.

5 You have to watch a member of your family doing their first parachute jump.

7 Compare your answers in small groups. If your answers are different, ask why.

read on

1 You're going to read about a woman who participated in a scientific experiment. Put these paragraph topics in a logical order. Compare with a partner.

a the conditions she lived in for a month

b the purpose of the experiment

c the after-effects of the experiment

d how scientists created the conditions for the experiment

e her feelings during the experiment

2 Read the article and complete the glossary. Was your order of paragraphs the same?

Excuse me, is it day or night?

Bestselling author, Dava Sobel, looks back on a distressing month spent in a windowless room for a scientific experiment.

As a science writer on the New York Times, I was invited to participate in an experiment. It was an attempt to explore how the body changes during a day: what it is that makes you wake up, get hungry or tired. If doctors could understand the body's clock, they could determine ideal times for administering treatments for **life-threatening diseases** – they could even cure jet lag.

I was warned that I'd be living in a laboratory for a month without knowing whether it was day or night outside. There would be no natural light, no clocks, no television, or radio. The only people I'd speak to

glossary	
life-threatening disease (para 1) very serious illness	
_____ (para 4) make sth out of wool using two needles	
_____ (para 5) confused; not understanding what's happening	
your own new words:	
_____ (para ___) _____	
_____ (para ___) _____	

natural English
spoken v. written English

You can use phrasal verbs and idioms more in spoken English. In written English, there's often a more formal equivalent.

more formal	more informal
Your telephone has been **disconnected**.	Our phone's been _____.
They **abolished** the old system.	They _____ the old system.
The boy was **reprimanded** by the teacher.	Joe was _____ by the teacher.

Fill the gaps with these phrasal verbs.

got rid of	told off	cut off

3 Where in the article could you use these phrases and phrasal verbs?

(para 1) *take part in, find out, work out*

(para 3) *turn out*

(para 4) *take up*

(para 5) *come to an end*

it's your turn!

1 **Think!** Read questions 1 to 4. What's your opinion?

1 Would you be prepared to do this experiment for nothing? Or if you were paid? Why / why not?

2 How do you think you'd react in these conditions?

3 What would you take with you to occupy your time?

4 What three things would you miss most, and why?

2 Compare your ideas in small groups.

would be doctors and technicians, all trained to say, 'hello' rather than 'good morning' or 'good afternoon'. After a while, I wouldn't know if it was day or night, and I'd have to create my own day by choosing when to go to bed and when to eat.

When I got there, I discovered that my accommodation consisted of two rooms, one with a desk and chair, the other with a bed and exercise bike, and a bathroom. I was wired up, and the doctors told me that they would be taking blood samples 'from time to time'. But what would you think 'from time to time' meant? I thought a couple of times a day; as it transpired, it was every 20 minutes, round the clock.

Optimistically, I'd thought the month would be a great opportunity for study. Before the experiment, I'd been learning German, so I brought along some tapes and books, and enough wool to knit two sweaters. In actual fact, I couldn't do a thing because the experiment occupied all my time. I found it all so difficult that I tried to quit. I was feeling very low one day, and the lab assistant made a joke that hurt my feelings. My husband had written every day, and on the day a letter didn't arrive, he said something like: 'Nobody loves you'. He didn't mean to upset me, but I was vulnerable. 'That's it,' I said. 'I can't take any more. I want to go home.' The director came and explained how much they'd invested in me as a subject; they really couldn't afford to let me leave. So I stayed.

The experiment terminated in a very anti-climactic way. One 'evening' I was growing tired, they told me it was in fact morning, and the experiment was over. A reception for me was going on outside, but I was too confused and disoriented to enjoy it. It took me a few days to feel comfortable walking down the street with all these people, cars, noise, and everything. I felt frightened and overwhelmed. The reunion with my husband, however, was lovely.

extended speaking
Learn these phrases for later

fairly challenging	really stressful
absolutely appalling	pretty unpleasant

how to ...
emphasize what you feel

vocabulary anxiety

1 Look at the pairs of phrases. Is the meaning similar or different?

1 I was scared /skeəd/ stiff. I was petrified /ˈpetrɪfaɪd/.
2 He was relieved /rɪˈliːvd/. He was upset /ʌpˈset/.
3 I was dreading /ˈdredɪŋ/ it. I was looking forward to it.
4 They look very nervous. They look very anxious /ˈæŋkʃəs/.
5 She was in tears /tɪəz/. She was crying.
6 It gets on my nerves. It's nerve-racking /ˈnɜːvrækɪŋ/.
7 I was shaking. I was trembling.
8 I felt uneasy. I was panic-stricken /ˈpænɪkˌstrɪkən/.

2 With a partner, practise saying the phrases.

TV challenges

1 Some TV shows challenge a member of the audience to do something unusual or dangerous. Look at the example.

example picture 1: The challenge might be to stand up and sing a song unrehearsed in front of the audience.

With a partner, guess what 'challenges' 2 to 5 are.

 natural English
introducing and focusing

In spoken English, these phrases introduce a problem or reason for something.

The trouble is, it just makes me very anxious.
The thing is, I'm scared stiff of heights.
The problem was, I'm not very strong.

Practise saying the phrases, stressing the underlined verb.

2 Which challenge(s) would you find easy or difficult? Tell the class, using the **natural English** phrases where appropriate.

example I'd find the first challenge quite difficult. I'm not shy, but the thing is, I'm hopeless at singing.

3 (5.4) Listen to Lucy and David describing their TV challenges. Which 'challenges' did each one have, and did they do them?

listening booklet *p.18 and p.19 for tapescripts and exercise*

vocabulary adding emphasis

1 Look at two ways of adding emphasis. What are the words in **bold** emphasizing?

I wasn't anxious about the challenge **at all**.

I **did** get worried about the bunjee jump beforehand.

Lucy

David

2 Look at these extracts from Lucy and David's descriptions. Complete the gaps with a suitable word which adds emphasis. Compare with a partner.

1 I was _____ more nervous than last time.

2 I was _____ petrified.

3 It was _____ a relief to be back down on the ground.

4 I wasn't _____ nervous.

5 The spider was _____ gigantic.

6 I was _____ relieved to get it over with.

3 Listen to Lucy and David again and check your answers.

go to **language reference** *p.160 and p.161*

go to **language reference** *p.160 and p.161*

---

natural English
not that + adjective

5.5

In spoken English, you can use *that* to emphasize that something is less funny/stressful, etc. than expected. *That* is usually stressed here.

Surprisingly, I **wasn't that nervous** before the exam. (= not as nervous as I thought) The food **wasn't that good**, when you consider the price.

Listen and practise saying the sentences, stressing *that*.

---

4 Complete the dialogues using *not that* + a suitable adjective.

1 A Did you enjoy the film?
  B Yeah, but _____ .

2 A I can't afford to eat there.
  B Oh, come on, _____ .

3 A Did you understand that joke?
  B Yeah, but _____ .

4 A I can't do this exercise.
  B Oh, come on, _____ .

5 Practise the dialogues with a partner. Remember to stress *that*.

6 **Think!** Choose one or two situations where you have felt anxious.

the first day of a new job
going to your first language class
a visit to the dentist
going on a first date with someone
doing a dangerous sport for the first time
being in a dangerous place
your own situation

7 Move round the class and tell other people how you felt.

example
I had a tooth taken out last month. I was absolutely dreading it but it wasn't that bad and it was such a relief to get it over with.

it's your turn!

1 Work with a partner. Devise two challenges for a TV programme. Think of a suitable prize for each one.

2 Move around the class and talk about your challenges and prizes. What do the others think? Would they be prepared to do them?

extended speaking
Learn these phrases for later
I was absolutely dreading it.
It was such a relief to get it over with.
It was really nerve-racking.
I was nearly in tears.

you're going to:

collect ideas
listen to someone's
experience of exams

think back
prepare and describe
your own experience
of taking exams

evaluate
compare your views
on taking exams

write your opinion
summarize what you
think about exams

but first ...
Look back at the
extended speaking
boxes in this unit.
You can use this
language in the
activity.

collect ideas

1   With a partner, write down all the different exams you can think of. You have one minute!

example   end of year school exams

2   Listen to **part 1** of a woman's story. What exams is she describing? How many were there?

3   Listen to **part 2** of the story. Are these sentences true or false?

1   The first exam went well.

2   In the second, she started screaming.

3   She felt relieved at the end of the exams.

4   She got the results by post.

5   She isn't very positive about exams.

think back

4   **Think!** Remember an exam experience you've had. Use the story framework and read the checklist.

checklist
– Use a dictionary to check any words you need.
– Go over the story in your head in English before you tell it.
– Make notes if you like.
– Don't read from your notes when you are telling your story.

language reminder *manage to / could*

I managed to get through the first exam.
  (= it was difficult but I succeeded)

I managed to (NOT ~~could~~) pass my driving test, and I was very relieved.

5   Tell your stories in small groups. Say how you feel about other people's stories.

STORY FRAMEWORK

setting the scene
What exams were they?
When did you do them?
How important were they?

lead-up to the exams
How hard did you work?
Did you have a revision programme?
How were you feeling around this time?
Were your teachers supportive?

the exams themselves
How did you feel the day of the (first) exam?
How did it go?
Did you have any little rituals in the exams?
Did anything unusual happen during the exams?

after the exams
What did you do at the end of the exams?
How did you feel?

the results
How did you get them?
What were your results, and how did you feel?

 evaluate

6 **Think!** Prepare to answer these questions.

1 Think about the experiences you described to each other. What things did they have in common? What does this tell you about examinations?

2 What do you think about oral exams? How are they different from written ones?

3 Examinations put people under a lot of stress. Is this good preparation for life?

4 What alternatives are there to formal examinations, and what are the advantages and disadvantages of these?

7 Discuss the questions in your group.

 write your opinion

8 Write your opinion of questions 3 or 4 above in not more than 100 words. Here are some link words and phrases you may need:

Personally, I feel that … because / as …

Another point is that … / In addition, …

However, … / On the other hand, …

good news, bad news

how to ... react to a joke

That's clever.

That's very funny.

Oh, that's horrible!

I don't get it.

do you get it?

with a partner ...

Imagine you're going to hear some good news and bad news.
Which would you prefer to hear first, and why?

joke time

Look at the pictures. Who and where are the people?
What could they be talking about?

 Listen and react to the joke. Did you get it?
Go to *p.20* of the listening booklet and listen again.

---

natural English
worth / value

What's the house **worth** /wɜːθ/?   **It's gone up / down (in value)** since last year.
It's worth $500,000.   That painting **is worth a fortune** now.
That restaurant is **good value** /ˈvæluː/ **(for money)**.

Complete the dialogues with appropriate phrases.

1 A Did you enjoy the package holiday?
   B Yes, we had fun and it was _____ .
2 A I bought this clock for €50, but now _____ €80.
   B That's the great thing about antiques – they usually _____ .
3 A Her jewellery must be _____ !
   B Yes, that's why she's afraid to wear it in public.

feelings and emotions

Which phrases could you use if you got a) good news or b) bad news?

over the moon ☺	really fed up ☹	thrilled to bits ☺
heartbroken	let down	really ecstatic /ɪkˈstætɪk/

How would you feel in these situations? Use the phrases.
   The football team you've supported for years is bottom of the league.
   Your best friend's getting married.
   Your best friend's getting married to your ex-boyfriend / -girlfriend.
   You win the lottery.
   You win the lottery but can't find the ticket.

natural English
worth / value ☐
talking about needs ☐
you get ... ☐
apparently, it appears / seems that ☐
getting sb's attention ☐
passives in news reporting ☐

grammar
past simple and present perfect passive ☐
indirect questions ☐

vocabulary
feelings and emotions ☐
collocation ☐
expressing opinions and interest ☐

wordbooster
dangers and disasters ☐
knowing your prepositions ☐

# reading
trouble spots

lead-in

1 Think! Prepare to answer these questions.

1 What important events are in the news at the moment?

2 What do you know about some of the world's trouble spots?

2 Compare your ideas in small groups.

3 Read the description of the contents of a foreign correspondent's survival case. Look at the photo below and identify the items.

World Affairs correspondent, DAVID LOYN, says:

❝ My ready-packed bag is a great comfort. I couldn't manage without it. ❞

A short-wave radio, three tape recorders, a microphone, a camera, cash, and a Bible: these are the essentials.

With his cup, water filter, and kettle, Loyn can make himself a hot drink wherever he is. A hip flask of whisky proves useful too.

Malaria tablets, vitamin pills, antibiotics, and mosquito repellent are essential for maintaining good health; the cigarettes are a useful bribe.

Peanut butter and *Vegemite*: if Loyn can get his hands on some bread, he can live on this for two weeks.

Radio Times 14–20 August 1999

---

natural English 6.2
talking about needs

I couldn't _____ / live / survive without _____ .
_____ would be absolutely essential
in the Amazon.
I'd have to have / take _____ .

Listen and complete the sentences. Practise saying them. Tell a partner:

1 three items you couldn't live without in a trouble spot in Africa.

2 three items you would take to San Francisco on a business trip.

vocabulary collocation

1 Choose the correct word.

1 The area is now totally / extremely dangerous.

2 The soldiers were strongly / seriously injured.

3 The city was badly / extremely damaged by fire.

4 Parts of the town were completely / fully destroyed.

5 The near / surrounding area is now controlled by the rebels.

6 The last / latest information is that the radio station is on fire.

7 People are concerned about possible terrorist / terrorism attacks.

8 The situation is now under / in control.

9 The fighting could escalate / go up and get out of / over control.

10 The capital is now in / on fire.

2 Think! Imagine you're reporting from a trouble spot. Complete the report using the collocations in **exercise 1**.

Last night, the roads leading out
of the city _____ . The
airport _____ and two
other reporters _____ .

The latest information we have
is that the political situation
_____ and the villagers
_____ .

read on

1 Foreign correspondents are given training before they go to trouble spots. Read these extracts. How do you think they finish?

1 You learn basic and advanced first aid, how to treat gunshot wounds and burns, and how to prepare for extreme _____ .

2 There's nothing optional about the training – if you haven't done the course, you _____ .

3 I've reported a lot from trouble spots around the world and the one thing I've learnt is that getting out can be more difficult than _____ .

4 When reporting somewhere for the first time, it's often worth contacting the aid agencies, religious communities, and any other _____ .

2 Read the article and check your answers. Then complete the glossary.

3 Read the article again, then tell a partner:

1 four things you have to learn before you go to a war region.

2 why Bosnia was significant for all foreign journalists.

3 why moving from one region to another is difficult.

4 why life can be dangerous for the 'fixers'.

Training
by Rageh Omaar

Every region in the world is given a danger rating. Before going anywhere, you have to go through the relevant **hostile** environment training; this is
05 provided not only by people with military backgrounds, but also by doctors, psychologists, and so on. You learn basic and advanced first aid, how to treat gunshot **wounds** and
10 burns, and how to prepare for extreme hot and cold climates. And if you're in danger, how to get out of it. Naturally you're also updated on the latest information about the specific region.
15 It all began really with Bosnia, where something like 50 journalists lost their lives – that's more than in the whole Vietnam war. There's nothing optional about the training – if you haven't
20 done the course, you aren't allowed to go.

Radio Times 14–20 August 1999

Understanding the territory
by George Alagiah

I've reported a lot from trouble spots around the world and the one thing I've learnt is that getting
25 out can be more difficult than getting in. The situation can escalate so quickly that the route you used to enter can be completely blocked a few days
30 later, so you need to do a lot of homework about the region.

Getting the right local people on your side is essential. You often find that different people control
35 different parts of a region, so you have to know where you part with one set of **bodyguards** and pick up another.

Then there are the 'fixers'. These
40 are local people who understand the situation and your safety will often depend on their judgement. In one conflict, we were captured by soldiers on the losing side. Soldiers
45 on the winning side can be quite generous, but a defeated army is often dangerous. I wasn't hurt, but

our fixer **got** badly **beaten up**. We pay them very well but sometimes
50 they too become **casualties** of war.

When reporting somewhere for the first time, it's often worth contacting the aid agencies, religious communities, and any other
55 organizations that have knowledge of the region. Taxi drivers can also be a very useful source of information, but it's necessary to know whose side they're on.

glossary

hostile /ˈhɒstaɪl/ unfriendly and _____

wound /wuːnd/ injury from a knife or _____

bodyguard person whose job is to _____

get beaten up ⑥ be _____

casualties /ˈkæʒʊəltiːz/ people who are killed or _____ in accidents or war

it's your turn!

1 Think! Read the questions and prepare to discuss them.

1 Would you be a good foreign correspondent? Why / why not?

2 What would you like / dislike about the work?

3 What areas in the world wouldn't you be prepared to go to? Why?

4 How would you feel about appearing on TV as a foreign correspondent?

5 How might the job affect your social / family life and your personality?

2 Compare your ideas in small groups.

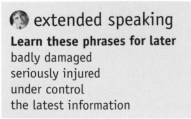

extended speaking

Learn these phrases for later
badly damaged
seriously injured
under control
the latest information

wordbooster

dangers and disasters

1 Match the definitions a to f with words in the table.

a catch and keep a person prisoner illegally, especially to get money

b promise to do something unpleasant if you don't get what you want

c hurt in an accident or attack

d manage to exist in a difficult / dangerous situation

e take control of a place, or take a person prisoner

f move people from a dangerous place to a safer one

verb	general noun	verb	general noun
warn	*warning*	attack	
explode		survive /sə'vaɪv/	
escape		capture /'kæptʃə/	
accuse		damage /'dæmɪdʒ/	
kidnap		threaten /'θretən/	
arrest		destroy	
injure /'ɪndʒə/		evacuate /ɪ'vækjʊeɪt/	

2 Complete the 'general noun' columns.

test your partner
– What's the noun form of 'destroy'?
– That's right.
– destruction

3 Complete sentences 1 to 5 using appropriate verbs from exercise 1 in the past simple. You can use the same verb more than once.

1 The bomb _____ .

2 Nobody _____ / _____ .

3 Terrorists _____ / _____ / _____ the politician's family.

4 The police _____ / _____ / _____ / _____ the young man.

5 The soldiers _____ / _____ / _____ / _____ / _____ the building.

knowing your prepositions

Good dictionaries tell you if a noun, verb, or adjective is often followed by particular prepositions, or if a preposition comes before or after a noun in special phrases.

> **fire** /ˈfaɪə/ [U, C] flames that are out of control and destroy buildings, trees, etc: *The car was now on fire.* ◊ *The warehouse had been badly damaged by fire.* ◊ *fire-fighting equipment* ◊ *Several youths had set fire to the police car (= had made it start burning).*

entry from *Oxford Advanced Learner's Dictionary* ISBN 019431510-X

1 Use a dictionary to complete these sentences with the correct preposition.

1 They **accused** the boy _____ stealing.

2 He was **arrested** _____ dangerous driving.

3 The soldiers will **protect** the women and children _____ attack.

4 The police **evacuated** the residents _____ the area.

5 One of the prisoners who escaped is still _____ **the run**.

6 The police were stopping cars _____ **random**.

7 After the recent terrorist attack, most people believe they are still _____ **danger**.

8 The village is desperately _____ **need** _____ medical supplies.

When you note down phrases with prepositions, you can test yourself later if you write them like this:

verb phrase	preposition
to accuse sb ___ doing sth	of
to be ___ fire	on

listening
have you heard?

lead-in

1 Think! Prepare to answer these questions.

> # TV NEWS
>
> ● Do you find out the news mainly from TV, radio, the Internet, or the press? Which do you prefer, and why?
>
> ● In your country what time do TV channels broadcast the news in the evening? What do you think is the best time for TV news, and why?
>
> ● Are there different styles of TV news programme? For example, for younger or older viewers? Quick headline news or more analytical in-depth news? Which style do you prefer?
>
> ● What do you think of the TV newsreaders in your country? How important is their appearance and personality?

2 Compare your ideas in small groups.

listen to this

tune in

1 🔊 **6.3** You're going to hear a journalist, Willie Ward, talking about TV news in one country. Read the extracts from his talk.

> There are ¹ _____ main, er, channels, television channels …

> They both have their news at ² _____ o'clock …

> You get really a ³ _____ news service on different channels …

> Probably the best time, er, for ⁴ _____ social life for news is in fact eight o'clock …

2 Listen and fill the gaps in the extracts.

listen carefully

3 Listen to **part 1.** Complete the sentences.

　1　You can watch the news from
　　 _____ to _____ .

　2　Eight o'clock is a good time for news
　　 because _____ .

4 Listen to **part 2.** Circle the correct word /
phrase.

　1　The news programmes are all
　　 politically similar / different.

　2　The analysis of the news is in the same
　　 programme / a different programme.

　3　The female newsreaders are low-key /
　　 very glamorous.

　4　The personality of the male
　　 newsreaders is important / not important.

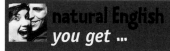

natural English
you get ...

In spoken English this common phrase can
mean that something happens or exists.

What **you get** in France is ... (= What happens in
　France is ...)
You get lots of traffic jams on the coast road in the
　summer. (= There are lots of traffic jams.)

Underline all the examples of *you get* ... in the
tapescript on *p.20* of the **listening booklet.**

listening challenge

5 **6.4** Listen to Bridget talking about TV
news in Australia. Why is there so
much international news there, and what
special channel do they have?
Tell a partner.

Bridget

listening booklet *p.20 and p.21 for tapescripts
and exercises*

grammar past simple and present perfect passive

1 **Think!** Read the opening sentences of some news stories and
prepare to answer these questions.

　1　Which of these stories could happen in your country? Can you
　　 think of examples?

　2　If the story's unlikely in your country, where could it happen?

> **❶** Parts of the countryside have been cut off by heavy snow.

example　Story 1 is very unlikely in our country because we hardly
　　　　 ever have snow. It could happen in places like Scandinavia
　　　　 or Canada, which are very cold in the winter.

> **❷** Thousands of people have been evacuated after floods destroyed
> several villages and left many homeless.
>
> **❸** Two people have been killed and several injured in a terrorist attack in
> the centre of the city.
>
> **❹** An important conservation area in the south has been badly damaged
> by forest fires.
>
> **❺** The seven tourists taken hostage last Friday have just been released.
>
> **❻** The son of a wealthy banker has been kidnapped near his home.
>
> **❼** A large explosion has been reported at a nuclear power station in the
> north of the country.
>
> **❽** A minister has been accused of lying to parliament about government
> contracts.

2 Compare your ideas in small groups.

3 Underline the examples of the present perfect passive in the
sentences in **exercise 1.** Why is the passive form used? Why is the
present perfect used?

4 Read the continuation of one of the stories. Which one is it?

> The eleven-year-old son of Francis Loubet was pushed into the back
> of a car when he was on his way to school this morning and driven
> away. A man accompanying him, thought to be his bodyguard, was
> seriously injured as he tried to protect the boy. Since then, there
> has been no news of him.

5 Answer these questions about the text in **exercise 4.**

　1　Which passive tense is used in the first two sentences?

　2　Why's this tense used?

　3　Why's the last sentence in the present perfect?

go to **language reference** *p.162 and p.163*

6 Complete the story using an active or passive form of these verbs.

injure	evacuate	spread
discover	bring	call out

A conservation area in the south has been badly damaged by forest fires. The fire brigade ¹ _____ this morning and people living in the surrounding area ² _____ immediately. The fire ³ _____ to Conway, an area of outstanding beauty much loved by walkers, but eventually it ⁴ _____ under control by a specialist team of fire fighters and nobody ⁵ _____. So far, the source of the fire ⁶ _____ not _____.

how to ...
be an ace reporter

vox pops

1 TV and radio reporters sometimes ask people for their reactions to events. Read the 'vox pops'. What topics do you think the reporter asked about?

2 It doesn't bother me actually – if people want to spend a fortune on a beautiful nose or perfect teeth, that's up to them. It's not really my business, is it?

1 Yeah, I feel quite strongly about that, actually. I think they should ban it in all public buildings – it's a disgusting habit anyway.

3 It's a difficult issue, really – I mean, on the one hand, we need more housing, but at the same time, I can see why people get upset about losing all our green spaces.

7 Work with a partner. Use the phrases in the **natural English** box to introduce and respond to these news stories.

examples **PRISONER RECAPTURED**

A I see that the escaped prisoner has been recaptured.

B Yes, that's right. **Apparently**, he was stopped at the station.

Art gallery destroyed

CITY CENTRE EVACUATED

MILLIONAIRE KIDNAPPED

GOVERNMENT BUILDING DAMAGED

your own story

extended speaking
Learn these phrases for later
The prisoner has been recaptured.
He was arrested earlier today.
The house was badly damaged.
Several people have been injured.

2 🔊 6.5 Listen to the vox pops. Were you right?

3 Listen again. Which phrases in the **natural English** box below does the reporter use, and in which order?

grammar indirect questions

1 Read the direct questions, then look at the tapescript on *p.22* of the **listening booklet**. Write down how the reporter asks the questions in an indirect way.

direct questions	indirect questions
How do you feel about the proposed ban?	
What do you think about people who have cosmetic surgery?	
Are you worried about the amount of housing available?	

2 With a partner, answer the questions.

1 What changes are there from direct questions to indirect questions? What has been added or removed?

2 Which questions sound more polite: direct or indirect ones?

3 Transform these direct questions into indirect questions.

1 What do you feel about free school meals for young children?
I'd like to know _____ .

2 What do you think about football hooligans?
Could you tell me _____ ?

3 Do you agree with random drug testing for car drivers?
Could I ask you _____ ?

4 Are you concerned about genetically modified food?
I'd be interested to know _____ .

4 Ask and answer with a partner, using the indirect questions.

go to **language reference** *p.163*

vocabulary expressing opinions and interest

1 Divide sentences 1 to 9 into these three groups:

strong opinions   'sitting on the fence'   lack of interest

1 I feel quite <u>strongly</u> about that.
2 I can see <u>both</u> <u>sides</u>.
3 I'm very much a<u>gainst</u> it.
4 It doesn't <u>bother</u> me <u>that</u> <u>much</u>.
5 I <u>would</u>n't like to <u>say</u>.
6 I'm not really <u>bothered</u>, to be <u>honest</u>.
7 I'm not all that <u>inter</u>ested in it.
8 I'm not at <u>all</u> in <u>fa</u>vour of it.
9 There's no easy <u>ans</u>wer to that.

2 Say the sentences, stressing the underlined words / syllables.

OPEN 24-7
ARMY BOARDING SCHOOL

it's your turn!

1 Work with a partner. You're going to collect five vox pops from your classmates. Choose one topic together.

– military service for women
– shops opening 24 hours a day
– footballers being paid so much money
– boarding schools (where children study and live away from home)

your own topic

2 Split up and interview five different classmates each. Use this framework:

– request someone's attention
– ask your question
– listen and note the answer
– thank them

3 Compare your interviews with your partner. Make a poster. Write your question and choose three or four of the answers.

4 Show your poster to the class. Vote for the most interesting one.

🔵 extended speaking

Learn these phrases for later
Could you tell me what you feel about ...?
I'd like to know if you agree with ...
I feel quite strongly about that.
It doesn't bother me that much.

extended speaking

you're going to:

collect ideas
listen to some local news reports from the *one o'clock news*

update the stories
develop two stories for the *six o'clock news*

prepare a bulletin
write out the two updated news stories

read the news
follow some expert advice and read your news stories to the class

role play
conduct vox pops on issues related to your news stories

but first ...
Look back at the **extended speaking** boxes in this unit. You can use this language in the activity.

 collect ideas

1   In small groups, look at the pictures from three news stories. What do you think they're about?

2   Listen to the *one o'clock news*. Make notes in the table. **6.6** Were your predictions about the pictures correct?

story 1	story 2	story 3
Who?	Who?	What's happened?
What's happened?	What's happened?	Where?
What's the situation now?	What's going to happen?	Why?

3   The newsreader made six changes to her stories as she was presenting the news. Look at the tapescript in the **listening booklet** on *p.22*. Listen to the *one o'clock news* again and find the differences.

natural English
passives in news reporting

News reports often use the verbs *know*, *believe*, *say*, and *think* in these patterns:

He's known to be dangerous.   **It's thought that** the children are safe.
She's believed to be in the States.   **It's said that** he has several wives.

Transform these sentences from active to passive, using the patterns above.

1   People say she's very rich.   She _____.
2   People think the children are out of control.   It _____.
3   People know she's very mean.   She _____.
4   People believe that the President is unwell.   The President _____.

update the stories

4 **Think!** Decide how <u>one</u> of the three stories could develop. Use the questions below to help you, but don't write yet.

5 Compare your ideas with a partner who chose a different story.

STORY ONE

- Has anyone seen these men?

- Do you know where they are now?

- Have the police caught them?

- Do you have any more information?

STORY TWO

- Do you know why Walker was arrested?

- Have Canfield Football Club made a statement?
  If so, what did they say?

- Do you have any more hard facts about the rumours?

STORY THREE

- Do you know why the explosion happened?

- Was anybody killed or injured?

- What damage was caused?

- Do you have any more information?

prepare a bulletin

6 Read the checklist. With your partner, write the updated bulletin for the *six o'clock news*.

checklist

- Decide which story is now the most important and should come first.
- You need to make changes to both stories, but some will change more than others, and you can still repeat some of the language from the earlier news broadcast. Look at the tapescript on *p.22* of the listening booklet to help you.
- If you like, you can add breaking news about a new story.
- Write the stories together.
- Edit your stories at the end.

read the news

7 Read the quotes from professional newsreaders and tick ✓ the most useful information. With a partner, practise reading your stories. Try to suggest improvements.

> **❝** I read it through first and think where I'm going to pause: between sentences, and sometimes in the sentences themselves. I often mark the pauses on the script. **❞**

> **❝** A good newsreader spends a lot of time going over the news again and again – if you're well-informed about the story, it makes a difference. **❞**

> **❝** You've got to practise: it takes time to do it well. You need to take a deep breath before each story or each long sentence. Don't let people hear that, though! **❞**

> **❝** It's only human to make mistakes when you read the news. Don't worry! The listeners don't mind the occasional mistake. **❞**

> **❝** If I don't know how to pronounce something, like someone's name or a place, I ask an expert. **❞**

8 Read your stories to the rest of the class.

9 Which stories were the most interesting and well-delivered?

10 (6.7) Listen to the *six o'clock news* update. How are these stories different from yours?

role play

11 Imagine you and your partner are reporters. Think of an issue relating to your news broadcast. Collect three or four vox pops from members of the public.

possible issues

- Should prisons be close to residential areas?
- Should parents be sent to prison for leaving children at home alone?
- What should happen to sportsmen and women who accept bribes to change the result of a game?

your own ideas

---

worries

life with Agrippine

in groups ...

What kind of things do parents worry about when their children are ...

| babies? | about seven? | teenagers? |

What worries do you have, if any, about your parents?

cartoon time

Read the cartoon. Have you had similar arguments in your family about going out in the evening?

 7.1 Listen and follow the cartoon. Then test your partner on the glossary words.

natural English
what / how / where on earth ...?

In spoken English, you can use *wh / how* questions + *on earth ...?* to express surprise or anger.

Where on earth have you been?   **What on earth** are you doing?
Why on earth did she leave him?   **Who on earth** made that mess?

You can also use *what / where / how the hell ...?* but it's stronger.

be worried sick be very worried

be supposed to /sə'pəʊzd tə/ be expected to (see **language reference** *p.164*)

hitchhike /'hɪtʃhaɪk/ get a free ride in a car from a stranger

get mugged /mʌgd/ be attacked in public and have money / valuables stolen

have a go at sb Ⓢ criticize sb or complain about sth

in unit seven ...
tick ✓ when you know this

natural English
what / how / where on earth ...? ☐
degrees of willingness ☐
that appeals to me ☐
putting people at ease ☐
linking reasons together ☐
ending an interview ☐

grammar
present perfect and past simple ☐
do, will, or *would* ☐

vocabulary
voluntary work ☐
success and failure ☐

wordbooster
conservation ☐
uncountable and plural nouns ☐

reading
caring for others

lead-in

1 Ask your partner these questions.

1 If you're feeling ill, who looks after you?

2 Are you a good patient, or a difficult one?

3 Who do <u>you</u> look after when they're ill?

2 **Think!** Which of these would you be prepared to do in your free time? Put a tick ✓, a cross ✗, or 'maybe'.

– Help a child who has problems with reading.

– Take an elderly person's dog for a walk two or three times a week.

– Give up a weekend to clear waste land which will be used for a children's playground.

– Take a small group of teenagers camping for a weekend.

– Babysit three small, noisy children regularly for a neighbour.

grammar present perfect and past simple

1 Choose the correct form. In one sentence, both forms are correct.

1 To be honest, I never did / I've never done anything like that before.

2 As a matter of fact, I just did / I've just done something like that.

3 I didn't do / I haven't done that sort of thing recently.

4 Actually, I've done / I've been doing that sort of thing before.

5 In fact, I've been doing / I've done that for years.

6 When I was younger, I've always wanted / I always wanted to do that.

7 Ever since I was a child, I've always hated / I always hated that sort of thing.

8 I did / 've done that as a kid, but I didn't do / I haven't done anything like that lately.

2 Explain your answers to a partner.

go to **language reference** *p.164 to p.166*

---

natural English
degrees of willingness

I'd be willing / prepared to do that.	**I'd be (a bit) reluctant** /rɪˈlʌktənt/ **to** do that.
I wouldn't mind doing that.	**I'd find it (a bit) hard to** do that.

Which responses are positive and which are negative? Practise saying the phrases.

---

3 Tell your partner what you'd do in **lead-in exercise 2**, and say why.

examples I'd be willing to help a child to read – it would be fun.

I'd find it hard to look after small children. I've always hated that kind of thing.

4 Listen to three people talking about the same topics. Complete the table.

	topic	willing to do it?	why? / why not?
Gareth	1 help a child to read		
	2		
DeNica	1		
	2		
Derek	1		

read on

1 English teacher Liz Inman was ill while working in China. Read her story and match the words and definitions in the glossary.

2 Match these headings with the paragraphs in the article.

taking care of my diet

providing physical help

life in a typical hospital

emotional support

how I ended up in hospital

3 What do you think of her students? Tell a partner.

4 With your partner, try to remember five duties the students performed. Then check your answers in the article.

5 Think of three other ways of helping somebody who is ill.

example doing their shopping for them

6 In what ways are hospitals in your country similar or different? Tell a partner.

it's your turn!

1 Write down the names of two people you know:

a relative _____
a colleague or classmate _____

2 Work with a partner. Imagine those people were ill. Talk about the duties you would perform.

examples Would you be willing to cook for your grandmother?

Would you be prepared to cook for your boss?

🔊 extended speaking

Learn these phrases for later
I've always loved that sort of thing.
I haven't done anything like that lately.
I'd be very willing to do that.
I wouldn't mind doing that.

caring students watch over teacher

 It was the end of my first term teaching English at Lanzhou University in China and I was looking forward to a winter break in Shanghai where it was warmer. Three days before departure, however, I spent a bad night alternately **shivering** and **sweating**, and finally I called a doctor. He diagnosed pneumonia, so that put an end to my travel plans, and instead I spent just over a week in a small three-bed **ward** in the university hospital.

 Nursing in China does not include personal care. Injections, intravenous drips, and medicines are administered by the nurses, and doctors check progress as in western countries. But food, washing, **laundry**, and night attendance must all be taken care of by the patients' relatives or friends. In fact, the medical care I received was competent, thorough and – once the staff became used to the presence of a foreigner – friendly.

 Although it was the exam period for the students, as soon as they were informed I was ill, they all came to visit me. Food appeared from all sides. Local students' parents cooked dishes for me; students delivered dishes of pears or delicious soups cooked in their dormitories over spirit stoves, or in one case in the chemistry laboratory. When I mentioned that I fancied some locally-made drinking yoghurt, 20 bottles appeared.

4 One of my second year students organized a rota of attendance at my bedside, including two or three students sleeping in the spare beds in my ward. For the whole time I was in hospital, I was only alone for two hours. The students would not let me do a thing, and someone always escorted me to the toilet. If I coughed at night, my 'minders' immediately woke up and came to make sure I was OK. It was all very gentle and loving. They filled bowls with boiled water so I could wash, and even washed my feet for me at night. One student painstakingly washed my long, thick hair in only two bowls of water.

5 My visitors all came prepared to cheer me up and help me make the best of things. Student after student expressed the view that since I should not travel, I could participate in the Chinese Spring Festival with a Chinese family. What an opportunity! I **was** also very **touched** by the way in which students, with so few resources at their disposal, thought of ways to amuse me. I hope that I've been able to give something back to them during this period. Of course, when I thank them, they merely reply, 'It is our duty'.

glossary			
1	**shiver** (para 1)	a	hospital room with beds for patients
2	**sweat** /swet/ (para 1)	b	feel grateful because of sb's kind actions
3	**ward** (para 1)	c	shake because of cold, or illness
4	**laundry** /ˈlɔːndri/ (para 2)	d	lose water from your body through your skin
5	**be touched** (para 5)	e	washing and ironing clothes, bedding, etc.

listening
was it successful?

vocabulary voluntary work

1 Complete the text using the correct form of these words.

volunteer /ˌvɒlənˈtɪə/	voluntary /ˈvɒləntri/	fund-raising
charity /ˈtʃærəti/	prize /praɪz/	the disabled /dɪsˈeɪbld/
raise (v)	donate (v)	conservation

Worldwide _charity_ organizations such as the *Red Cross* and *Oxfam* spend their time trying to ¹ _____ money to help the victims of war and natural disasters. Money is often collected by ² _____ who give up their time for nothing. However, there are thousands of smaller ³ _____ groups, often in local communities, who organize ⁴ _____ events such as music festivals, sponsored walks, or lotteries with attractive ⁵ _____ . The proceeds from these events are then ⁶ _____ to various projects: for instance, wildlife ⁷ _____ , or providing free local transport for ⁸ _____ .

2 Practise your pronunciation. Read the text aloud with a partner.

lead-in

1 **Think!** Have you ever raised money for charity? If so, which one, and how? If not, what kind of charity would you support?

2 Compare your ideas with a partner.

3 A local charity is planning a small event. Discuss the questions, using phrases from the **natural English** box.

  1 Which prizes below would appeal to most people?

  2 Which ones appeal to you, and why?

  – free car hire for a week (to be taken within a three-month period)
  – six free meals at a local restaurant (to be taken within a three-month period)
  – four free visits to a hairdresser
  – a chance to be interviewed about your hobby by a local radio station
  – a course of instruction in water-skiing
  – six free driving lessons

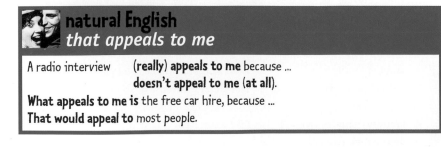
natural English
that appeals to me

A radio interview	**(really) appeals to me** because …
	doesn't appeal to me (at all).
What appeals to me is the free car hire, because …
That would appeal to most people.

listen to this

tune in

1 🔊 7.3 Listen to **part 1** of the conversation. What charity event does the man describe? What was the aim of it?

listen carefully

2 Listen to the whole conversation. What is the significance of 1 to 5 in the story?

  1 the marquee (tent)
  2 the lights and equipment
  3 the DJ
  4 the young people
  5 the older people

listening challenge

3 🔊 7.4 Listen to another man describing an event. What was it, and was it successful? What happened at the end? Tell a partner.

4 Do you think the events described would work well in your country? What would make them more successful?

listening booklet *p.24 to p.26 for tapescripts and exercises*

vocabulary success and failure

1 Think! Read the questionnaire, choose the correct words in **bold**, and answer the questions.

would you make a good **fund-raiser**?

1 You've organized a large event to raise money. If it fails, your charity will lose a great deal of money. Are you good at **coping / managing** with this kind of pressure?

2 You've invited a famous person to start a sponsored walk you've organized. The day before the event your secretary tells you the celebrity has decided not to come because they are too busy. How would you **handle / solve** this situation?

3 You and your friends organize a street party or carnival to raise money for a local park. Unfortunately, you only manage to sell 40 advance tickets and it looks as though the event is going to be a **fail / fiasco**. What would you do?

4 Your class decides to organize a lottery in your school to raise money for a children's charity. Do you think you could **do / make** a success of it? Why / why not?

5 A charity you support needs $5,000 to **realize / achieve** their target. What kind of local event could raise this much money?

6 In your opinion, what are the most important qualities you need to **succeed / success** as a fund-raiser?

2 In groups, compare your answers and ideas.

🗣 extended speaking

Learn these phrases for later
What appeals to me is …
I've done some voluntary work before.
I think I could cope with that.
I'd be able to handle that.

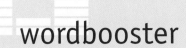

wordbooster

conservation

1 Match the words in bold in the texts with these words / phrases.

endangered species /ˈspiːʃiːz/	captivity	feed	dug up /dʌg ˈʌp/
buried /ˈberɪd/	site /saɪt/	the wild	breeding
reptiles /ˈreptaɪlz/	remains		

2 In A / B pairs, A shut your book and B read one text aloud. Pause after the phrases in bold and ask A to replace them with words / phrases from exercise 1. Then swap roles.

It's true that zoos keep animals in ¹**cages or enclosures**, but one reason for this is that they want to help ²**animals that soon may no longer exist**, and many have ³**reproduction** programmes to increase numbers. In some cases they can then return animals to ⁴**free and natural conditions**.

Some zoos specialize in ⁵**snakes, lizards, crocodiles, etc.** and it's particularly important that the public do not ⁶**give food to** these animals as they have very special diets.

Archaeologists have ⁷**excavated** part of a medieval village. They've discovered many things that were ⁸**hidden in the ground**, including 9th century ⁹**ruins**, which could become a major historic ¹⁰**place**.

uncountable and plural nouns

1 Correct any mistakes in these sentences. (Some are correct.)

1 His knowledge of the topic are limited.

2 Has she got enough work experiences?

3 We always give the proceeds to charity.

4 They found the remains when they started digging.

5 We always provide a training for successful applicants.

6 We are doing more researches.

7 Did you make use of the facilities?

8 Everyone loved the accommodations.

9 The company will provide travel expenses.

10 Do they have the funds to buy the new equipments?

test your partner
– *His knowledge of the topic are limited.*
– *That's wrong. It should be 'is limited'.*

2 Organize the nouns in the sentences in exercise 1 into two lists, plural and uncountable. Add three more words to each list.

how to ...
have a successful interview

what <u>not</u> to say or do

Read what some interviewees did.
What do you think? Tell a partner.

In a survey, employers were asked about the most bizarre events that occurred during a job interview. Here are some of their answers:

1 The interviewee wore a Walkman, explaining that she could listen to the interviewer and the music at the same time.

2 The candidate announced she hadn't had lunch and proceeded to eat a hamburger and French-fries in the interviewer's office.

3 The applicant insisted on being interviewed standing up.

4 A job applicant challenged the interviewer to an arm wrestle.

5 The candidate explained that her long-term goal was to replace the interviewer.

6 The candidate asked whether the company would pay to relocate her horse.

7 The applicant interrupted the interview to phone her therapist for advice on how to answer specific interview questions.

8 The candidate brought a large dog to the interview.

greet and make small talk

1 Imagine you're going to interview a candidate for a job. What can you do to put them at ease? Tell a partner.

   example   greet them in a friendly way

2   Listen to the beginning of two interviews. Which interviewer is more welcoming?

3 Listen to the second interview again. Tick ✓ the phrases in the **natural English** box that you hear. They must be exactly the same.

> ### natural English
> ### putting people at ease
>
> | | |
> |---|---|
> | Hello, it's (Catherine Walker), isn't it? | Do have a seat. |
> | It's very nice to meet you. | Can I take your coat? |
> | Did you have any problems getting here? | Did you find us OK? |
>
> How could you reply to these phrases? Practise the phrases and your responses with a partner.

4 With a partner, turn to the tapescript in the **listening booklet** on *p.26* and practise the second conversation.

5 Do job interviews start like this in your country? If not, how are they different?

grammar *do, will,* or *would*

1 The interviewee is asking about the job. Look at *do / am, will,* and *would* in the questions.

   a Which form(s) sound(s) as if they have definitely not been offered the job yet?

   b Which form(s) sound(s) as if the person has already got the job?

Do	I have to work at the weekends?
Will	
Would	

Am I	expected to wear a uniform?
Will I be	
Would I be	

Do	I need to have any special training?
Will	
Would	

go to **language reference** *p.167*

2 Write down one similar question to ask in a first interview for each job below.

   – staff at the check-in desk at an airport
   – farm worker during the summer
   – waiter / waitress in a five-star hotel
   – entertainments manager on a cruise ship

sell yourself

1 **Think!** Choose one job from **grammar exercise 2**. Prepare three reasons why you're the right person for the job, using the phrases in the **natural English** box below.

> **natural English**
> **linking reasons together**
>
> **There are several reasons why** I'd like the job / I'd be good at the job.
> **First of all,** I've had experience in dealing with the public.
> **Secondly,** I'm very patient.
> **And another thing is that** I'm very fond of travelling.

2 Compare your ideas with your partner.

end the interview

> **natural English**
> **ending an interview**
> 7.6
>
> At the end of the interview, the interviewer should thank the candidate and tell them what will happen next.
>
> 1 **Thank you very much for coming.** ... **I'll let you know** as soon as possible.
> 2 **It was very nice meeting you.** ... **I'll be in touch** by the end of the week.
>
> Listen. Underline the stressed words. Practise the sentences. Practise the end of an interview with a partner, starting ...
>
> | Interviewer | Right. Do you have any further questions you want to ask? |
> | Interviewee | No, I don't think so. |

Work with a partner. Choose either A or B.

   A Write the beginning of an interview dialogue. Put the greetings, introductions, and the first question about the job.

   B Write the end of an interview dialogue. Write the final question from the interviewee and the answer, then the ending to the interview.

> 🙂 extended speaking
> **Learn these phrases for later**
> Did you have any problems getting here?
> Would I be expected to ...?
> There are several reasons why I'd like the job ...
> I'll be in touch ...

extended speaking

you're going to:

collect ideas
read adverts for voluntary work and prepare to be interviewed

first interview
have an interview for the job of your choice

second interview
interview a partner for a different job

evaluate
think about the performance of the interviewer and interviewee

but first ...
Look back at the **extended speaking** boxes in this unit. You can use this language in the activity.

 collect ideas

1   **Think!** Read the three adverts for voluntary work. Choose one that interests you.

2   Find someone who chose the same job. Together, write three reasons why you would be good at the job.

APPOINTMENTS VOLUNTEER WORK

 NATIONAL ARCHAEOLOGICAL SOCIETY

VOLUNTEERS WANTED

We're looking for weekend helpers to work over the summer period on a recently discovered historic site in the local area. You'll be part of a large team excavating the remains of a 1,000-year-old civilization.

No previous experience required. This project is being filmed as part of a TV documentary to be shown in the autumn.

All transport and meals provided.

Interested volunteers should e-mail us on: digsforfree@eserve.com

zooscape
children's zoo charity

Can you give up two weeks a month for the summer period?

As a member of a team in a local children's zoo, you'll be involved in caring for the birds, reptiles, and small mammals in the centre. You'll also be expected to help with educational visits for young children. The charity is also involved in important conservation projects. No previous experience is necessary.

Food and travel expenses provided.

For further information, please contact us at zooscape **on:** 5644 306 276

 **THE WINGED FELLOWSHIP TRUST**

HOLIDAY HELPERS NEEDED

Have you got a weekend to spare? We need volunteers to help out in centres where we offer **respite care** and holidays for people with physical disabilities. Your role will be to enhance the fun holiday atmosphere.

We welcome applicants of all ages over 16. Previous experience is not essential, and training will be provided.

Travel expenses, and board and lodgings are provided.

For further information please ring our volunteer department on: **0111 787 865**

glossary **respite** /ˈrespaɪt/ **care** looking after people who are disabled, elderly, etc. so that their usual carers can have a rest

first interview

3 Find a partner who chose a different job. Decide who will be the interviewer and the interviewee for the first interview.

Interviewer   Turn to the role cards on *p.148*.

Interviewee   Look at the role card below.

INTERVIEWEES

Be prepared to talk about the following:

- your reasons for wanting the job
- why you would be good at it
- any relevant experience you have

Look at the advertisement again. Think of two or three questions to ask the interviewer, e.g. about training.

---

checklist
- Begin the interview only when you're well prepared. Don't read from your role card; take in as much information as you can beforehand.
- Remember to make the volunteer feel at ease.
- Both the interviewer and the interviewee will sometimes have to answer a question they didn't expect. Be ready to invent a sensible answer.

4 Conduct the first interview.

---

 second interview

5 **Think!** Change role cards, and prepare your answers.

6 Conduct the second interview.

---

 evaluate

7 How did the interviews go? Discuss these questions.

As the interviewer …

- Did you relax the candidate?
- Did you succeed in making the candidate talk at length?
- Did you ask the right kind of questions, or were there other questions you could have asked?
- Did you end the interview clearly and effectively?
- Would you give the candidate the job?

As the interviewee …

- Do you think you showed the right attitude?
- Which questions did you answer clearly and well?
- Did you ask the right questions, or were there any other questions you wish you'd asked?
- Would you be happy to do the job? Why / why not?
- Do you think you'd get the job?

---

test yourself!

How well do you think you did the extended speaking? Mark the line.

0	10

From this unit, write down:

1 three plural nouns, e.g. *clothes*, and four uncountable nouns, e.g. *advice*.

2 five words or phrases to do with zoos / conservation.

3 three words or phrases to do with charity work, e.g. *raise money*.

Complete the sentences. The meaning must stay the same.

1 Where the hell have you been?
   Where on _____ ?

2 I'd be reluctant to do that.
   I wouldn't _____ .

3 I'll let you know as soon as possible.
   I'll be in _____ .

4 Did you find us OK?
   Did you have _____ ?

Correct the errors.

1 I wouldn't mind to work with snakes.

2 I didn't see her lately.

3 Do you think you can cope this job?

4 If they offered you the job, do you accept it?

Look back at the unit contents on *p.81*. Tick ✓ the language you can use confidently.

eight

snails for dinner

how to ... react to a joke

do you get it?

with a partner ...

In your family or circle of friends, who is usually late? Are <u>you</u> ever late for things? How do you feel about people being late?

joke time

Look at the pictures. Who are the people and what's happening in each one? What's going to happen next?

Listen and react to the joke. Did you get it?
Go to *p.28* of the listening booklet and listen again.

all over the ...

This means everywhere on a surface or in a place. Stressed words are underlined.

He dropped them **all over the floor**. (= everywhere on the floor)
People came to the concert from **all over the world / country**.
The documents were **all over the place**.

Where might you find these?

litter	fast food restaurants	an untidy person's clothes
graffiti	people who can speak English	

ways of walking

'Anyway, eventually he **staggers** out of the bar ... '
What do you think 'stagger' means? Use one of the verbs below to say how you would move if ...

1 you didn't want anyone to hear you.
2 you were out in the country having a nice, relaxed walk.
3 you were carrying something very heavy.
4 you had hurt your foot.
5 you couldn't walk.
6 you were on a military exercise.

stroll /strəʊl/	limp	stagger
crawl /krɔːl/	march	tiptoe

test your partner
– (do one of the actions)
– Yes!
– You're staggering across the room.

in unit eight ...
tick ✓ when you know this

natural English
all over the ... ☐
making threats ☐
apologies and excuses ☐
linking events in a sequence ☐
repeated comparatives ☐

grammar
verb patterns ☐
linking ideas ☐

vocabulary
ways of walking ☐
expressing anger ☐

wordbooster
neighbours ☐
word building ☐

91

listening
confrontation

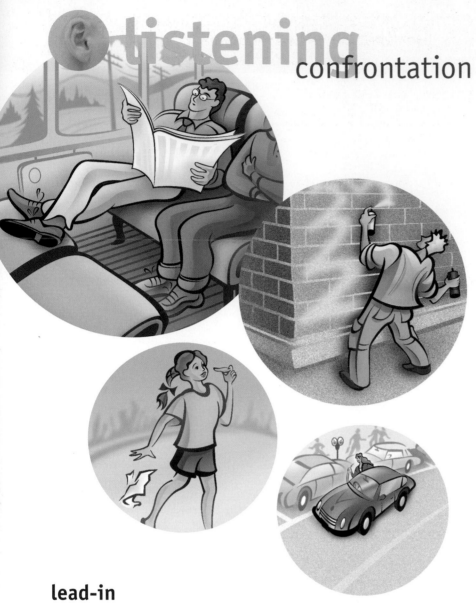

lead-in

1 Work with a partner and look at the pictures. What can you see?

2 With your partner, order the actions in the pictures from the most to the least annoying.

3 What would you say to these people? Tell another pair.

natural English
making threats 8.2

Put those apples back **or I'll** _____ ! (= if you don't put them back, I'll ...)
Tidy your room, **otherwise** /ˈʌðəwaɪz/ **I won't** _____ .

Listen and complete the sentences. Practise the intonation.

4 Use the phrases in the **natural English** box to tell the people in the pictures what to do.

vocabulary expressing anger

1 Match phrases 1 to 6 with responses a to f with a similar meaning. Put the ⊚ symbol next to the two most informal phrases.

1 Did you **get very angry**?
2 Did you **get your own back**?
3 Did you **quarrel** /ˈkwɒrəl/ **with** them?
4 Did you **shout abuse** /əˈbjuːs/?
5 Did you **control your temper**?
6 Did you **find it irritating**?

a Yes, I **swore** /swɔː/ at him.
b Yes, I **completely lost my temper**.
c Yes, it **got on my nerves**.
d Yes, I **got my revenge** /rɪˈvenʒ/.
e Yes, we **had a big row** /raʊ/.
f Yes, I managed to **keep calm**.

test your partner
– *Did you get very angry?*
– *Yes, I completely lost my temper.*

2 **Think!** In A / B pairs, cover the phrases in **exercise 1**. A fill the gaps in the A questions, and B in the B questions.

A Do you often _____ your temper?
What gets on your _____ ?
Do you ever _____ rows with your best friend?
Do you ever _____ at people when you're angry?

B When did you last _____ very angry?
Do you find it easy to _____ your temper when you're angry?
Do you like to _____ your own back if someone upsets you?
How often do you _____ with members of your family?

3 Check your phrases and ask your partner the questions.

listen to this

tune in

1 **8.3** Julia Weeks is preparing a radio report on anti-social behaviour. Listen to the beginning of her first interview. Where is she, and what's she waiting for?

listen carefully

2 Listen to the interviews and answer the questions.

first interviewee
1 What did she do wrong?
2 What was her excuse?
3 What action did she take?

second interviewees
1 What did they do wrong?
2 What action did they take?
3 What was their attitude?

listening challenge

3 **8.4** Listen to Julia confronting another person in the street. What did he do wrong? What's his excuse and attitude? Tell a partner.

4 **Think!** If you were stopped in these situations, what would you say and do? Do you ever confront people in situations like these?

5 Compare your answers with a partner.

> **listening booklet** *p.28 and p.29 for tapescripts and exercises*

natural English   apologies and excuses

I didn't intend to.
I'm sorry, I didn't mean to take it.
I'm really sorry, I didn't do it on purpose ...

I didn't know.
I'm so sorry, I didn't realize (that you couldn't park here).
I'm sorry, I wasn't aware /ə'weə/ **that** (it was private).

Practise saying the apologies and excuses with a partner.

6 **Think!** Invent apologies or excuses for these situations.

1 You knock a small statue off a coffee table in a friend's house.
2 At work, you go into your boss's office to make a phone call. In the middle of your call your boss comes back.
3 You're at a coffee machine, and you drop a cup of coffee. Some of it spills onto a colleague / classmate's shoes.
4 You're in a coffee bar and you pick up a newspaper. The person next to you says, 'Hey, that's my paper'.
5 You open a classroom door thinking it is empty; in fact, two people are having a private conversation in the room.

7 With a partner, make excuses and responses using phrases from the **natural English** box.

it's your turn!

1 You're going to do an interview similar to Julia Weeks's in **listen to this**. With your partner, invent a situation like the ones in the tapescript. Complete the table.

your situation
What was the situation? *e.g. someone smoking in a no smoking area*
Where did it take place? *e.g. railway station*
Possible excuse? *e.g. wasn't aware you couldn't smoke there*

2 Act out your situation. Then swap roles and repeat, but with a different excuse and attitude.

extended speaking

Learn these phrases for later
He completely lost his temper.   It got on their nerves.
They had a big row.   He decided to get his revenge.

reading too close for comfort

grammar verb patterns

1 Complete the sentences using the correct form of these verbs.

claim   suspect   deny   attempt   pretend   admit   threaten   resent

1 She _____ to be happy with the results, but I'm sure she was disappointed.

2 He _____ that he was a millionaire, but I don't believe him.

3 Eventually she _____ breaking the mirror.

4 She _____ that her colleague was telling stories about her behind her back, but she couldn't prove it.

5 He _____ stealing the money, but his fingerprints were all over his boss's desk.

6 He _____ doing all the work when it's his boss who gets all the credit.

7 All the climbers _____ to reach the summit but only two succeeded.

8 The bus drivers _____ to go on strike unless their conditions were improved.

2 With a partner, put these verbs in the correct column. Some can go in more than one.

promise   suggest   offer   claim   deny   pretend
agree   attempt   threaten   admit   suspect   resent

verb + (*not*) + infinitive	verb + (*that*) ...	verb + *-ing*
promise (*not*) *to do*	promise (*that*)	—
—	suggest (*that*)	suggest *-ing*

3 Think! Read this situation. What would you do?

> You share a flat with another person. One evening, a guy you met on holiday a few years ago knocks on your door. He's just arrived in town and is looking for somewhere to stay. You let him stay at your flat for a few days, and tell him to help himself to anything he needs. Unfortunately, however, he helps himself to huge quantities of food and drink. Money belonging to you and your flatmate starts to disappear as well.

4 Compare your ideas with a partner.

5 Complete options 1 to 8 in an appropriate way.

example   You suspect *that your flatmate has taken some money.*

1 You could pretend _____.

2 You could attempt _____.

3 He could claim _____.

4 He may deny _____.

5 He could offer _____.

6 He could promise _____.

7 He could agree _____.

8 You could threaten _____.

go to **language reference** *p.167 and p.168*

read on

1 **Think!** Prepare your answers.

   1 Who would you most like to share a flat with? Why?

   2 Who would you <u>not</u> like to share with? Why?

2 Compare your ideas with a partner.

3 Read Michelle's story and complete the glossary.

4 With a partner, decide which of Sophie's actions are harmless, and which would worry you.

5 Write *Sophie* or *Michelle* in the gaps.

   1 _____ invited _____ to move in with her.

   2 _____ was worried because _____ refused to compromise about the decorating.

   3 _____ started getting nosy and interfering in her flatmate's life.

   4 _____ tried to ruin _____'s dress in the washing machine.

   5 _____ found washing-up liquid in the food.

   6 _____'s friends were told that she had lots of boyfriends.

   7 _____ moved out.

   8 _____ probably made _____ jealous of her.

---

linking events in a sequence

When you want to link a series of bad events in a story to show how a situation got worse and worse, you can use these phrases:

At first …
As time went by (however,) …
The situation deteriorated (when) …
Things got much worse (when) …
Eventually, things came to a head (when) …

Find words / phrases in the text with the same meaning as the phrases above.

SINGLEWHITEFEMALE

AS IN THE MOVIE STARRING BRIDGET FONDA, MICHELLE BAKER, 35, FOUND HERSELF SHARING WITH THE FLATMATE FROM HELL.

"When I moved into a two-bedroom flat with Sophie, I imagined we'd
05 get on really well. I couldn't afford the place by myself, but after meeting Sophie at a local wine bar, I thought she seemed quite a nice person to join me.

I had my first **doubts** about her the
10 day we went to choose paint to **do up** the flat. I wanted bright colours, but she insisted on very plain shades and wasn't prepared to compromise at all. I thought: 'What am I getting myself
15 into?' Unfortunately we had already signed the contract by then, so it was too late to **pull out**.

Initially, everything else seemed fine. Then as the weeks passed, things
20 began to change. When I went out, she'd ask me why I was wearing so much make-up, or she'd want to know where I was going or where I'd been. Gradually, I began to realize that she
25 was jealous of me and my social life.

However, when I bought a new white dress, things took a turn for the worse. I was just about to put the dress in the washing machine when I noticed a
30 **speck** of orange. I put my hand into the machine and a whole load of orange **turmeric** powder fell out. It would have ruined my dress. I suspected that

Sophie had done it. When I confronted
35 her, she denied it, but I was so angry I even threatened to call the police.

Another night I came in and found a curry that Sophie had made, so I thought I'd taste it. After one mouthful
40 I realized it had washing-up liquid in it. It made me terribly ill.

Things went from bad to worse. I had a large collection of framed family photos which were very important to
45 me. I came home one day and found all the pictures had been turned upside down. When I asked Sophie who had done it, she claimed that it was nothing to do with her and just
50 shouted abuse at me.

It was the last straw, however, when she started spreading rumours; she told my friends, including my boyfriend, that I was going out with
55 other boys, which just wasn't true. But eventually, I began to lose confidence and after almost a year of this I had to move out. **In retrospect**, I think she wanted to be like me, but when that
60 proved impossible, she tried to make my life hell. She nearly did, too. I have never bumped into her again and, to be honest, I'd be horrified if I did. "

---

glossary

Match the words and definitions.

1	**doubt** /daʊt/	a	thinking back to the past
2	**do up**	b	powder which gives colour / flavour to food
3	**pull out**	c	decorate
4	**speck**	d	uncertainty
5	**turmeric** /ˈtɜːmərɪk/	e	get out of a situation / agreement
6	**in retrospect**	f	very small mark / piece of sth

it's your turn!

Bridget Fonda and Jennifer Jason Leigh in *Single White Female*

1 With a partner, choose two famous people and imagine they decide to share a flat. Invent a story about their relationship which starts well, but gets worse.

Use linking phrases from the **natural English** box or the article, like this:

_____ and _____ decided to rent a flat together. **Initially**, they got on very well, and _____ was a great cook, which _____ appreciated. **As time went by, however**, …

2 With a new partner, tell your story. Are they similar? Are they believable?

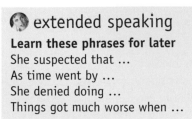

extended speaking

Learn these phrases for later
She suspected that …
As time went by …
She denied doing …
Things got much worse when …

wordbooster

neighbours

1 Complete the phrases with an appropriate word. Sometimes, there's more than one answer.

opposite	penthouse	down	corridor	across	next
upstairs	basement	door	downstairs	top flat	

1 my neighbour _____ the road
2 my _____ door neighbour
3 the person in the flat _____
4 the person across the _____ from me
5 the person in the flat _____ me
6 the person next _____ but one
7 the person in the _____

2 Work with a partner. Ask and answer about the people in the picture using phrases from exercise 1.

example   **A**   Who's Carlo?
   B   He's my next-door neighbour.

3 Draw a plan of your block of flats / neighbourhood. Write the names of a few neighbours. Tell your partner about them, giving a little extra information.

example
OK, My next door neighbour is Mr Villa, and he's an old friend of ours. The people in the flat opposite are very strange and never speak to us.

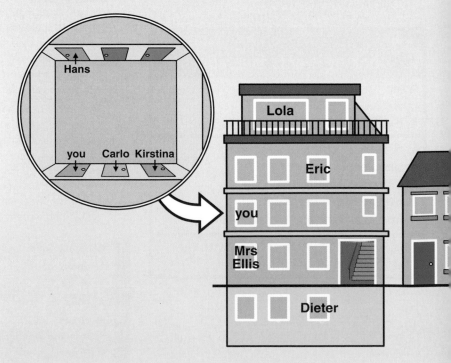

word building

You can expand your range of expression quickly by learning the other parts of a word family.

example   Did they **solve** the problem?
Yes, they found a **solution**.

Complete the dialogues with nouns formed from the verbs in bold.

1 A Did they **complain**?
   B Yes, somebody made a _____ .

2 A Didn't they **behave** well?
   B No, their _____ was terrible.

3 A Can they **prove** it?
   B No, they haven't got any _____ .

4 A Has his condition **deteriorated**?
   B No, there's been no _____ .

5 A Did they **threaten** anybody?
   B Yes, there were several _____ .

6 A Are they willing to **compromise**?
   B No, they can't reach any _____ .

7 A Do they **suspect** your neighbour?
   B Yes, there's a _____ it was him.

8 A Did you **remind** him?
   B Yes, I gave him a _____ .

test your partner

– *Did they complain?*

– *Yes, somebody made a complaint.*

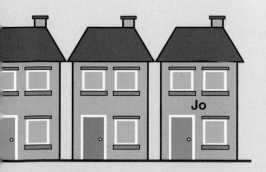

how to ...
write a letter of complaint

style and layout of a formal letter

1 **Think!** You want to write a letter of complaint to a travel company. Which approach is more effective: A or B?

A Show how angry you are in the letter.
   Give as much detail as possible.
   Describe how the problems of the journey affected you personally.
   Demand that they take particular action.

B Be polite in the letter.
   Keep to the main facts about what went wrong.
   Avoid mentioning how the problems affected you personally.
   Say what you would like to happen next.

2 Compare your ideas with a partner, giving your reasons.

3 Read the letter. Is it effective?
Why / why not?

4 With a partner, answer the questions.

1 Where is the sender's address and date?

2 What is on the left-hand side above the greeting?

3 Why does the greeting say 'Sir or Madam'?

4 Why does the writer end 'Yours faithfully' and not 'Yours sincerely'?

5 What information is in each of the first three paragraphs?

6 In what way are letters like this similar or different in your language?

natural English
repeated comparatives

You can use these with *get* and *become* to emphasize that something is increasing.

Football is **getting more and more popular**.
  (= increasingly popular)
The noise **became louder and louder**.
The problems with the rubbish **got worse and worse** as time went by.

Find an example of this structure in the letter. Then complete the sentences using the structure.

The roads are getting _____ .
Fashion _____ .
Trains _____ .
Television _____ .

28 Maldon Rd
Glasgow GS3 2DP
Tel: 0141 236 4982

12 July

Customer Services
Silverline Ltd
Petersham House
London WC1 6DR

Dear Sir or Madam,

Last Thursday, I travelled on the 8.40 a.m. train from Glasgow to London King's Cross and I was very unhappy with the service provided by your company.

The train was forty minutes late leaving Glasgow, and although the guard apologized, we were not given a satisfactory reason for the delay. We then had further delays when the train crew changed at Preston and had to wait another thirty minutes. As a result, I missed my flight from London Heathrow to Frankfurt and had to wait for several hours.

The service on the train was also very poor. Despite the fact that the journey takes over five hours, there was no restaurant car on the train and only a bar with poor quality snacks. Worst of all, the air conditioning broke down half-way through the journey and the carriages just got hotter and hotter. However, there was no apology for this, and by the time we reached King's Cross, the temperature was unbearable.

In view of the poor service, I feel I am entitled to compensation.

I look forward to hearing from you.

Yours faithfully,

David Robertson

grammar linking ideas

Certain link words / phrases show a contrast:

within one sentence
He won the match **in spite of the fact that** he was injured.

between two sentences
We know the children are safe there.
Nevertheless, we still worry about them.

1 Underline three more link words / phrases in the letter that show a contrast.

2 Fill the gaps using *although, however, nevertheless, despite,* or *in spite of.*

  1 _____ the fact that I complained about the service, it didn't improve.

  2 _____ we got on the train early, we still couldn't find a seat.

  3 The train service has been bad for years. _____ , people still have to use it.

  4 The train was on time _____ the terrible weather.

  5 The first class carriage was very comfortable, _____ it was incredibly expensive.

  6 _____ booking a month in advance, I still couldn't get the seats I wanted.

3 Complete the table using the link words / phrases in **exercise 2**.

within one sentence
_____ it was very cold, we went out.
_____ the fact that it was very cold, we went out.
_____ feeling very cold, we went out.
_____ the cold (noun), we went out.

between two sentences
It was very cold. _____ , we went out.

go to **language reference** *p.168*

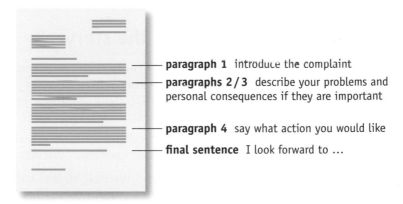

write a letter

1 Work with a partner. You're going to write a letter of complaint to an airline or a hotel. Decide together, and make notes on three things you were dissatisfied with.

2 Organize your ideas for your letter, as in the model.

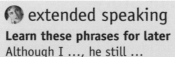

paragraph 1 introduce the complaint
paragraphs 2 / 3 describe your problems and personal consequences if they are important
paragraph 4 say what action you would like
final sentence I look forward to ...

3 On your own or with your partner, write your letter.

4 Look back at **how to ... write and edit e-mails,** on *p.51*. Then with your partner, see if you can improve your letter.

5 Exchange your letter with another pair who chose a different topic.

🎧 extended speaking

Learn these phrases for later

Although I ..., he still ...   They kept having parties, despite ...
The situation got more and more ...   Everything seemed OK. However, ...

extended speaking
nasty neighbours

you're going to:

collect ideas
read an episode from a new TV series about problems between neighbours and decide on a conclusion

develop the story
plan the next episode around a different set of neighbours and problems

tell your story
tell your story and decide which group has planned the best episode

write your story
use the model in **collect ideas** to write your episode

but first ...
Look back at the **extended speaking** boxes in this unit. You can use this language in the activity.

 ## collect ideas

1 Read the story below, then tell a partner what you know about ...

– the Carters.
– Paul Beck.
– the reasons for the conflict.

2 In small groups, decide how the episode ends. Then tell the class.

3 **8.5** Listen to the ending. Is it similar to yours?

 # nasty neighbours

Eve and David Carter had been living in a quiet area on the edge of town for several years when **Paul Beck** moved from the city and bought the house next door to them. At first, they seemed to get on quite well, until the Carters' cat came in one day with a nasty injury. Although he didn't see the incident, Carter believed Beck's dogs were responsible, and spoke to him about it. Beck was furious to be accused of this without any evidence.

As the weeks passed, the relationship between the neighbours began to deteriorate after repeated complaints by Carter about Beck's noisy dogs. Things got much worse when Beck bought himself a big, old van and several motorbikes and kept them in his front garden. When Carter complained that it looked very ugly, Beck just laughed and refused to do anything about it. Eventually things came to a head when Beck started doing car repairs and revving up the engine late at night. This time, Carter threatened to go to the police. Beck just lost his temper ...

 ## develop the story

4 In your groups, you're going to invent another *Nasty Neighbours* story with a new set of neighbours, and a different dispute. First, think of two more causes of disputes.

examples people leaving litter outside their house
neighbours parking obstructively

5 In groups, choose two neighbours from the photos. Decide who they are and where they live.

6 Develop your story around the framework on the right. Make notes but don't write the story in full.

7 Practise telling your story together.

STORY FRAMEWORK

Who was living there first?

Who moved in?

How did they get on initially?

What event or incident caused the first problem?

What other incidents caused the relationship to deteriorate?

What was the climax to the events?

How did the dispute end, and how do the neighbours feel about it now?

 ## tell your story

8 Find a partner from a different group and tell them your story. At the end, decide which would make the best episode for a TV series.

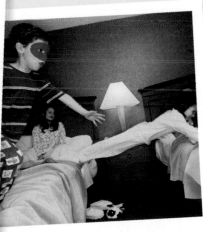

write your story

9 In your own time, write your episode, using the story about the Carters and Beck as a model.

book signing

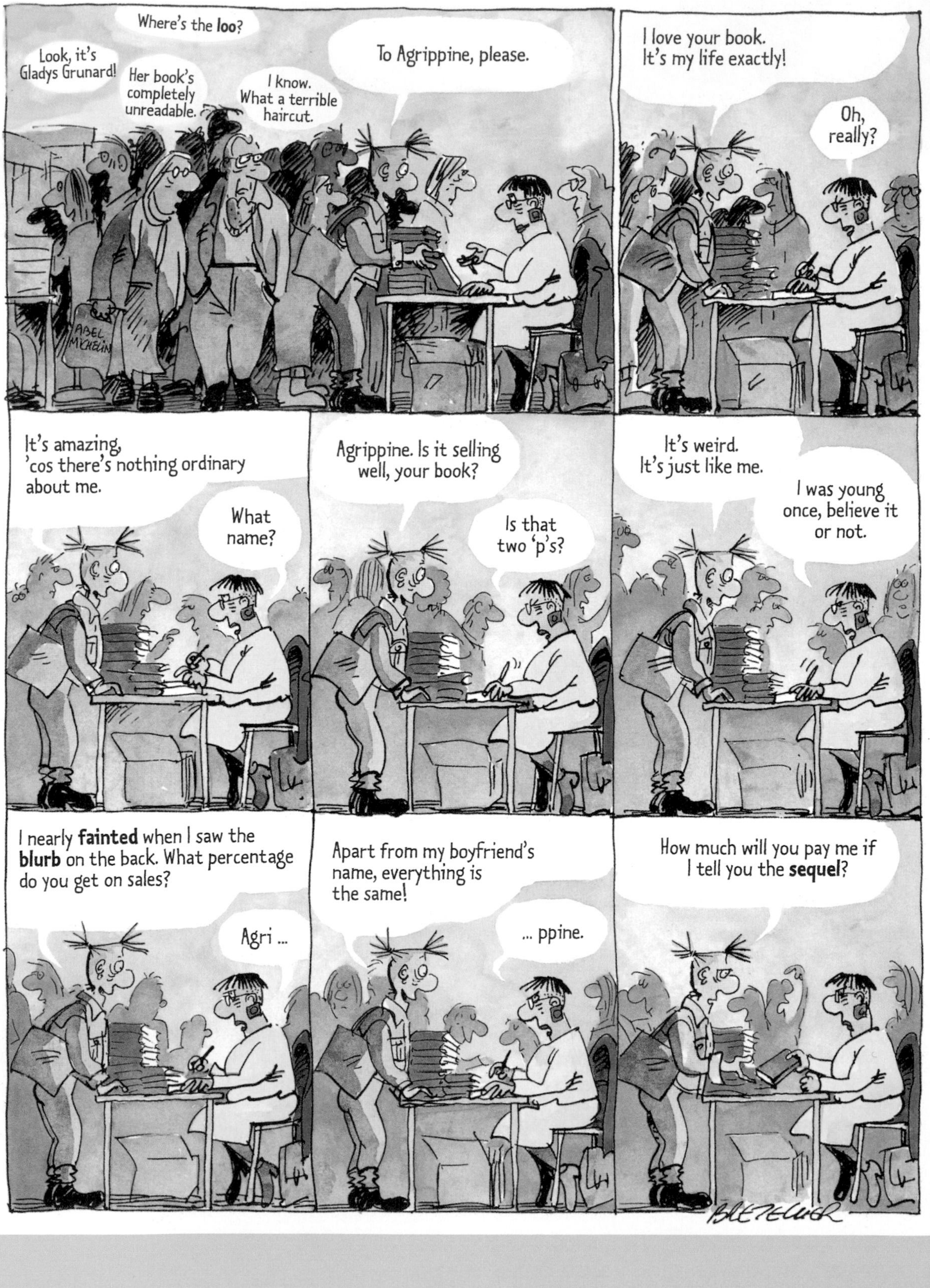

life with Agrippine

in groups ...

Do you have booksignings in your country? Have you ever been to one, or been given a signed book as a present?

cartoon time

Read the cartoon about a writer signing her latest novel in a bookshop. Why does Agrippine ask a lot of questions? Why does the writer say very little?

 Listen and follow the cartoon. Then test your partner on the glossary words.

natural English
expressing great surprise

These phrases are used figuratively when you're telling a story:

I nearly	fainted.	I couldn't believe my eyes/ears!
	died.	I couldn't believe it!

Listen. In each phrase, underline the main stress. Practise saying the phrases.

books and publishing

Answer the questions about <u>this</u> book.

1 What is the title and who is it published by?
2 When did it come out?
3 Is it a hardback or a softback?
4 What's on the front cover and the back cover?
5 Is there an index or a contents page?
6 How many copies are there in your class altogether?

glossary

loo ⑥ toilet

faint (v) lose consciousness

blurb /blɜːb/ description/information on the back cover of the book

sequel /ˈsiːkwəl/ book or film that continues the story of an earlier one

in unit nine ...
tick ✓ when you know this

natural English
expressing great surprise ☐
whenever, wherever, etc. ☐
reacting to ideas ☐
the + comparative, *the* + comparative ☐
superlative + *ever* ☐

grammar
making comparisons ☐
linking words ☐

vocabulary
books and publishing ☐
advertising ☐

wordbooster
literal and figurative meaning ☐
affixes ☐

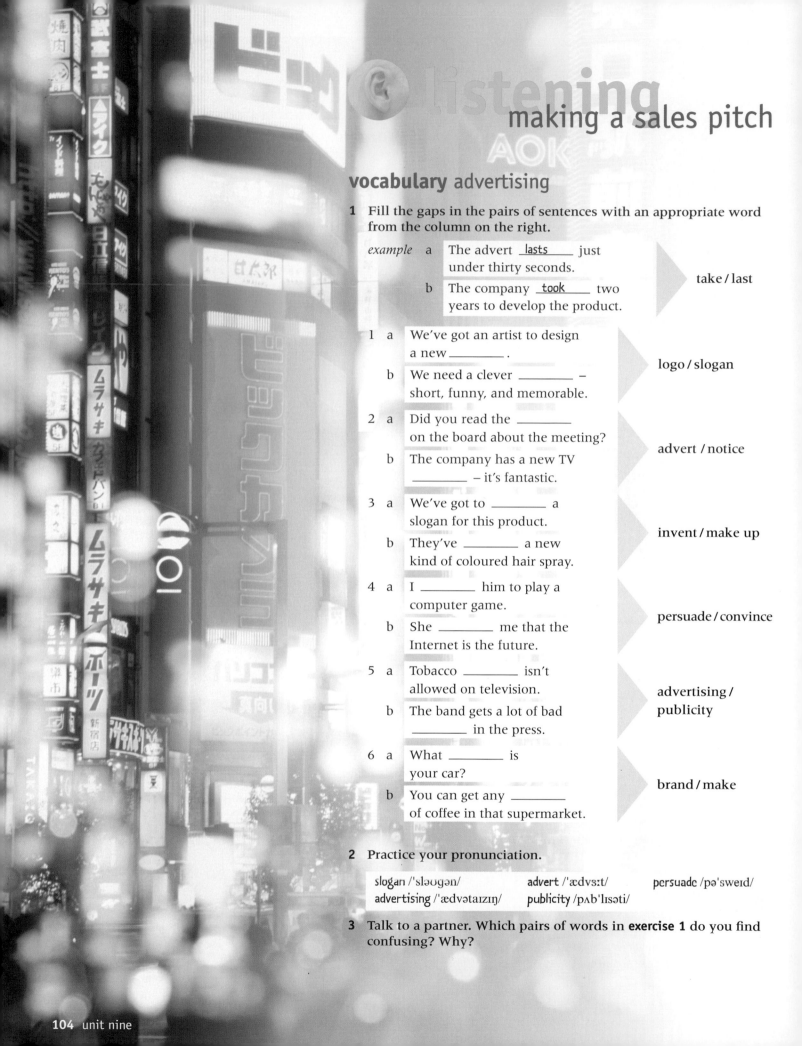

listening
making a sales pitch

vocabulary advertising

1 Fill the gaps in the pairs of sentences with an appropriate word from the column on the right.

example   a   The advert <u>lasts</u> just under thirty seconds.

   b   The company <u>took</u> two years to develop the product.

▷ **take / last**

1   a   We've got an artist to design a new _____ .

   b   We need a clever _____ – short, funny, and memorable.

▷ **logo / slogan**

2   a   Did you read the _____ on the board about the meeting?

   b   The company has a new TV _____ – it's fantastic.

▷ **advert / notice**

3   a   We've got to _____ a slogan for this product.

   b   They've _____ a new kind of coloured hair spray.

▷ **invent / make up**

4   a   I _____ him to play a computer game.

   b   She _____ me that the Internet is the future.

▷ **persuade / convince**

5   a   Tobacco _____ isn't allowed on television.

   b   The band gets a lot of bad _____ in the press.

▷ **advertising / publicity**

6   a   What _____ is your car?

   b   You can get any _____ of coffee in that supermarket.

▷ **brand / make**

2 Practice your pronunciation.

slogan /ˈsləʊɡən/   advert /ˈædvɜːt/   persuade /pəˈsweɪd/
advertising /ˈædvətaɪzɪŋ/   publicity /pʌbˈlɪsəti/

3 Talk to a partner. Which pairs of words in **exercise 1** do you find confusing? Why?

listen to this

1 What are the advantages of buying goods and services on the Internet? Tell a partner using phrases from the **natural English** box.

natural English
whenever, wherever, etc.

Call me **whenever you feel like it**. = at any time
You can do it **whenever it suits you**.
We can go **wherever you want**. = any place
Eat **whatever you like**. = anything

tune in

2 **9.3** Read the text opposite and look at the picture. Listen to **part 1**. What kind of e-business does Joe Rajko want to start up?

listen carefully

3 Read the sentences. Listen to the whole extract and correct any factual errors.

   1 5% of the population are disabled.
   2 The site is only for disabled people.
   3 You can find holiday homes for the disabled on the website.
   4 You can buy specialist equipment on the website.
   5 You'll be able to find out what facilities hotels provide for the disabled.
   6 This website would be the only one of its kind.

listening challenge

4 **9.4** Now listen to a sales pitch from another finalist, Michelle Richie. What is her website for? Remember three things you can get from it, then tell a partner.

5 **Think!** What do you like about each idea? Which do you prefer, and why? Tell a partner.

listening booklet *p.30 and p.31 for tapescripts and exercises*

7,000 Internet business ideas were presented to a television channel as part of a competition to find the **best new e-business website**. The entries were then reduced to **15** finalists, who were given the chance to convince the judges on TV. **Two** winners received **£1m** each to turn their idea into reality.
Joe Rajko was one of them.

it's your turn!

1 You're going to give a mini-presentation of a new e-business idea. In A / B pairs, A turn to *p.148* and B to *p.150*.

2 Present the idea to a partner. What do you think of each other's e-businesses? Use the phrases in the **natural English** box below.

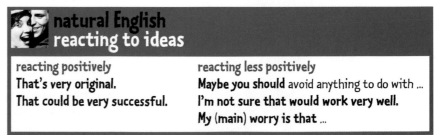

natural English
reacting to ideas

reacting positively
That's very original.
That could be very successful.

reacting less positively
Maybe you should avoid anything to do with ...
I'm not sure that would work very well.
My (main) worry is that ...

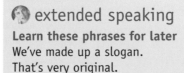 **extended speaking**

Learn these phrases for later
We've made up a slogan.
That's very original.

Our advert is for a brand of cat food.
Have a snack whenever you feel like it.

reading
accentuate the positive

lead-in

Ask and answer with a partner.

1   What kinds of TV adverts do you like most?
2   Which ones do you hate? Why?
3   Can you describe one TV advert that you feel strongly about?

grammar making comparisons

1   In which of the examples 1 to 4 below ...

a   are the two products the same in a particular quality?
b   is there a large difference between the products?
c   is there a small difference between the products?

1   A dishwasher **is just as easy to use as** a washing machine.
2   An ordinary razor **isn't quite as practical as** an electric razor.
3   Personal stereos **aren't nearly as expensive as** CD players.
4   Laser printers **are twice as fast as** ink jet printers.

2   Practise saying the phrases in **bold**. Stress the underlined words/syllables and remember that *as* is pronounced /əz/.

3   With a partner, write down two brand names for each product.

clothes	fizzy drinks	cars	fast food restaurants	trainers	video games

4   Together, make sentences comparing the brands. Use the phrases from **exercise 1**.

5   Tell another pair. Do they agree with you?

go to **language reference** *p.169*

read on

1   **Think!** Read the statements and complete the columns.

statement	why might it be true?	why might it be false?
1 On average, single men earn more than married men.	*Single men might be more interested in their career and have more time for work.*	
2 Single men are healthier than married men.		
3 Single men score more highly on happiness tests than married men.		

Let's make marriage more attractive

When your image is poor, you need to call in the professionals. This week's case for treatment: marriage.

The problem

Marriage is in a bad way. The number of people taking the plunge has dropped by 20% over the last decade, and recent figures showed that Britain has practically the highest divorce rate in the Western world, and the highest number of single mothers.

The Advertising Agency

The professionals called in to tackle the problem were the Yellow Grey group, which is part of Grey Advertising, with many clients in both Britain and the US.

The solution

'There are all kinds of reasons for the unpopularity of marriage,' says Kate Munson, group planning director at Grey. 'For one thing, women have greater financial independence than in the past; for another, there is the decline in the traditional view that the man should go out to work and bring in the money, while the woman is the homemaker.'

In view of these various difficulties, Grey realized that they needed something with impact. They decided, therefore, on a campaign that would give men a short sharp shock, and make them think about marriage in ways they hadn't considered before. And what could grab their attention more effectively than this poster?

'Research suggests that married men earn more and achieve more in the workplace than single men,' says Munson. 'They score more highly on tests of psychological well-being, are happier, and lead healthier, longer lives. No surprise then that they are also less likely to commit suicide or die violently.'

'It is an equally telling fact,' says Munson, 'that around 40% of marriages today are between couples where at least one partner has been married before. And men are much more likely to take the plunge a second time than women.'

The ads are meant for intelligent people in their mid- to late twenties, and are intended as a shared joke. 'If you choose an image of a loving couple to promote marriage, nobody's going to notice it.' Munson is aware that it may be necessary in future to build more serious ideas into the campaign, but for the moment it's important to get across the idea that marriage isn't a terrible burden or responsibility. It's a simple message: 'the happier you are, the longer you live – and marriage can make you happy.'

Which box would you rather be in?

Single ⬡

Married ☐

Married men live healthier, longer lives.
MARRIAGE IS GOOD FOR YOU

---

glossary

Complete the verb phrases.

_____ **the plunge** /plʌndʒ/ (para 1) decide to do something important

_____ **a problem** (para 2) deal with and solve a problem

_____ **sb's attention** (para 4) get / attract someone's attention

_____ **suicide** (para 5) kill oneself

_____ **an idea** (para 7) communicate an idea

your own new words _____ _____

---

2 Compare your ideas in small groups. Then choose two statements from the table on *p.106* and change *men* to *women*. Would the reasons be different?

3 Read the article and complete the glossary.

4 Which statements in **exercise 1** are true?

---

natural English
the + comparative, *the* + comparative

We use this structure to show how two things change together.

The older you get, **the happier** you become.
The more money you earn, **the more** you want.
The sooner we leave, **the better**.
The harder you work, **the more** you earn.

Find an example in the article. Complete these sentences.

1 The more you eat, the _____
   _____.

2 The sooner you give up smoking, the _____
   _____.

3 The _____,
   the easier it is to speak English.

4 The _____,
   the more likely you are to win the lottery.

---

it's your turn!

1 **Think!** Work with a partner. You are going to interview others in your class. Write down three questions to find out their opinion of marriage.

2 Circulate and find out what others think. Then tell the class your most interesting answer.

🔊 extended speaking

Learn these phrases for later
It's just as cheap as …
It's twice as nice as …
It's not nearly as … as you think.
The more you … the better …

literal and figurative meaning

Many words have a literal and figurative meaning.

examples
Babies crawl before they can walk. (= move forward on hands and knees)
Traffic was crawling through the town centre. (= moving slowly)

1 Check you understand these 'water' words and phrases. Use a dictionary if necessary.

sink (v)	stream	float (v)	flood /flʌd/ (v)
wave	leak (v)	the deep end	out of one's depth

2 What do the words and phrases in bold mean in these examples?

1 At the beginning of the troubles there was already a steady **stream** of refugees, but now that civil war has broken out, people are just **flooding** across the border.

2 The Prime Minister is said to be very angry that details of the confidential report have been **leaked** to the press.

3 We employ a number of graduates and our policy has always been to throw them in at **the deep end**. That way we quickly find out if they're going to **sink** or swim.

4 As he ran towards them, a **wave** of panic ran through the crowd.

5 The dancer seemed to **float** across the stage.

6 I've just got a new job. It's really hard – I feel quite **out of my depth**.

affixes

Certain prefixes and suffixes are often used to describe features of products.

affix	meaning	other examples
fat-<u>free</u> yoghurt	= no fat	sugar-free, alcohol-free
home-<u>made</u> bread	= made at home	hand-made
locally-<u>grown</u> fruit	= produced locally	home- / organically-grown
<u>non</u>-iron shirt	= you don't iron	non-stick, non-slip
a water-<u>proof</u> watch	= not damaged / affected by water	bullet-proof, sound-proof

1 What features could these products have?

a chocolates *hand-made chocolates*   e beer

b a raincoat   f cola

c cherries   g frying pan

d a recording studio   h shoes

2 What do the prefixes in bold mean?

mini-disc	**micro**film	**multi**-media	**pre**-cooked

3 Use your dictionary to find more examples for these prefixes.

grammar linking words

1 **Think!** Have you ever given a presentation?

If so, when, and what was it about? Who was the audience? How did it go?

If not, how do you think you would feel about giving one?

2 Compare your ideas with a partner.

Eye contact establishes positive rapport with the audience.

successful presentation

3 Form sentences using the table.

example Prepare a written outline as this will help you clarify the structure of your talk.

Prepare a written outline	so that	you lose one.
Put your main points in a logical sequence	as	memorize the content and feel confident.
Keep the notes short and simple	in case	this will help you feel less nervous at the beginning.
	otherwise	
Write your first two sentences and memorize them	in order to	this will help you clarify the structure of your talk.
Rehearse as much as possible		you can read them easily at a glance.
Have an extra copy of your talk		the audience won't be able to follow.

4 With a partner, practise saying the sentences. Which are the best pieces of advice?

Stand behind or lean on something to make you feel relaxed.

Open-hand gestures emphasize key points.

Relaxed body language conveys confidence.

5 Complete the table below with the link words from **exercise 3**.

1	*in order to* + verb	= for this purpose
	_____ + clause	
2	_____ + clause	= because
3	_____ + clause	= if not / if you don't …
4	_____ + clause	= because it's possible that …

go to **language reference** *p.169 and p.170*

6 With a partner, complete the advice in a suitable way.

1 Stick to three or four main points, otherwise _____ .
2 End on a strong point so that _____ .
3 Tell the truth, as _____ .
4 Number the pages in your notes in case _____ .
5 Get a good night's sleep the night before in order to _____ .

give your talk with confidence

1  **(9.5)** Look at the pictures, then listen to the recording. Which advice in the pictures do you hear?

2 Listen again. What <u>other</u> advice do you hear? Make notes.

> **natural English**
> **superlative +** *ever*
>
> It's **the best talk I've ever been to**.
> That was **the funniest film I've ever seen**.
> She gave me **the most useful advice I've ever had**.
>
> Find an example of this structure in the tapescript on *p.32* of the listening booklet. Tell your partner about …
>
> a the best film you've ever seen.
> b the hardest thing you've ever had to do.
> c the nicest thing anyone has ever said to you.
> d the worst meal you've ever eaten.

3 What are the three most important things to remember about preparing and giving a presentation? Tell a partner.

> **extended speaking**
> **Learn these phrases for later**
> We chose this product as …
> We wanted to make it funny so that …
> Always … in case …
> It's the best … you've ever …

extended speaking
advertise it!

you're going to:

collect ideas
listen to and evaluate adverts

produce an advert
choose a product and prepare your advert

give a presentation
present your advert to the class

but first ...
Look back at the **extended speaking** boxes in this unit. You can use this language in the activity.

 ## collect ideas

1 Listen to two radio adverts.

  1 What product are they advertising?
  2 Which do you prefer, and why?

2 TV adverts are often based on a simple situation, and include dialogue and a slogan. Read the example below, then tell a partner what you think of it.

3 **Think!** What is this company trying to say about itself?

  1 'We're calm.'
  2 'We're an old, established company.'
  3 'We're friendly.'
  4 'We're efficient.'
  5 'We're good value for money.'

4 Compare your ideas with a partner.

Man in living room. Metre-deep water, furniture is floating. Water gushing from a burst pipe. Man on the phone to insurance company.

VOICEOVER: Man: "... it was terrible! I woke up and my living room was full of water."

At the insurance company call centre.

VOICEOVER: Woman: "Don't worry Mr. Brown, we'll take care of everything. I'm sending someone to you right now ..."

Man still on phone. Premier Insurance van arrives.

VOICEOVER:
Man: "Wow! They're already here!"

Some time later, everything is fixed. Man looks happy.

Premier Insurance 0800 1234527

VOICEOVER: "Don't get out of your depth. Ring Premier Insurance. The sooner you call us the sooner we bail you out."

PREMIER INSURANCE television advertisement – spring 2003   ref: PIZ30774

produce an advert

5 Think! Choose one product that you'd like to advertise.

- something to eat
- a cut-price airline
- *your own idea*
- a flu remedy
- cat food

6 Compare your ideas in groups. Agree on one product to advertise on TV. Give it a brand name.

7 Look at the checklist and produce your advert together.

checklist

- Your advert should be based on a situation and have at least two characters.
- It should not last longer than one minute.
- It should have a storyline, with some dialogue between the characters.
- Think about the tone or style of the advert: humorous / mysterious / dramatic / romantic / other?
- At the end, there should be a slogan.
- You could include a 'voice-over' which gives some factual information.
- Write out the advert, with the dialogue and slogan, as in the example.

give a presentation

8 You're going to present your advert to the class. First, decide in your group who will …

1 introduce the advert: say what the product is, and say what style your advert is.
2 tell the class what the different scenes are in the advert.
3 act out any dialogue.
4 read the voice-over and slogan at the appropriate moments.

9 Rehearse your presentation.

10 Present your advert to the class. Vote for the best advert.

test yourself!

How well do you think you did the extended speaking? Mark the line.

0 ————————————————— 10

From this unit, write down:

1 five words / phrases to do with water which have a literal and figurative meaning, e.g. *stream.*
2 two more ways of expressing surprise, e.g. *I nearly died.*
3 two examples for each of these suffixes: ___-proof, __-free, ___-made.

Complete the sentences. The meaning must stay the same.

1 Come whenever you feel like it.
   Come whenever it ——————— .
2 I've never heard such a funny joke.
   That's the ———————————— .
3 Take it with you because you might need it.
   Take it with you in ——————— .
4 The book is much better than the film.
   The film isn't ————————————— .

Correct the errors.

1 She's just as intelligent than her brother.
2 More you work, more you earn.
3 Leave early, otherwise you are late.
4 Big companies do a lot of publicity on TV.

Look back at the unit contents on *p.103*. Tick ✓ the language you can use confidently.

absent-minded

glossary

absent-minded forgetting things easily

how to react ... to a joke

do you get it?

with a partner ...

Are you a forgetful person? Do you forget people's names / birthdays? Do you forget where you left your keys or glasses?

joke time

Look at the pictures. What's happened, and why?

 10.1 Listen and react to the joke. Did you get it? Go to *p.34* of the listening booklet and listen again.

natural English
things like that / that sort of thing

In spoken English, you can list one or two examples, and finish with these expressions.

They serve coffee, juice, and **that sort of thing**.
I need soap, shampoo, and **stuff / things like that**.
She keeps rabbits, mice, and **animals like that**.
We discussed organic food, and **issues like that**.

Complete these sentences.

1 They've got a pool, a squash court, and ...
2 You can buy vegetables, fruit, and ...
3 I've worked in Chad, Malawi, and ...
4 We talked about ...
5 My suitcase ...
6 I love ...

memory

Fill the gaps with these words to give a phrase of a similar meaning.

by heart   tongue /tʌŋ/   absent-minded   vague /veɪg/   bell   blank

1 His name is very familiar. = His name rings a _____ .
2 I only remember a bit about it. = I've got a _____ memory of it.
3 We had to memorize the poem. = We had to learn the poem _____ .
4 He's very forgetful. = He's very _____ .
5 Suddenly I couldn't remember a thing. = Suddenly my mind went _____ .
6 I know this, but I can't quite remember it. = I know this; it's on the tip of my _____ .

test your partner
– *His name is very familiar.*
– *His name rings a bell.*

113

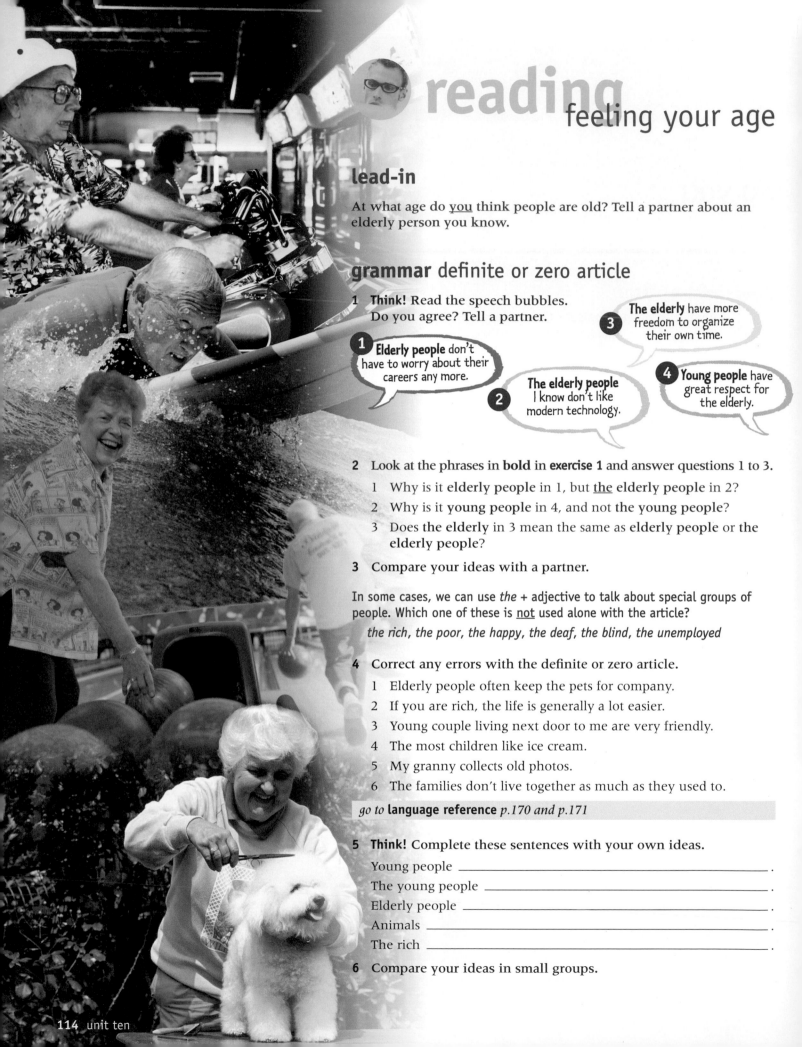

reading
feeling your age

lead-in

At what age do you think people are old? Tell a partner about an elderly person you know.

grammar definite or zero article

1 **Think!** Read the speech bubbles. Do you agree? Tell a partner.

> 1 **Elderly people** don't have to worry about their careers any more.

> 2 **The elderly people** I know don't like modern technology.

> 3 **The elderly** have more freedom to organize their own time.

> 4 **Young people** have great respect for the elderly.

2 Look at the phrases in **bold** in **exercise 1** and answer questions 1 to 3.

 1 Why is it **elderly people** in 1, but <u>the</u> **elderly people** in 2?

 2 Why is it **young people** in 4, and not **the young people**?

 3 Does **the elderly** in 3 mean the same as **elderly people** or **the elderly people**?

3 Compare your ideas with a partner.

In some cases, we can use *the* + adjective to talk about special groups of people. Which one of these is <u>not</u> used alone with the article?

the rich, the poor, the happy, the deaf, the blind, the unemployed

4 Correct any errors with the definite or zero article.

 1 Elderly people often keep the pets for company.

 2 If you are rich, the life is generally a lot easier.

 3 Young couple living next door to me are very friendly.

 4 The most children like ice cream.

 5 My granny collects old photos.

 6 The families don't live together as much as they used to.

go to **language reference** *p.170 and p.171*

5 **Think!** Complete these sentences with your own ideas.

Young people _____ .

The young people _____ .

Elderly people _____ .

Animals _____ .

The rich _____ .

6 Compare your ideas in small groups.

read on

1 **Think!** What problems might an elderly person have when they go out shopping?

2 Compare your ideas with a partner.

3 Read the text and complete the glossary.

4 Why did the writer wear gloves, ear plugs, and goggles? How did he feel?

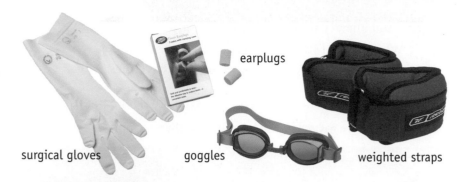

surgical gloves   earplugs   goggles   weighted straps

MY DAY AS A 75-YEAR-OLD

WHAT'S IT LIKE TO BE 75? I RECENTLY TOOK PART IN AN EXPERIMENT IN WHICH ANN PARR, AN EXPERT ON AGEING, TRANSFORMED ME FROM A FIT 37-YEAR-OLD MAN INTO SOMEONE WITH THE PHYSICAL ABILITY OF A PERSON TWICE MY AGE.

05 She started with the eyes, fitting me with a pair of goggles which gave me **tunnel vision**, a common problem for elderly people. To this, she added weighted straps round 10 my wrist and another round my ankle. This was to make me both weaker and slower.

Wearing two pairs of surgical gloves helped me to appreciate the poor 15 sense of touch that comes with age, and finally, she gave me some ear plugs. 'From the age of 25,' explained Ms Parr, 'there is a slight deterioration, but it is so gradual 20 that you don't notice it.' I certainly noticed it. The conversation around me was **muffled** and I felt cut off from Ms Parr and the photographer. I understood the conversation 25 about as well as if I was lying head down in the bath.

Starting to feel my new age, we set out for a department store in the city centre, where I tried to buy a 30 scarf as a Christmas present for my 78-year-old father. It was frightening to step out, like the first time you let go at the side of a swimming pool. The goggles made 35 everything seem so bright, a complaint many older people have, which is why they often wear shaded glasses. With my restricted vision and poor hearing, the world 40 seemed unsafe. I can understand why many elderly people stay in their homes, while a few brave ones go out into the busy world that young people **take for granted**.

45 Going on public transport was dreadful. Feeling **disorientated**, I was **jostled** by young people in a hurry. Even finding the right money for the ticket was a problem, as my 50 gloved hands couldn't distinguish the coins in my pocket.

When we reached the department store, Ms Parr had to guide me to the men's clothing department. 55 When we got there, it was hopeless. I couldn't tell, by touch, the difference between a silk scarf and an acrylic one. 'Can we stop for coffee?' I asked, echoing my father's 60 words whenever he goes shopping. It was such a relief to sit down and stay in one place.

Ms Parr uses this equipment on company executives to help them 65 understand their elderly customers. 'It isn't quite this bad to be elderly,' she said. 'It happens slowly, so gradually you adapt.'

glossary	Circle the correct definition.		
	tunnel vision (para 2)	a wide vision	b restricted vision
	muffled (para 3)	a unclear	b clear
	take (sth) for granted (para 4)	a enjoy	b accept without thinking
	disorientated (para 5)	a confused	b disorganized
	jostle /ˈdʒɒsəl/ **sb** (para 5)	a help	b push

5 Ask and answer with a partner.

1 What facts did you learn from the article?

2 Do any of the elderly people you know have these kinds of problems?

3 Is this kind of training useful? If so, who would it help?

6 Complete the **natural English** box with a phrase from the text.

natural English
expressions with *tell* (*recognize*)   10.2

_____ a silk scarf and an acrylic one.
I can't tell one type of beer **from** another.
Can you tell what someone's nationality is, just by looking at them?
Can you tell the difference between one type of mineral water and another?

In A/B pairs, ask/say something about:

A – decaffeinated coffee and ordinary coffee
  – someone lying or telling the truth
  – different brands of fruit juice
  – a crocodile and an alligator

B – different brands of pasta
  – someone's job and their appearance
  – real leather and fake leather
  – good wine and cheap wine

grammar definite or indefinite article

1 Read the rules. Look at the four underlined examples in the text on *p.115* and decide which rule applies to each one.

1 We use the definite article *the* when we know which one(s) we are talking about. We know this because:

  a we have heard about it/them before, e.g. *I saw a dog, ... Later, the dog ran towards ...*

  b we say which one we mean, e.g. *I gave some money to the child who came to see me.*

  c it is the only one in existence, e.g. *The sun's hot today. We went to the lake in the park.*

2 If people or things are not defined or we haven't heard about them before, we use *a/an*, e.g. *Yesterday I saw a squirrel in the back garden.*

2 Put *the* or *a/an* in gaps 1 to 5 below.

When we reached ¹_____ department store, Ms Parr had to guide me to ²_____ men's clothing department. When we got there, it was hopeless. I couldn't tell, by touch, ³_____ difference between ⁴_____ silk scarf and ⁵_____ acrylic one.

3 Compare your answers with lines 53 to 58 in the text on *p.115*.

go to **language reference** *p.171*

👤 **extended speaking**
Learn these phrases for later
People who ...
The people I know ...
Keeping animals in zoos is ...
Pets are important for ...

listening
there's no easy answer

lead-in

1 Ask and answer in small groups.

1 In your country, do you have TV programmes where the audience are invited to give their opinions? If so, what do you think of them?

2 Which of these topics would <u>you</u> give your opinion on?

drugs   spending on the arts   aid for developing countries
sex education   street crime   money paid to sports professionals
your own topic

listen to this

tune in

1 **(10.3)** You're going to hear members of a studio audience giving opinions. Listen to the first part of **interviews 1** and **2**.

1 Is the presenter calm or excited?

2 Is the man confident or nervous?

3 Is the woman enthusiastic or angry?

listen carefully

2 Listen to the whole extract and answer the questions.

interview 1

1 What does the presenter ask the man about?

2 Why is he against it?

3 What is the presenter's second question about?

4 What's his answer?

interview 2

1 What does the presenter ask the woman about?

2 Why is she in favour of it?

3 What is the presenter's second question about?

4 What's the woman's answer?

listening challenge

3 **(10.4)** Listen to a member of the audience talking about a different topic. What's the topic, and what's his opinion? Tell a partner.

listening booklet *p.34 to p.37 for tapescripts and exercises*

vocabulary making judgements

1 With a partner, match phrases 1 to 10 with a to j.

1 It's immoral.

2 It's a shame.

3 It's ridiculous /rɪˈdɪkjələs/.

4 It's a nuisance /ˈnjuːsəns/.

5 It's harmful.

6 It's upsetting.

7 It's cruel /ˈkruːəl/.

8 It's inevitable /ɪnˈevɪtəbl/.

9 It's justifiable /dʒʌstɪˈfaɪəbl/.

10 It's illegal.

a It's damaging.

b It's against the law.

c It's annoying.

d It's a pity.

e It's bound to happen.

f It's stupid and absurd.

g It's wrong and unacceptable.

h There's a good reason for it.

i It makes you sad or angry.

j It causes pain and suffering.

test your partner

– *It's immoral.*

– *It's wrong and unacceptable.*

– *That's right.*

it's your turn!

1 **Think!** Choose three topics from the table and make notes on your opinion. The phrases in **vocabulary exercise 1** will help you.

topic	your opinion	reasons
the use of live animals for testing cosmetics		
eating fruit and vegetables (from other continents) out of season		
raising the price of petrol to pay for health and / or education		
keeping people alive on life support machines		
spending money on designer clothes		
body piercing		
women in their fifties and sixties giving birth		

natural English
buying time to think

When you are asked your opinion, you can give yourself time to think, like this:

Let me think ...	I've never really thought about that.
That's an interesting question, um ...	I'll have to think about that.

Practise saying the phrases.

2 Work in small groups. Choose topics and start the discussion.

3 Tell the class which topic caused the most discussion and why.

extended speaking

Learn these phrases for later
I think it's justifiable in some ways.   It's immoral and illegal.
I've never really thought about that.   Let me think ...

wordbooster

animals

1 **Label the pictures. How are the words pronounced?**

2 **Answer the questions with a partner and compare with another pair.**

Which animal(s) in the pictures:

1   can **poison** you with a **bite**?
2   can poison you with a **sting**?
3   is **covered in spots**?
4   have thick **fur**?
5   is found in China but rarely **breeds** in captivity?
6   have **skin** which is used in expensive shoes and handbags?
7   has **stripes**?
8   live as part of a **herd**?
9   are **in danger of extinction**?
10 has a **beak** and **hunts** at night?

3 **Think! Prepare three questions about animals using the vocabulary in bold in exercise 2. Then test your partner.**

example   Can you name another animal which is in danger of extinction?

word building

There are few rules about word building, but there are common patterns which can help you to guess what kind of word it is.

1 **Complete the table.**

noun	adjective
_____	captive
_____	attractive
_____	cruel
_____	persuasive
_____	hungry
_____	harmful / harmless
_____	(un)justifiable
_____	disgraceful
_____	(in)sensitive
_____	destructive
_____	stressful
_____	protective

2 **Ask and answer with a partner.**

1   If an adjective ends *-ful* and has a related noun, what is the most likely form of the noun? Can you think of three more examples that follow this rule?

2   If an adjective ends in *-ive* and has a related noun, what are the two most likely forms of the noun? Can you think of one more example for each?

how to ...
write a human interest story

look at issues behind a story

1 **Think!** Look at the headlines.

1   Which story would you read first, and why?
2   What might be in the story?

MAN BITES PARROT

Wife walks away with $10m

WOMAN CONFRONTS NAKED BURGLAR IN HER LIVING ROOM

Thousands wait for world to end

KILLER SHARK EATEN BY VICTIM'S FAMILY

2   Compare your ideas with a partner.

3   Look at the photo. What's unusual about the woman's face?

4 Read the article and complete **part 1** of the table.

part 1	
Jean's reasons <u>for</u> cosmetic surgery before the operation.	
Bernie's arguments <u>against</u> cosmetic surgery.	
The benefits she felt after the operation.	
part 2	
<u>Your</u> arguments for cosmetic surgery.	
<u>Your</u> arguments against cosmetic surgery.	

5 With a partner, discuss **part 2** of the table and write down your ideas. Do you sympathize more with Jean or Bernie?

6 Compare your ideas with another pair.

'This was money which we'd put aside for our daughter's education, and now she has spent it just to make herself look more glamorous. I can't believe it!' John also believes it is against the laws of nature to turn the clock back in this way.

Jean, whose confidence has improved enormously, has no regrets. Before the operation, she had become very depressed, but now she not only looks better, she feels more energetic as well. 'I'm a better wife and mother now,' she says, 'and if the technology is there to make the improvements, why shouldn't I benefit from them?'

SURGEON'S KNIFE THREATENS MARRIAGE

JEAN HUMPHRIES LIVES IN CHESHIRE WITH HUSBAND, BERNIE, AND 13-YEAR-OLD DAUGHTER MIRIAM. AN ATTRACTIVE WOMAN IN HER MID-FORTIES, SHE SEEMED TO HAVE EVERYTHING, YET ONE DAY, SHE PHONED A COSMETIC SURGEON AND BOOKED HERSELF IN TO A PRIVATE CLINIC FOR A FACELIFT.

'My husband is seven years younger than me, and many of his friends are even younger,' she said. 'What's more, at 46, I suddenly found I didn't recognize myself in family photos.'

Her husband, who knew nothing about the operation, agrees that she looks fabulous after the surgery, but is horrified at the cost.

THE DAUGHTER MIRIAM

THE HUSBAND BERNIE

grammar relative clauses

Relative pronouns, e.g. *who, which, whose ...*

1   say <u>which</u> person or thing you mean (defining relative clauses; *that* can also be used in place of *who* or *which*).
He was the surgeon who performed the operation, i.e. not any other surgeon.

2   give <u>extra information</u> about a person or thing (non-defining relative clauses; these clauses have commas before and after. *That* cannot be used in these clauses.)
The daughter, who was only thirteen at the time, refused to comment.

1   Fill the gaps with *who, which, that,* or *whose*.

1   Miriam, _____ mother had the operation, refused to comment.

2   Jean, _____ is in her mid-forties, feels better and more positive.

3   The decision, _____ came as a surprise to everyone, was Jean's alone.

4   The husband, _____ friends were younger, didn't understand.

5   She spent the money _____ they had been saving.

6   Bernie was the person _____ she should have asked first.

7   The surgeon _____ she phoned was the one who performed the operation.

8   People _____ confidence is low shouldn't automatically opt for cosmetic surgery.

go to **language reference** *p.171 and p.172*

plan and write your human interest story

1   Look at the photo, then read the synopsis and the questions.

Carl Zola recently returned from holiday with a tattoo on his arm. His boss, **Marina Epstein**, was horrified, and told him to keep it covered up during working hours. Carl refused, and so Marina has sent him a warning letter saying that unless he agrees to cover the tattoo, he will lose his job.

1   What kind of company do you think it is, and what is Carl's job?
2   What are the issues from Carl's point of view?
3   What are Marina's arguments against the tattoo?
4   What happens next? How is the situation resolved?
5   Where do your sympathies lie?

2   With a partner, use the questions above to plan your story.

3   Look again at the article on *p.120* and find examples of ...

– the use of link words to add new ideas.
– the use of direct speech to bring the characters and arguments to life, and add human interest.
– how it gives both points of view, but favours one over the other.
– how non-defining clauses add extra information efficiently.

4   Write your story in your own time. Give it a headline. Show it to your partner in the next lesson.

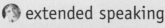 extended speaking

Learn these phrases for later
It's cruel, and what's more I think ...
It's not only ..., it's ... as well.
People who ... should ...
Animals which are kept ...

extended speaking

you're going to:

collect ideas
listen to some people talking about pets

prepare your argument
consider some statements about animals in society and add your own

share your views
agree or disagree with the statements and identify the most controversial one

write a summary
choose one statement and write your arguments for and against

but first ...
Look back at the **extended speaking** boxes in this unit. You can use this language in the activity.

 ## collect ideas

1 Find out how many people in your class have pets. What kinds of pets are they, and why do they have them?

2 Read the arguments for and against the idea that all children should have a pet.

3 Listen to the speakers and tick ✓ the arguments they mention.

4 Which arguments do you agree with? Tell a partner.

a Children learn to be responsible if they have a pet.

b It can be dangerous or unhygienic for children to have pets.

c They like the pet at first, but then don't bother to look after it.

d It's fun for children to have a pet.

e Children can grow up with a pet and establish a close relationship.

f Children treat the pet like a toy, which can be bad for the pet.

prepare your argument

5 Read the statements below. In small groups, choose <u>one</u> of the categories you'd like to discuss, e.g. 'Animals as pets'.

6 **Think!** Prepare your arguments <u>for</u> and <u>against</u> each statement. Add one more statement of your own to discuss.

ANIMALS AS **PETS**

- People shouldn't be allowed to keep any animal as a pet which has to be kept in a cage or tank, e.g. birds, fish, or snakes.
- Cruelty to pets is as serious as cruelty to children, and punishments should be much tougher than they are at present.
- *your own statement*

ZOOS

- Keeping animals in zoos for human entertainment and education is justifiable.
- Zoos are essential to protect and breed endangered species.
- *your own statement*

share your views

 natural English
clarifying your position

If someone hasn't understood your argument, you can say:

That's not what I meant.	No, what I meant was ...
That's not what I was trying to say.	What I'm trying to say is ...

7   In your group, agree or disagree with the statements from your category.

8   Tell the class the most controversial statement for your group.

 ## write a summary

9   In your own time, write down the arguments for and against one of the statements you discussed. Use the words for adding ideas on *p.120*.

ANIMALS FOR FOOD&CLOTHING

- If you aren't prepared to kill an animal, you shouldn't eat it.
- Wearing animal fur and skin is immoral.
- *your own statement*

USING ANIMALS FOR WORK & ENTERTAINMENT

- Guide dogs for the blind and deaf are fine for the owners, but not the animals.
- It is immoral to make money from horse racing and dog racing, because the animals have no choice.
- *your own statement*

saying the right thing

life with Agrippine

in groups ...

Which words are fashionable with young people in your language at the moment? Which words were fashionable ten or twenty years ago?

cartoon time

Read the cartoon. How would you say *brill*, *cool*, and *fab* in your language? Do you agree with Agrippine's advice in the last picture? Why / why not?

11.1 Listen and follow the cartoon. Then test your partner on the glossary words.

---

natural English
exaggerating
11.2

There are some common phrases for exaggerating in spoken English.

I've got a million things to do!	It weighs a ton!
I wouldn't do that in a million years!	I could eat a horse!
I've told you a hundred times!	It cost a fortune!

Listen and repeat the phrases.
Practise dialogues using these questions and the phrases.

Is that bag heavy?	Was that jacket expensive?
Are you hungry?	Would you do a bungee jump?
What's your phone number?	Will you give me a hand?

---

glossary

brill Ⓢ brilliant, great (1980s)

cool Ⓢ great (1960s and 1990s)

fab Ⓢ great, fabulous (1960s)

backside Ⓢ part of the body you sit on

stick to sth continue doing sth

---

in unit eleven ...
tick ✓ when you know this

natural English
- exaggerating ☐
- imagining someone else's situation ☐
- letter writing clichés ☐
- reacting to ideas ☐
- informal and formal language ☐

grammar
- past conditionals ☐
- mixed conditionals ☐
- reporting what people say ☐

vocabulary
- describing character ☐

wordbooster
- phrases and phrasal verbs ☐
- use your dictionary ☐

listening
making the right decision

lead-in

1 Think! Look at the **natural English** box and the people in the pictures indicated with an arrow. What would <u>you</u> do in each situation, and why?

natural English
imagining someone else's situation

In his / her shoes, I'd probably do nothing.
(= if I were in his / her situation)
In his / her position, I might intervene.
If that were me, I'd definitely say something.

2 Compare your ideas in small groups.

grammar past conditionals

1 Read the situation. Tick ✓ sentences 1 to 5 that you agree with and compare your ideas with a partner, giving your reasons.

> Last weekend, an eighteen-year-old woman left a friend's party at midnight, but missed the last bus home. She didn't have enough money for a taxi, so although it was three kilometres, she decided to walk.

1 If that had been me, I would have done the same.

2 If that had been me, I wouldn't have walked home alone.

3 If that had happened to me, I would have phoned my parents.

4 In her shoes, I'd have gone back to the party and borrowed money for a taxi.

5 In her position, I might have tried to hitch a lift.

2 With a partner, answer the questions.

1 Compare sentences a and b below. Which one means 'in general', and which means 'on a specific occasion in the past'?
   a If that were me, I'd do the same.
   b If that had been me, I would have done the same.

2 Sentence a has the form *If* + past simple, *would* + verb. What is the form of sentence b? *If* + _____ .

3 Which sentence types are 'second' and which are 'third' conditional?

4 Look at sentences 2 to 5 in **exercise 1**. What other forms are used in the conditional clause?

3 Say the phrases.

If that had /ˈðætəd/ been me …

I would have /ˈwʊdəv/ done …

I wouldn't have /ˈwʊdəntəv/ walked …

I'd have /ˈaɪdəv/ gone back.

I might have /ˈmaɪtəv/ tried …

4 Change the sentences in **exercise 1** to make them true for you. Say them to a partner.

go to **language reference** *p.173*

listen to this

tune in

1 **11.3** Listen to **part 1** of the woman's story in **grammar exercise 1**. What do you think happened next? Tell a partner.

listen carefully

2 Listen to the whole story. Were you right?

3 Listen again and complete the sentences.

1 The people in the car looked _____ .

2 She felt _____ .

3 When they arrived at her village, she

_____ .

4 They _____ .

5 She felt _____ .

6 Eventually, they _____ .

7 They said to her, '_____ .'

listening challenge

4 **11.4** Listen to Mike talking about a difficult situation. What happened? Tell a partner.

5 **Think!** What would you have done in the two situations you listened to? Write three sentences for each situation, using these sentence structures.

1 If that had been me, I'd (probably) have _____ .

2 If that had happened to me, I wouldn't have _____ .

3 In his / her shoes / position, I might have _____ .

6 Find other students with similar sentences.

listening booklet *p.38 and p.39 for tapescripts and exercises*

grammar mixed conditionals

1 Read the situation.

Stefan (17) met Anna (18) and asked her to go out with him. When Anna asked him about his age on their first date, he lied and said he was 20. Several weeks later, they arranged to go on a short trip. However, Stefan realized he would have to show his identity card with his true age on it, and now he's worried that Anna might find out.

2 Decide which sentences are grammatically correct.

If Stefan had told Anna the truth in the first place,

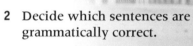

   → she wouldn't have gone out with him.

   → it would've been sensible.

   → she might go out with him.

   → he wouldn't be worried now.

   → she would accept it.

   → he wouldn't have this problem with his ID card.

go to **language reference** *p.173*

3 Complete these sentences with a past consequence and a present consequence.

1 If I'd married him / her, → I _____ .
                  → I _____ .

2 If we'd gone on holiday last month, → we _____ .
                                   → we _____ .

3 If I hadn't gone to the bank this morning, → I _____ .
                                   → I _____ .

4 Think of something that you did or didn't do that has consequences for you now. Write a sentence, and tell a partner.

example If I'd saved more money this year, I'd be on holiday now.

🌐 extended speaking

Learn these phrases for later

If that had been me ...   In his shoes, I'd have ...

In her position, I might have ...   If that were me, I wouldn't ...

a time to forgive

lead-in

1 **Think!** A prison near you is looking for people to go and meet prisoners who never get any visitors. Would you go? Why / why not? If so, what would you talk about?

2 Compare your ideas with a partner.

3 Read the introduction to the letters. Close your book and tell your partner what you remember.

4 Read the letters. Put them in the correct order and complete the glossary.

5 Discuss these questions with a partner.

1 Does Craig sound truly sorry, or are you suspicious of his reasons for writing?

2 Is it right for Mrs Robinson to forgive Craig so easily?

3 If you were in Mrs Robinson's shoes, could you forgive Craig? Why / why not?

natural English
letter writing clichés

These phrases are very common in informal letters.

I hope you're well.
Sorry I haven't written for a while but I've been ...
It was lovely to hear from you.
I was so pleased to hear that ...

6 Work with a partner. Write a short reply to Mrs Robinson's last letter. Use the **natural English** phrases.

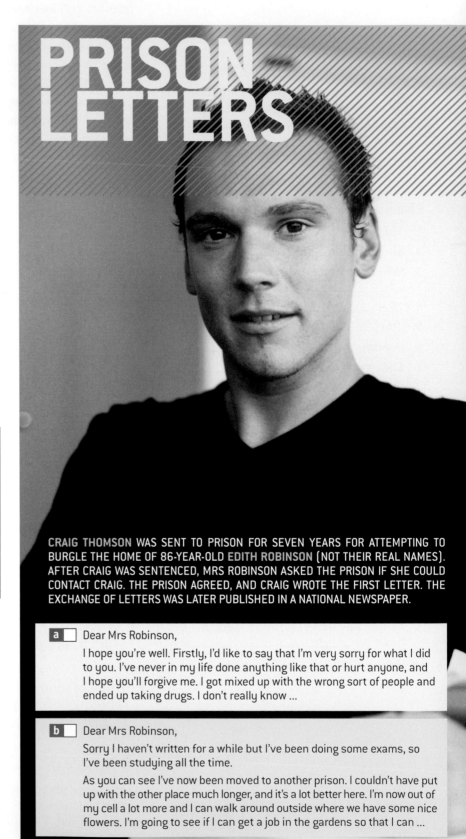

PRISON LETTERS

CRAIG THOMSON WAS SENT TO PRISON FOR SEVEN YEARS FOR ATTEMPTING TO BURGLE THE HOME OF 86-YEAR-OLD EDITH ROBINSON (NOT THEIR REAL NAMES). AFTER CRAIG WAS SENTENCED, MRS ROBINSON ASKED THE PRISON IF SHE COULD CONTACT CRAIG. THE PRISON AGREED, AND CRAIG WROTE THE FIRST LETTER. THE EXCHANGE OF LETTERS WAS LATER PUBLISHED IN A NATIONAL NEWSPAPER.

a   Dear Mrs Robinson,
I hope you're well. Firstly, I'd like to say that I'm very sorry for what I did to you. I've never in my life done anything like that or hurt anyone, and I hope you'll forgive me. I got mixed up with the wrong sort of people and ended up taking drugs. I don't really know ...

b   Dear Mrs Robinson,
Sorry I haven't written for a while but I've been doing some exams, so I've been studying all the time.
As you can see I've now been moved to another prison. I couldn't have put up with the other place much longer, and it's a lot better here. I'm now out of my cell a lot more and I can walk around outside where we have some nice flowers. I'm going to see if I can get a job in the gardens so that I can ...

c Dear Craig,

Such a nice letter. I was planning to write to you this week even if I hadn't received your letter.

I'd like you to confide in me and regard me as a friend, not a victim. I have great faith in you and feel there's a lot of good in you. I was so pleased to hear that your education is going well. Do try hard – it's your only hope of a decent life when you're released.

Choose your friends with care. I'm so afraid of you being influenced by the wrong sort of people. Your sentence was harsh but it may be that it was meant to save your life. If you'd continued on drugs, you could have died. Remember …

d Dear Craig,

It was lovely to hear from you, and I'm so pleased you're in better surroundings. I do hope you'll be able to work in the garden – it's hard work but very rewarding. If you could get some proper training, this might be a good career for you …

Take care, Craig. I want to live long enough to see you make a success of your life.

With best wishes and very kind regards,

Edith

e Dear Mrs Robinson,

I hope you're feeling OK. I'm doing OK myself.

Well, so far everything's going well, and my education's going OK. I'm going for some exams as I want to be in a better position when I get out. I've made quite a few friends but they're not the sort of friends I want when I'm back out there.

I'd like to say thank you for being so understanding. You're a really nice person and I wish I'd never done what I did. I'm glad that you've forgiven me. I just cannot forgive myself.

f Dear Craig,

Thank you for your very nice letter. I know it wasn't an easy letter for you to write, and I do appreciate the effort you made. Of course I forgive you. I've done many things in my 86 years which I'm ashamed of, and it isn't for me to judge you.

I'm very pleased you've now given up taking drugs and feel so much better …

The Guardian

vocabulary describing character

1 Complete the definitions using these words / phrases.

understanding	full of remorse
(in)sincere /(ɪn)sɪnˈsɪə/	vulnerable /ˈvʌlnərəbl/
open-minded	(un)wise /(ʌn)waɪz/
kind-hearted	easily led
naive /naɪˈiːv/	reckless
courageous /kəˈreɪdʒəs/ / brave	
(un)trustworthy /(ʌn)ˈtrʌstwɜːði/	

1 If you're _____, you're caring and generous.

2 If you're _____, you show sympathy to other people's feelings.

3 If you're _____, you're easily hurt emotionally or physically.

4 If you're _____, you don't show that you are afraid when facing danger.

5 If you're _____, you feel very sorry for what you've done.

6 If you're _____, your actions are often influenced by others.

7 If you're _____, people think you're honest and dependable.

8 If you're _____, you're happy to listen to and accept people's ideas.

9 If you're _____, you have experience of life, and make good judgements.

10 If you're _____, you genuinely believe what you say.

11 If you're _____, you don't care about danger and its consequences.

12 If you're _____, you have little experience, and believe people are kind and honest when they aren't.

test your partner

– *You are caring and generous.*

– *kind-hearted*

2 Decide with a partner whether the words in exercise 1 describe …

Craig   Mrs Robinson   neither of them

it's your turn!

1 **Think!** Prepare your answers to the questions below.

WHAT'S YOUR VERDICT?

1 If more criminals came face to face with their victims and talked to them, would they be less likely to commit the same crime again?

2 If criminals met other criminals and took part in group counselling sessions with a psychologist, would this have a beneficial effect?

3 If people were sentenced to life in prison for committing robbery or assault three times, would it deter other criminals?

4 If we used electronic tagging on all criminals, would it be better for them to spend less time in prison and more time in the community?

natural English
reacting to ideas

That sounds like a great / an interesting idea.
I've got mixed feelings about that.
I'm completely against that idea.

2 Compare your ideas in small groups, using phrases from the **natural English** box.

extended speaking

Learn these phrases for later

He's rather reckless.
She's very vulnerable.

She's easily led.
He's a bit naive.

---

wordbooster

phrases and phrasal verbs

Many words frequently combine together in collocations. It is important to notice these combinations and learn them as phrases.

1 **Which word completes the phrases and phrasal verbs in bold?**

in	of	by	out	up

1 Have you any idea why she tried to **cover** _____ the truth ?

2 Pat spoke to her teacher about the problem but wouldn't **confide** _____ her parents.

3 Martha never understood how her son **got mixed** _____ **with** criminals.

4 She never takes friends back to her house: I think she's **ashamed** _____ it.

5 We forgot to take the chairs so we **ended** _____ sitting on the floor.

6 I hadn't seen him for years, then _____ **of the blue**, he **turned** _____ on my doorstep.

7 I gave her the wrong change _____ **mistake** and she complained.

8 I don't know how you **put** _____ **with** that noise. It would drive me mad.

2 **Memorize the phrases in bold. Then shut your book and write them down.**

use your dictionary

It isn't always easy to find the meaning of a phrase in a dictionary. Start with the first content word (noun, verb, or adjective).

> **blue** *noun* **1** [C,U] the colour that is blue. **2 blues** [pl] a sad, slow, style of music that came from the southern US: *a blues singer –* (see also RHYTHM AND BLUES) **3 the blues** [pl] (*informal*) feelings of sadness: *Don't be surprised if you get the blues for a while after your baby is born.* **4 out of the blue** (*informal*) unexpectedly: *A phone call from Jane right out of the blue.* (see also A BOLT FROM THE BLUE / OUT OF THE BLUE ⇨ BOLT³)

Longman Dictionary of Contemporary English

If you wanted to check the meaning of 'out of the blue' in the sentence *He turned up on my doorstep out of the blue*, you would first look at the entry for *blue*.

But if you wanted to check 'a bolt from the blue' in the sentence *It arrived like a bolt from the blue*, you should look under *bolt*.

1 Underline the words in each sentence which form a set phrase.

examples

If you fail the test, it'll be <u>your own fault</u>.
<u>With a bit of luck</u>, he'll pass the exam.

1 I have no sympathy for those two boys: they're selfish and stupid.

2 He's 19 years old, but his mother still treats him like a child.

3 Several children were injured but we don't know who's to blame.

4 I think he was wrong to buy the flat in the first place.

5 I don't see the point of trying to help them if they don't want it.

6 Put yourself in her shoes – what would *you* have done?

7 Well, to cut a long story short, I asked her to marry me and she said yes.

8 He's in a bad mood today – don't take any notice of him.

2 In the phrases in exercise 1, which word would you look up in a dictionary to find the phrase? Circle it. Use a dictionary to check the meaning of any new phrases.

how to ...
write an apology

say sorry

1 Are these true for you? Tell a partner.

> I often have to apologize /əˈpɒlədʒaɪz/ for being late.

> I get annoyed if people don't apologize when they bump into me.

> I sometimes apologize even if something is not my fault /fɔːlt/.

> If someone apologizes to me, I always accept their apology.

> In a relationship, 'sorry' is the hardest word to say.

2 **Think!** Nicola went to Germany on business. Before she left, she asked her husband, Darren, to buy a book for her mother's birthday and send it to her. What three things could have gone wrong?

Nicola

Darren

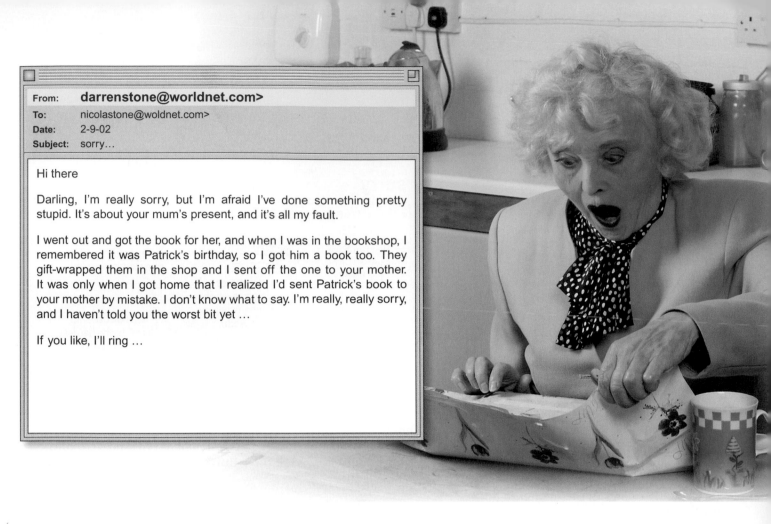

From: darrenstone@worldnet.com>
To: nicolastone@woldnet.com>
Date: 2-9-02
Subject: sorry...

Hi there

Darling, I'm really sorry, but I'm afraid I've done something pretty stupid. It's about your mum's present, and it's all my fault.

I went out and got the book for her, and when I was in the bookshop, I remembered it was Patrick's birthday, so I got him a book too. They gift-wrapped them in the shop and I sent off the one to your mother. It was only when I got home that I realized I'd sent Patrick's book to your mother by mistake. I don't know what to say. I'm really, really sorry, and I haven't told you the worst bit yet ...

If you like, I'll ring ...

3 Read Darren's e-mail to Nicola. Were your predictions right?

4 (11.5) Darren abandoned the e-mail and decided to speak to Nicola directly. Listen and answer the questions.

1 Which book did Darren buy for his mother-in-law?
2 Which book did he buy for Patrick?
3 How does Nicola react at first?
4 How does she react at the end?
5 What does Darren promise to do?

5 In A / B pairs, prepare to role play.

A You are Darren. Telephone your mother-in-law. Apologize and explain what happened.

B You are Darren's mother-in-law. You've just received the book. How do you feel? How will you react to Darren's apology and explanation?

6 Act out your telephone conversation.

grammar reporting what people say

When we report what people said, after *said*, *told*, *admitted*, etc., we often move the tense form one tense back in written English and careful spoken English.

1 Complete the table.

direct speech	reported speech
'I feel tired.'	She said she _felt_ tired.
'I made a mistake.'	He admitted he _____ a mistake.
'We were waiting for ages.'	He explained they _____ for ages.
'I've lost the tickets.'	She told him she _____ the tickets.
'I'll ring you later.'	She said she _____ me later.
'I'd been there before.'	He told me he _____ there before.

2 Change these examples of direct speech from the tapescript to reported speech.

1 'There's a bit of a crisis.' Darren said _____ .
2 'I've done a very stupid thing.' He admitted _____ .
3 'They gift-wrapped both books in the shop for me.' He explained _____ .
4 'I've sent your mother the wrong book.' He told _____ .
5 'You can swap them over.' Nicola suggested _____ .
6 'I'm going to call her now.' He told _____ .

go to **language reference** *p.174*

formal letter of apology

1 Look again at Darren's apology in his e-mail. How would a formal letter be different? Think of three differences.

2 Read the formal letter of apology below. Complete the column for the letter. Would a letter of apology have a similar structure in your language?

structure of the writing	Darren's e-mail	formal letter
apologize	1	
admit responsibility	2	
explain what happened	3	
apologize again	4	
say what will happen next	5	

CROFT OFFICE SUPPLIES
238 MERTON WAY • BEDFORD • BD3 6PJ

Mr Simon Gray
International Holdings
Bristol House
Cowley Rd
Oxford OX4 3DR

2 June 2002

Dear Mr Gray,

Further to our telephone conversation yesterday, I must apologize for the delay regarding the delivery of the office desks you ordered. This was caused by a computer error and we accept full responsibility.

I can now confirm that your order has been re-processed and we will contact you to arrange delivery within seven days.

Once again, we apologize for any inconvenience caused.

Yours sincerely,

Peter Baker

3 In A / B pairs, role play the situation.

A You are Simon Gray. Tell your boss what the letter said. Where appropriate, use reported speech.

B You are Simon's boss. You know Simon has had a problem with the office furniture. Ask him if he has any news.

4 In your own time, write one of these:

A an informal letter from Darren to his mother-in-law, explaining what's happened.

B a formal letter of apology. You have a bookselling business, and a language school ordered some dictionaries from you which didn't arrive. Apologize, explain, and say what action you're taking.

extended speaking
Learn these phrases for later
He explained he'd been having problems.
She told them she had …
They said they would …
It's all his own fault.

extended speaking

you're going to:

collect ideas
read a case study and decide on your response to it

analyse
discuss your case study and react to a different one

evaluate
reflect on the different stages of the **extended speaking** and decide what you found difficult

but first ...
Look back at the **extended speaking** boxes in this unit. You can use this language in the activity.

 collect ideas

1 **Think!** Remember an occasion where you had an argument or problem with a good friend. What caused the problem, and what happened?

2 Describe what happened to a partner.

3 Work in two groups, A and B.

Group A read case study A.

Group B turn to *p.150*.

Christopher and Jeff

CASE STUDY A

CHRISTOPHER and JEFF had known each other since childhood. One day, Jeff told his friend that he'd fallen in love and planned to get married the following month. He asked Christopher to lend him £1,000 for the wedding reception, but promised to pay him back a month later when he started his new job. Christopher knew that Jeff was not very good with money, but he still agreed. As they were old friends, they didn't put anything in writing.

A month later, Christopher hadn't heard from Jeff or received any money, so he phoned him. Jeff was very apologetic and said he would definitely pay him back within a month.

Six weeks later, Christopher tried to phone Jeff and discovered he had moved and left no forwarding address. By this stage, he was very angry.

Then, one month later, out of the blue, Christopher received a cheque for £100 from Jeff and a letter giving his new address. He explained that he'd been having financial problems, and wouldn't be able to pay back the remaining £900 for some time. Christopher wrote back telling Jeff to forget the rest of the money and never to contact him again.

4 Think! Decide how you'd answer these questions.

1 What was the first problem, and who was responsible? What could people have done at that stage, and why?

2 What problems arose later? What should they have done, and why?

3 Is there <u>one</u> person who is totally to blame?

4 Do you know anyone who has been in a similar situation?

language reminder

Remember that when you want to criticize what someone did, you can use *should / shouldn't have done.*

> He said nothing, but he **really should have thanked** them.
>
> I don't think she **should have spoken** to her mother like that.

 analyse

5 Work with two or three people who read the same case study. Compare your ideas on the questions in **exercise 4.**

6 You're going to tell your case study to someone who hasn't read it. First, practise telling the story in your group. Just tell the story; don't give your opinion.

7 In A / B pairs, read the A or B checklists below.

checklist A
– Tell your partner what happened in your case study. Answer any questions they have about it.
– Ask them what they think the problems were, what people should have done, and why.
– At the end, tell them any other ideas your group discussed.

checklist B
– Listen to A's story. If you don't understand something, ask them to explain it again.
– Tell your partner what you think the problems were and what people should have done, and why.
– At the end, read A's case study if you like.

8 Swap roles, and B tell A about your case study.

9 As a class, vote on who you think was to blame in each story.

 evaluate

10 Think! Which of these did you find easier / more difficult?

– Discussing the first case study in a group.

– Telling the whole story to a new partner.

– Giving immediate opinions on the second case study.

11 Compare your ideas with a partner. What do you feel you need to practise most?

Sherlock Holmes

twilight /ˈtwaɪlaɪt/ the time when day starts to become night

sleeping bag large bag for sleeping in when camping

glossary

how to ... react to a joke

She tells it very well.

That's hilarious!

Do you get it? I don't.

That's silly.

do you get it?

in unit twelve ...
tick ✓ when you know this

natural English
phrases with *mean* ☐
phrases with *go* ☐
rephrasing an idea ☐
saying how easy something is ☐
fronting ☐

grammar
reported questions ☐
like, as, such as ☐

vocabulary
sleep and times of day ☐
games ☐

wordbooster
collective nouns ☐
attitude adverbs ☐

with a partner ...

Make a list of real or fictional people famous for their intelligence, e.g. Sherlock Holmes. You have one minute! Compare your ideas with other people's lists.

joke time

Look at the pictures. Where are Sherlock Holmes and Dr Watson? Describe what you can see.

 12.1 Listen and react to the joke. Did you get it? Go to *p.42* of the listening booklet and listen again. Which phrase from the **natural English** box do you hear?

---

natural English
phrases with *mean*

What does that mean to you? (= What does that information tell you?)
Does the name Carlo Sanchez **mean anything to you?** (= Do you know who he is?)
That present **meant a lot to me.** (= was very important)
Success **means nothing to him.** (= has no importance)

Practise saying the phrases. What means a lot / nothing to you?

---

sleep and times of day

Put the words in the appropriate column.

fall asleep	dusk	doze /dəʊz/ off	fast asleep	have a nap
sunrise	yawn /jɔːn/	daydream	wide awake	snore
noon	half asleep	dawn /dɔːn/	insomnia	twilight

times of day	sleep	awake
	fall asleep	

Write four questions to ask your partner, using the words.

examples   Do you ever get up at dawn?
            Do you ever doze off while you're watching TV?

reading
questions! questions!

50:50		
15	£1	MILLION
14	£500,000	
13	£250,000	
12	£125,000	
11	£64,000	
10	£32,000	
9	£16,000	
8	£8,000	
7	£4,000	
6	£2,000	
5	£1,000	
4	£500	
3	£300	
2	£200	
1	£100	

The letter PL is the international car registration for which country?

A Poland

B Portugal

C Philippines

D Peru

lead-in

1 Look at the scoreboard above from a game show. What do you think happens?

2 What do the symbols at the top mean? What's the right answer to the multiple choice question?

3 [12.2] Listen to a description of the game. What are the three ways contestants can get help?

4 **Think!** Prepare to answer these questions.

   1 Would you like to take part in this show? Why / why not?

   2 How might you prepare for the quiz?

   3 Who would you phone for help on one question?

   4 How would you feel during the show, and at the end?

   5 If you won, how might it change your life?

5 Compare your ideas with a partner.

read on

1 Read the article and complete the glossary.

2 How would Alli answer the questions in **lead-in exercise 4**?

---

natural English
phrases with *go*

Let me have a go. (= let me try, in a game)
It's your go. (= it's your turn)
I ate all the chocolates **in one go.** (= all at the same time)
Go for it! ☺ (= Go on! You can do it!)

Practise dialogues using these prompts and the phrases.

I've got the chance of going round Thailand on a bike!
I can't open this jar of coffee.
You don't look well.
Whose turn is it?

MILLIONAIRE HOPEFULS — GO FOR IT!

31-year-old single mother, **Alli Hamilton**, took part in 'Who wants to be a millionaire?'

" I like quiz shows that **stretch your mind**, which is why 'Millionaire' **appealed to** me – that, and the fact that I have two children and had
05 real financial problems. When you phone to try and get on the show, they ask you a single question. Mine was 'What's the capital of Peru?' I got that right, and then they asked me some contestant checks,
10 such as, 'Do you have a criminal record?' and, 'Are you related to anyone employed on the programme?' After that, I had to answer one more question which no one could possibly know the correct answer
15 to, but they take the ten people who get closest. I got 'What's the height of the Eiffel Tower?' Miraculously, I got through, and I had 12 hours to find someone to look after
20 my children – but obviously, no time to swot up on any facts!

They told me that I could bring one guest
25 with me. I was also given instructions about which train I should catch, who I would be met by and what sort of thing to wear (avoid black and white, evidently).

30 I then had to decide which friends I should phone for help during the show. I worried that an old person might panic or not hear the question properly, so I went for younger people. One of them
35 was my boyfriend, Wayne, who knew about sport.

When the programme started, I managed to do well by staying calm. I had decided if I could just make it to £16,000 and was
40 70% sure of the next question, I'd gamble. All I wanted to do was **pay off my debts**, get a house to give the children security, and something for myself – a green Kawasaki motor bike.
45 When I passed the £16,000 mark, I could see the motorcycle in my head.

I had to phone a friend at £16,000. I'd known Wendy for 26 years. I trust her, and knew she'd keep her nerve. The next
50 question for £32,000 was on maths. I work in an accounts department, so that was okay. I thought, 'It's a miracle.' That £32,000 meant I could pay off my debts, get a mortgage on a house and get my bike.

55 When I was at the £64,000 question, I really didn't know the answer, but I had a guess, which was correct; I had won £64,000. I hadn't a clue about the answer to the next question, so I kissed
60 the quizmaster, took the money, and came off stage in a daze.

Here was a chance to sort out and re-evaluate my life in one go. That meant splitting up with Wayne, my
65 boyfriend of more than four years, because I felt our relationship wasn't going anywhere. We parted on good terms. My advice to 'Millionaire' hopefuls is – go for it! "

glossary	
stretch your mind make the fullest use of your mind	
appeal to sb interest or attract sb	
_____ (para 1) Ⓖ learn / study for a test / exam	
_____ (para 4) take a risk	
pay off (your) debts pay money you owe people	
_____ (para 5) money you borrow to buy a house	
your own new words _____ (para ___) _____	
_____ (para ___) _____	

grammar reported questions

1 Underline the four direct questions in paragraph 1 of the article. Compare them with the reported questions below.

  a What differences are there in tense and word order?

  b When do we use *if / whether*?

  1 They asked me what the capital of Peru was.

  2 They wanted to know if / whether I had a criminal record.

  3 They asked if / whether I was related to anyone employed on the programme.

  4 They asked me what the height of the Eiffel Tower was.

2 Put the jumbled reported questions in the correct order.

  1 Japan asked the highest mountain he in was me what

  2 wanted Paris from she how was know Vienna to far it to

  3 fruit I asked a was of papaya whether kind was

  4 was the Wall asked ago came I long down how Berlin

  5 Swedish asked two the had colours more whether she me flag than

3 Rewrite the questions in direct speech. Can you answer them?

> *go to* **language reference** *p.174 and p.175*

it's your turn!

1 Work in A / B pairs.

A prepare to phone 'Who wants to be a millionaire?' and answer B's questions.

B turn to *p.149*.

2 Find a new partner. Report what happened in your conversation.

extended speaking

Learn these phrases for later
It's your go.
Go for it!
This programme would appeal to ...
We'd ask people if they knew ...

wordbooster

collective nouns

These refer to a group of people or things, e.g. *family, team, bunch (of flowers)*. You can use a singular or plural verb after these nouns. *The team is / are doing well*.

Complete the sentences using the correct collective noun.

audience /ˈɔːdiəns/	crew /kruː/	pile /paɪl/
congregation	herd	jury /dʒʊəri/
crowd	staff	gang
set	choir /ˈkwaɪə/	
series	public	

1 We walked through one field with a large _____ of cows.

2 Some people in the _____ threw things at the referee.

3 The _____ were upset when the head teacher was sacked.

4 The ship sank in minutes but the _____ were all rescued.

5 In the end, the _____ found both men guilty.

6 The police stopped a _____ of young boys who were obviously looking for trouble.

7 Could you do something with that _____ of books?

8 The _____ often think politicians are lying, even when they're telling the truth.

9 We bought them a _____ of wine glasses as a present.

10 Some members of the _____ walked out halfway through the play.

11 They're going to carry out a _____ of tests to find out what's wrong with her.

12 There's usually a big _____ in church when the full _____ is singing.

test your partner
– *What do you get a bunch of?*
– *Flowers.*
– *Where will you find an audience?*
– *In a theatre.*

attitude adverbs

1 Complete the sentences in a logical way.

example The tickets were on sale at half price, but **surprisingly**, _they still couldn't sell them all_ .

1 I lost my car keys on the beach. We searched for a while, and **miraculously**, _____ .

2 I've moved into a much bigger flat with all mod cons, but **funnily enough**, _____ .

3 I was in a terrific rush this morning, the weather was awful and I was in a bad mood. I got in my car and **predictably**, _____ .

4 When we arrived, they told us all the hotel rooms had been taken. **Luckily**, _____ .

5 The doctor was called out three times last night, for minor illnesses. **Understandably**, _____ .

6 I'd love to go and work in the United States. **Obviously**, _____ .

7 I haven't seen Jean and that boyfriend of hers together for ages. **Presumably**, _____ .

8 It's been raining all week and we're going walking at the weekend. **Hopefully**, _____ .

2 Work in small groups. Each choose two different adverbs from exercise 1. Write sentence beginnings for your adverbs, as in the exercise.

3 Pass them to others in your group to complete orally.

 listening

boost your brain power

lead-in

1 In small groups, try to solve the two mysteries.

A man walks to a bus stop and asks a woman there for directions. The woman has never seen this man before. There is nothing offensive in the man's actions, and he appears to be pleasant and smartly dressed. The woman suddenly turns to the other people at the bus stop and asks them to help her restrain the man, while she calls the police. For a little while, the other people in the queue are reluctant to get involved. However, once the woman explains her motive the others act quickly to restrain the man before he runs away.

Why did the woman want the man stopped?

CROWDS IN TEARS AS ONE MAN SHOT DEAD IN TRAGEDY

This headline appeared on the sports page in several newspapers. Although there was **mourning** for some time, there was no police investigation or murder enquiry. Nothing was heard of the story after that day.

What were the circumstances of this death?

glossary | **mourning** /ˈmɔːnɪŋ/ great sadness after a death

2 Compare your ideas with the solutions on *p.148*.

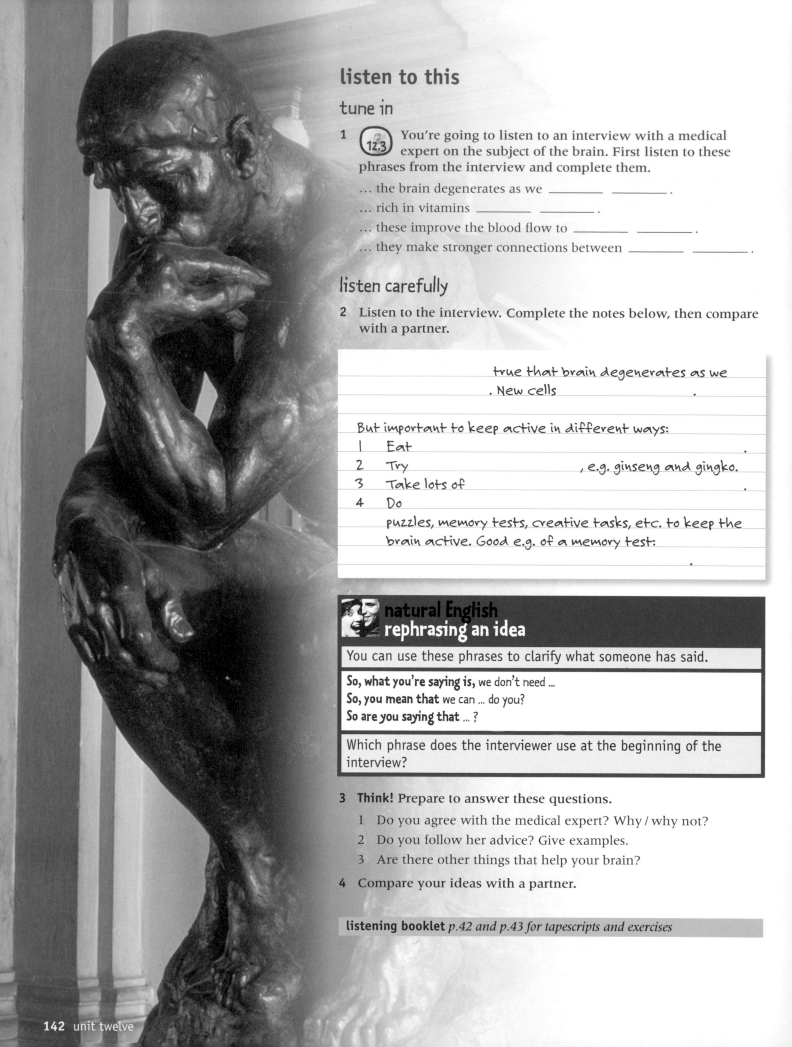

listen to this

tune in

1 **(12.3)** You're going to listen to an interview with a medical expert on the subject of the brain. First listen to these phrases from the interview and complete them.

… the brain degenerates as we _____ _____ .

… rich in vitamins _____ _____ .

… these improve the blood flow to _____ _____ .

… they make stronger connections between _____ _____ .

listen carefully

2 Listen to the interview. Complete the notes below, then compare with a partner.

> _____ true that brain degenerates as we
> _____ . New cells _____ .
>
> But important to keep active in different ways:
> 1 Eat _____ .
> 2 Try _____ , e.g. ginseng and gingko.
> 3 Take lots of _____ .
> 4 Do _____
>   puzzles, memory tests, creative tasks, etc. to keep the brain active. Good e.g. of a memory test: _____ .

3 **Think!** Prepare to answer these questions.

1 Do you agree with the medical expert? Why / why not?
2 Do you follow her advice? Give examples.
3 Are there other things that help your brain?

4 Compare your ideas with a partner.

listening booklet p.42 and p.43 for tapescripts and exercises

grammar *like*, *as*, *such as*

1 Match these examples with explanations
a to d.

1 We went to the pizzeria on Tuesday, **as**
we always do.

2 That suitcase is just **like** mine.

3 I had to use the empty bottle **as** a vase.

4 I got a job **as** a waiter for six months.

5 I love outdoor sports **like** tennis and
athletics.

a *as* + noun is used to say that sth or sb
has a particular job, role, or function.

b *as* + clause (NOT *as + noun*) means
'similar to the way …'

c *like* + noun / pronoun means 'similar
to'.

d *like* + noun is used when giving
examples, and means 'such as'.

2 Choose the correct form in each sentence.

1 He got a job like / **as** an interviewer.

2 You can use a watch like / **as** a compass.

3 Some people say the brain is **like** / as
a computer.

4 She arrived late for work, such as / **as**
she always does.

5 He said that activities as / **such as** memory
games were good for the brain.

6 The brain looks a bit as / **like** a sponge.

7 Follow the instructions such as / **as** I
showed you before.

8 One memory test is as / **like** any other.

go to **language reference** *p.175*

listening challenge

 Listen to more examples of activities
to stimulate the brain. Make notes
about the activities, then compare with a
partner. Listen again with the tapescript on
p.42 of the **listening booklet** if you need to.

it's your turn!

1 Try at least three of the activities below with a partner. Which is
the hardest?

BE A **BRAIN** GYMNAST!

1 Write your name and address
with your 'wrong' hand.

2 Throw something in the air
with your right hand and
catch it. At the same time,
throw and catch something
with your left hand.

3 Put the things on your desk
on the floor. Try picking
them up with your feet.

4 Look at the pictures on *p.136*
for one minute. Close your
book and tell your partner
how much you remember
about them.

5 Write a set of instructions
for putting on make-up or
having a shave.

6 Think up five uses for a ruler.

2 Tell another pair what you tried, and what your results were.

⊙ extended speaking

So what you're saying is, …
Games like … are very popular.
We could have activities such as …

how to ... explain the rules of a game

lead-in

12.5

natural English
saying how easy something is

It's _____ straightforward /streɪt'fɔːwəd/.
It's _____ easy / simple. ☺
It's easy _____ you get the hang of it.
It's _____ complicated.
The instructions are hard to _____.

Listen and complete the phrases.
Practise saying them.

1 **Think!** Prepare to answer these questions.

1 Do you recognize the games in the photos above?
2 Are the rules easy or difficult?
3 Do you enjoy any of them in particular?
4 What other games do you play / have you played? Are the rules easy or complicated?

2 Compare your ideas in small groups.

vocabulary games

1 With a partner, correct the errors in these sentences.

1 I like *Monopoly* – it's a very good play.
2 The contestants won a fantastic travel to the Bahamas.
3 If you get all the answers right, you win a present.
4 When you've decided your mind, you throw the dice.
5 Each team in the competition consists in five people.
6 You have to answer knowledge questions.
7 If you can't answer, you lose a turn.
8 A OK, next question. How far is Venus from Mercury?

   B I don't know ... can you tell me a clue?

2 Circle the words / phrases to do with games.

explain a word game

1 In A / B groups, A look at the set of rules on *p.149* and B on *p.150*.

2 Work with a partner who read the same rules. Practise explaining the game to each other, until you can do it without looking.

3 Find a pair who read the other rules. Take it in turns to explain your game. Then read their rules to see if they remembered everything.

3 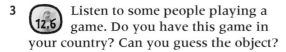 Listen to some people playing a game. Do you have this game in your country? Can you guess the object?

4 Put these rules in the correct order.

a **The winner is the person who** guesses correctly.

b Team members **take it in turns** to ask Betty questions to which the answer has to be 'yes' or 'no'.

c But If no one has guessed in twenty questions, Betty is **the winner**.

d In *Twenty questions*, one person (let's call her Betty) **competes against** a team.

e If they think they know what the object is, they can **have a guess**, but if they are wrong, they **are out** of the game.

f **The aim of the game is** for the team to guess what the object is in twenty questions.

g Betty has to think of an object, and not tell anyone what it is.

5 You have two minutes. Memorize the rules in the correct order. Then shut your book, and ask your partner to test you.

play the games

Play the two games in your groups of four. (For *Fives in sixty seconds*, the person who is the quizmaster will find the categories on *p.150*.)

 extended speaking

Learn these phrases for later

One person competes against a team.
You have to miss a turn if ...

You take it in turns to ...
The aim of the game is ...

extended speaking

you're going to:

collect ideas
read about and discuss some TV game shows

design a show
adapt one of the game shows or make up your own

give a presentation
present your game show idea to the rest of the class

play the game
write your own questions and play the game as a class

but first ...
Look back at the **extended speaking** boxes in this unit. You can use this language in the activity.

 collect ideas

1 Which TV game shows are popular in your country? Why? Tell a partner.

2 Read the descriptions of three game shows. Do you have similar games in your country?

3 **Think!** Which descriptions are true of the game shows you thought of?

fast-moving and exciting   fun and humorous
tedious and predictable   original
competitive and tense   *your own words*
appeal to a wide audience

4 Compare your ideas with a partner.

Friends like these

Two groups of five close friends (a male group and a female group) compete against each other in a series of tests: for example, playing an interactive computer game, memorizing and recalling a list of thirty names. When one group of friends has won (either the men or the women), they compete against each other to win a dream holiday. When one person is left, he or she can either accept the prize, or gamble and try to answer one last question to take their four friends on the holiday.

Ten to one

Ten contestants stand side by side facing the question master. They are asked an open-ended question such as 'give boys' names ending in -y' (Billy, Danny, Johnny, etc.), and each contestant in turn must give a correct response within three seconds. If they can't, or they repeat an answer already given, they are out, and another question is asked. When they are reduced to two contestants, they have to compete against each other in a final round of general knowledge questions, answering alternately until one fails to answer.

Mr & Mrs

Couples, either married or boyfriend and girlfriend, are invited to compete. One partner or spouse is taken to a soundproof booth so that they cannot hear their partner's answers. The partner is asked questions like, 'What is your husband's favourite pizza topping?' or 'What would your partner do if she was woken up by a burglar in your home?' The second partner is then asked the same questions, and if their answers are similar, they win a prize.

design a show

5 In your groups, you're going to design a game show. It could be an adaptation of one you know or a completely new idea. Look at the checklist.

> **checklist**
>
> Decide …
> – what the game will be and what it will be called.
> – what will make your game show different and original.
> – what kind of audience you're aiming at.
> – what kind of contestants you'll have and how you'll select them.
> – who your presenter will be – someone famous, perhaps?
> – on two or three typical questions, challenges, or activities for your show.

give a presentation

6 You're going to present your game show to the class. Divide up the presentation so that everyone has a chance to speak. Rehearse in your groups.

natural English
fronting

These introductory phrases help listeners to understand and be prepared for what you are going to say.

The thing I like about your show **is** …
The one thing that worries me is …
One thing I'd like to ask you is …

7 Give your presentation and listen to the others. At the end, ask any questions and tell them what you think, using the **natural English** box.

play the game

8 Look at *Ten to one* again. In your group, write down three or four open-ended questions such as 'types of vegetable' or 'reasons for being late for an appointment'.

9 Give the questions to your teacher, who is the quizmaster. Play the game with the whole class.

test yourself!

How well do you think you did the extended speaking? Mark the line.

0	10

From this unit, write down:

1 six collective nouns, e.g. *team*.
2 four words connected to sleep.
3 three phrases using *go* as a noun.

Complete the sentences. The meaning must stay the same.

1 'Do you know the answer?'
  He asked _____ .
2 'How long will the journey take?'
  He wanted _____ .
3 Do you know who Jim Carter is?
  Does the name _____ ?
4 I don't like that game much.
  That game doesn't _____ .

Correct the errors.

1 He got a job like an engineer.
2 So what you try to say is, we don't need the money.
3 You take in turns to answer.
4 If you don't know, make a guess.

Look back at the unit contents on *p.137*. Tick ✓ the language you can use confidently.

pairwork

three

wordbooster

student A Paraphrase these words.
Student B has to guess what they are.

impatient   colleague   honest   whisper

nine

listening

student A Read this e-business idea and
prepare to give a mini-presentation.

nonstopparty.com

On this website, you'll be able to organize and
order everything you need for any kind of party:
wedding parties, birthday parties, children's
parties – whatever you are celebrating.

You can get ideas for your party: for example, fancy
dress, and find out where to hire the clothes.

You can have direct links to companies who will
supply food, drinks or entertainments, such as
mobile discos, clowns, bands or comedians. We
can e-mail your friends and family with invitations
and tell them how to get there. We can arrange
accommodation for them if necessary too.

twelve

listening

Puzzle solutions:

A   The man was wearing the woman's
husband's clothes, which he had stolen
in a suitcase from their car, and the
woman recognized the clothes.

B   'One Man' was the name of a horse,
much loved by people who go horse
racing. The headline was on the sports
page of many newspapers the
following day.

seven

extended speaking

Read the role card for the job your interviewee chose and prepare to
interview them.

NATIONAL ARCHAEOLOGICAL SOCIETY

1   Welcome and relax the interviewee, and find out what they do.
2   You will also need to find out:
    – why the person is interested   – their special skills or abilities
    – their experience, if any   – how often they could help.
3   Give the information below <u>only</u> when you are asked about it.
    The work: The team is 25-30 people. Some of the work is physically
    demanding, and some is very slow, so volunteers need to be patient.
    The work involves digging or cleaning the objects most of the time.
    Hours: Work from 8 in the morning till 6 in the evening.
    Support and training: Volunteers will be given training in excavating
    and cleaning techniques, and will receive talks about the site and
    archaeology. They will learn about up-to-date technological advances
    which help with the excavation.
    The documentary makers will be on site all the time, and may film
    volunteers at work and interview them.
4   At the end, thank them and tell them what will happen next.

zooscape children's zoo charity

1   Welcome and relax the interviewee, and find out what they do.
2   You will also need to find out:
    – why the person is interested   – their special skills or abilities
    – their experience, if any   – how often they could help.
3   Give the information below <u>only</u> when you are asked about it.
    The work: Looking after and feeding the birds, reptiles and animals.
    Cleaning out the cages and enclosures. The educational talks will be given
    by experienced zoo keepers, but volunteers will talk to groups of children
    about some animals in the zoo such as rabbits and goats.
    Hours: 8.30 to 5.00. Could be one weekend or two separate days.
    Support and training: Volunteers will be trained how to handle and feed
    the animals, particularly snakes and spiders. None are dangerous. The zoo
    has some important breeding programmes for endangered species. There
    will be talks on the conservation element of the zoo's work. The zoo has
    spacious enclosures similar to the animals' conditions in the wild.
4   At the end, thank them and tell them what will happen next.

THE WINGED FELLOWSHIP TRUST

1   Welcome and relax the interviewee, and find out what they do.
2   You will also need to find out:
    – why the person is interested   – their special skills or abilities
    – their experience, if any   – how often they could help.
3   Give the information below <u>only</u> when you are asked about it.
    The disabled: Most are in their teens and twenties. Many are in
    wheelchairs, blind or partially sighted. Volunteers do not provide any
    specialist or nursing care.
    The work: Help the guests on day trips and outings; organize and
    participate in games and activities, e.g. musical evenings (do they play
    an instrument, can they sing or provide entertainment of this type?);
    listen to and talk to guests.
    Hours: On duty 9.00 to 9.00 but with rest periods during the day.
    Support and training: one-day training, the day before the guests arrive.
    This is to help prepare for possible problems, and how to handle them.
4   At the end, thank them and tell them what will happen next.

twelve

how to ...
explain the rules of a game

student A Read the rules of the game and prepare to explain it to a partner.

the 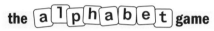 game

The players decide on eight categories, e.g. fruit, jobs, countries, vegetables, musical instruments, animals, clothes, parts of the body, and everyone writes these down in a list.

One player chooses a letter of the alphabet, e.g. S.

Then the players divide into two teams.

The aim of the game is to think up an example in each category beginning with the letter S. Both teams must finish in two minutes. The winner is the team with most correct answers.

twelve

reading

student B You work for 'Who wants to be a millionaire?' and you're going to speak to student A on the phone.

1 Greet student A, and ask their name and phone number.

2 Ask them a very easy general knowledge question (e.g. the name of the currency in a particular country; or the name of the president of a country near yours).

3 Ask them some 'contestant check' questions:
   – if they've ever been on a quiz before
   – whether they are over eighteen
   – whether they know anyone employed on the show.

4 Ask a final general knowledge question, e.g. the distance from one city to another in your country. You need to know the answer yourself! If they answer correctly, they can go on the show tomorrow.

one

reading

student B

HOW DO **YOU** MEASURE UP?

DO YOU WANT TO BE A TOP FOOTBALLER? AN OLYMPIC GYMNAST? Or would the simple act of being able to catch a ball fill you with joy? We offer tips and exercises to increase your physical confidence. And we've enlisted the help of ex-Chelsea and England
05 footballer, GRAEME LE SAUX.

FIELD OF VISION

Top rugby and football players can see the ball out of the corner of their eye, which means they have a good field of vision. We tested Graeme Le Saux using special apparatus. Most people have
10 a 180° field of vision (90° on either side.) Le Saux's was 100° on both sides – a powerful asset to a footballer.

You can do a simple version of this test at home. Tell a friend to sit down and stand behind them with your **index fingers** pointing upwards behind their head, at the same level as their eyes. Keep
15 your fingers 10 to 15 cm from their head, and move them round slowly to the front of their face. As soon as they see your fingers, they must shout 'stop'. If your fingers are level with their ears, they have a good field of vision.

LEG STRENGTH: THE JUMP TEST

20 We gave Le Saux a test of leg strength. He stood sideways against a wall, with the arm nearest the wall raised above his head. From that position, he had to jump as high as possible. Le Saux managed 55 cm, a typical score for a good footballer, and one that shows he has good leg muscles. A good basketball player is likely
25 to jump more than 70 cm. For most people, 20 to 40 cm is good.

You can do a version of this test at home. Stand sideways against a wall, and mark the height of your **outstretched** hand with some chalk. Then, with the chalk in your hand, jump as high as you can, and mark the point you reach. The distance between the two
30 chalk marks gives an indication of your leg strength.

glossary

Fill the gaps.

_____ (para 1) advice

_____ (para 2) something that is useful and helps you

index finger (para 3) the finger next to your thumb

outstretched /aʊtˈstretʃt/ (para 5) extended as far as possible

pairwork

nine

listening

student B Read this e-business idea and prepare to give a mini-presentation.

viewahotel.com

This website will give you all the information you need about any hotel in the country. You'll be able to see photographs of all the rooms in any hotel, and take a virtual tour around the rooms. You'll be able to see a typical meal, the hotel staff and find out the prices.

We can also suggest hotels in a particular location at a range of prices. Tell us how much you want to spend and we'll do the rest.

We can also tell you what entertainments and attractions there are in the area.

And of course, we can book for you free of charge.

twelve

how to ... explain the rules of a game

student B Read the rules of the game and prepare to explain it to a partner.

FIVES IN SIXTY SECONDS

There is a quizmaster and three or four players.

The quizmaster has sets of categories, e.g. Walt Disney films, breeds of dog, seaside towns, medical complaints, sports which use a ball, etc. and each player has to give five examples for the category they are given.

The player wins a point for each correct example, plus a bonus point if they name all five. If a player cannot name five in 60 seconds, the other players can suggest one more answer and win a bonus point each.

The next player is given a new category.

The winner is the person who scores the highest number of points.

Possible categories for Fives in Sixty Seconds:

- five medical complaints
- five sports which use a ball
- five ways of walking
- five adjectives ending in -ive
- five negative prefixes
- five adjectives describing character
- five phrasal verbs with *up*
- five verbs followed by -ing
- five verbs you can use with the noun *exam*

three

wordbooster

student B Paraphrase these words. Student A has to guess what they are.

popular   babysitter   reliable   crawl

eleven

extended speaking

group B Read the case study.

CASE STUDY B

Paula Lewis, 15, had been a perfect, well-behaved daughter, but then she started mixing with a group of teenagers who were a bad influence on her. Increasingly, she stayed out late and didn't take any notice of what her parents said. She was also worried about failing her exams, but was too frightened to confide in her parents.

There were other changes in her behaviour as well. A local shopkeeper had seen Paula stealing chocolates. He told her to put them back, but didn't take the matter any further. Not long after that, Paula's schoolteacher rang the parents to say she was worried about Paula's poor attitude and progress in her schoolwork. The teacher offered to meet them to talk it over, but the parents said they would deal with the problem themselves.

Their response was to get angry with Paula, and cut her pocket money to stop her going out. Paula went out a little less, but started coming home in expensive new clothes. When the parents asked her about this, she said that she'd borrowed them from friends.

One afternoon, her mother answered the door to find Paula with a policeman. She'd been caught shoplifting with her friends in a department store. Her mother was horrified.

language reference

-ing form v. infinitive

-ing forms

You can use -ing forms after certain verbs and expressions.

enjoy	keep	give up	finish
imagine	start	practise	mind
be / get used to	look forward to	avoid	involve

Verbs and phrases related to liking and hating are usually followed by -ing.

like	be fond of	loathe	can't bear
enjoy	be keen on	detest	can't stand
fancy	hate	resent	

You can use -ing forms after prepositions.

After meet**ing** him, we left.
I got in **by** climb**ing** through a window.
Before sett**ing** out, I checked the gas.
Instead of eat**ing** at home, we decided to go out.

To can be a preposition (e.g. I went **to** the bank; he looks up **to** her) and it can also be part of the infinitive form (e.g. I don't know what **to** do; I was happy **to** see him). When it's a preposition, it can be followed by -ing.

I'm looking forward **to** go**ing** there.
I can't get used **to** wear**ing** this uniform.
I don't object **to** tak**ing** the bus in the mornings.

You can use -ing forms as the subject or object of a sentence.

Jogging is fun.
The nicest thing in the summer is **drinking** ice-cold drinks in the shade.
Hang-gliding is more dangerous than **waterskiing**.

You can use -ing forms after certain expressions.

It's not worth go**ing** now – the film's already started.
Is it any good try**ing** to persuade him?
It's no use wait**ing**. The last bus has gone.
It's pointless sitt**ing** here. Let's go.

go to **exercises 1.1** *and* **1.2**

-ing form and infinitive

Some verbs can be followed by either the -ing form or the infinitive, with no difference in meaning.

We	**started** **began**	**collecting** stamps when we were children. **to collect**
They	**continued**	**talking** long into the night. **to talk**

cover & check exercises

1.1 Complete with a suitable -ing form.

1 Don't leave the flat without _____ the front door.
2 I can't stand _____ for buses.
3 _____ is a very active hobby.
4 In Britain, you have to get used to _____ on the left.
5 I've asked her at least ten times to buy some sugar, but she keeps _____ .

1.2 Complete the gaps with a suitable adjective or preposition.

1 Do you think it's _____ seeing his latest film?
2 You must be looking forward _____ going on holiday.
3 It's _____ telling him to work harder; he's just very lazy.
4 Instead _____ taking the train, we decided to go by bus.
5 It's no _____ trying to ring him; his phone's out of order.

> Cover the grammar, then try the exercise. Check the grammar again to help you.

Avoid using two -ing forms together.

> We were just starting to work ~~working~~ when the boss arrived.

A few verbs can be followed by either -ing or the infinitive, but the meaning changes.

> He **tried to open** the door, but it was stuck. = make an effort to do sth
> I've **tried jogging**, **weightlifting**, **cycling** – and I'm still unfit. = experiment in different ways

> I must **remember to ring** Bill. = make a mental note to do sth
> I **remember ringing** Bill last week. = I remember now sth I did before; recall

> I **regret to tell** you that we cannot offer you the job. = be sorry about sth you are about to say
> I **regret studying** sociology at university. = be sorry about sth that happened before

> She saw Jack, **stopped to chat**, then walked on. = stop doing one thing in order to do another
> I **stopped playing** tennis two years ago. = give up doing sth

> I **meant to ring** her, but I forgot. = intend
> If we buy this house, it'll **mean doing** a lot of decorating. = one thing will result in another

go to **exercise 1.3**

wishes and regrets

You can use *wish* + past simple to express regret about something in the present.

> I **wish I knew** Pete's address. = I don't know his address but I want it.
> I **wish it was / were** five o'clock. = It isn't five o'clock but I would like it to be.
> I **wish I could swim**. = I can't swim, but I would like to be able to.
> He **wishes he didn't have to** go away this weekend. = He has to go away, but doesn't want to.

natural English *wish + was / were*

After *I*, *he*, *she*, and *it*, you can use *was* or *were* in spoken English, but *were* is more correct in formal English.

> I wish I **was / were** on a beach right now.   NOT ~~I wish you was rich.~~
> I wish she **was / were** more confident.

You can use *wish* + past perfect (*had* + past participle) or *regret* + -ing to express regret about something in the past.

> I **wish I'd (had) gone** to university. = I didn't go and I regret it.
> I **wish they hadn't asked** us to help. = Unfortunately they did ask us to help.
> They **regret moving** to Scotland. = They moved to Scotland and they're sorry they did.

go to **exercises 1.4** *and* **1.5**

1.3 Tick ✓ the sentences which are correct and correct those which aren't.

1 Could you stop to talk please? I'm trying to work.
2 Will you remember to post this letter for me?
3 I think he regrets to buy that car.
4 There was a thunderstorm, but they continued working in the garden.
5 Did you mean breaking the window, or was it an accident?

Is this grammar the same in your language? If not, make a note of the difference.

1.4 Tick ✓ the correct paraphrase.

1 I wish I didn't have to do this exam.
  a I have to do an exam and I don't want to.
  b I had to do an exam and I didn't want to.
2 She wishes she could stay longer.
  a She has to go, but she'd prefer to stay.
  b She hopes to stay longer.
3 I wish you hadn't told me your secret.
  a I regret that you told me.
  b I don't want you to tell me.

1.5 Rewrite these sentences using *I wish* followed by the correct tense.

1 I can't read without glasses.
  I wish _____.
2 Unfortunately, I'm not on holiday.
  I wish _____.
3 I didn't bring my sunglasses.
  I wish _____.
4 I spent all my money on that camera.
  I wish _____.
5 They gave us that horrible vase.
  I wish _____.

should + verb, should have + past participle

You can use *should* + verb to talk about obligation or duty. It's less strong than *must / have to*.

> Children **should wear** a protective helmet if they're riding a bike.
> You **shouldn't leave** young children on their own.

We use *should* to give advice or make recommendations.

> That new exhibition is great – you **should** go and see it.
> If you have any problems with your work, you **should** go and talk to your boss.

We use *should* to say we think something is true, or will happen.

> A lot of people have recommended this restaurant, so it **should** be good.
> It's eight o'clock, so Mary **should** be here soon.

You can use *should* to say what is correct or appropriate in a particular situation.

> You've made a mistake – 'accommodation' **should** have two 'm's, not one.
> There **should** be at least twelve chairs in this classroom – why are there only eight?

You can use *should have / shouldn't have* + past participle to say that something did or didn't happen, but you wish it had / hadn't happened. It's often used as a criticism or regret.

> I **should have bought** that DVD player when it was in the sales – now I can't afford it.
> She **shouldn't have left** school without qualifications. She'll find it hard to get a good job.

go to **exercise 2.1**

although, though, and even though

These words all show a contrast between two clauses, with the second clause being unexpected or a surprise after the first. The meaning (i.e. 'but') is basically the same, but *though* is more common in spoken English and *even though* adds greater emphasis.

> **Although** the company has increased production, it's still not making a profit.
> The film had good reviews, **though** I didn't really like it.
> I wouldn't go to that place again, **even though** the food is excellent.

You can also use *though* as a sentence adverb to mean 'however'. It goes at the end of a clause and is in contrast with information in the previous sentence. It's very common in spoken English, often occurring in dialogue.

> I bought these trainers in a sale. They're not exactly what I want, **though**.
> **A** I like these biscuits.
> **B** Yeah. A bit sweet, **though**.

go to **exercise 2.2**

cover & check exercises

2.1 Rewrite the sentences using *should / should have*.

1 It's a good idea for you to borrow the extra money.

   _____

2 Carole didn't leave early enough.

   _____

3 The teacher didn't tell them off. That was stupid.

   _____

4 That's wrong – 'carefully' has got two 'l's, not one.

   _____

5 I forgot to warn the neighbours about the party and they were very annoyed.

   _____

When you've finished an exercise, say the sentences aloud.

2.2 Complete these sentences in a logical way.

1 Although we left early, _____

   _____ .

2 Everyone enjoyed the picnic, even though _____ .

3 My brother kept telling me I played well, though _____ .

4 It wasn't a particularly hard exam, although _____ .

5 **A** It's quite sunny today.
   B Yeah, _____ , though.

possibility and probability

You can express degrees of possibility and probability in a number of ways:

You can use modal verbs *might, may, could, will,* and *won't.*

He left early so he **might get** here soon. = it's possible
We **may finish** before 6.00 – it depends how hard we work.
It **could be** difficult to get tickets for the game.

She**'ll pass** the test, I'm sure. = it's certain
They **won't win** the tournament; their goalkeeper's been injured.

You can use the adverbs *definitely, probably,* and *well.* Notice the position of the adverbs.

She**'ll probably** ring me later. He **probably won't** be in time for dinner.
I**'ll definitely*** have the answer by then. You **definitely won't** enjoy that film.
*definitely = certain, sure

Well changes the meaning of the phrase from 'it's possible' to 'it's probable'.

That	**could well**	**be** true.
	might well	
	may well	

go to **exercise 2.3**

You can use adjectival phrases.

It**'s bound to rain** – don't forget your umbrella. = almost certain to happen
She**'s sure to know** the answer. = certain to be true
The concert**'s** **likely** /ˈlaɪkli/ **to finish** late. = will probably
 unlikely = probably won't
Do you think it'll snow? That**'s highly unlikely**. = it almost certainly won't
Is it likely that they'll get married? = is it probable?

You can use certain verbs.

I **doubt** /daʊt/ **(that)** she'll be here before ten o'clock. = she probably won't be
I **doubt if / whether** we'll be able to get into the stadium. = we probably won't be able to
I **don't suppose** /səˈpəʊz/ there will be any tickets left. = there probably won't be
I **dare say** /ˌdeə ˈseɪ/ the train will be late as usual. = it probably will be
I **shouldn't think** there'll be any delay. = there probably won't be

go to **exercise 2.4**

2.3 Do the pairs of sentences have a similar (S) or different (D) meaning?

1 a It might be nice tomorrow.
 b It'll probably be nice tomorrow.
2 a I definitely won't be able to help.
 b I'm certain I won't be able to help.
3 a It could be true.
 b It's probable that it's true.
4 a There may be a lot of people there.
 b It's possible there will be a lot of people there.
5 a She could well get here late.
 b She probably won't be on time.

2.4 Rewrite the sentences. Use the word in brackets.

1 I doubt if he'll come. (unlikely)
 _____
2 My bag is almost certain to be the last one off the plane. (bound)
 _____
3 They probably won't win. (suppose)
 _____
4 It'll probably start raining before lunchtime. (likely)
 _____
5 There are likely to be a lot people on that train. (dare say)
 _____

three

each other / one another / -self / -selves

reflexive pronouns

I	cut	myself	he	cut	himself	we	cut	ourselves
you		yourself	she		herself	you (pl)		yourselves
			it		itself	they		themselves

You can use reflexive pronouns when the object is the same person or thing as the subject. Compare:

Peter hurt **himself**. = the same person (Peter hurt Peter.)
Peter hurt **him**. = a different person (Peter hurt David.)

Reflexive pronouns are commonly used with certain verbs.

enjoy	introduce	hurt	injure	behave	(yourself, etc.)
teach	look after	help	cut	burn	

You don't usually use reflexive pronouns with these verbs (though it's common in other languages).

He had a shave. NOT ~~He shaved himself.~~
She had a wash. NOT ~~She washed herself.~~
I got dressed. NOT ~~I dressed myself.~~

These examples are only possible if the event is unusual, e.g. someone isn't usually able to do these things.

It's the first time she's **dressed herself** since the accident.

Certain verbs are reflexive in some other languages, but not in English.

relax ~~me / myself~~   feel ~~me~~   meet ~~us~~   concentrate ~~me~~

I often relax by going out walking. NOT ~~I often relax myself by going out walking.~~
John feels ill. NOT ~~John feels himself ill.~~

go to **exercises 3.1** *and* **3.2**

each other / one another

You can use *each other / one another* to say that two (or more) people do something to or for the other(s). They are interchangeable in meaning.

Jack and Jo bought **each other / one another** a gift.
  = Jack bought a gift for Jo, Jo bought one for Jack.

Certain verbs are often used with *each other / one another*:

agree with	disagree with	argue with	each other / one another
kiss	hug	love	
hate	talk to	listen to	
compete with	consult	fight	

cover & check exercises

3.1 Complete using the correct pronoun, reflexive pronoun, or nothing.

1 Ow! Stop it! You're hurting _____ !
2 Are you enjoying _____ here?
3 Janet and I first met _____ at a party in New York.
4 Are those children behaving _____ ?
5 I really need to relax _____ as I've been working very hard.

3.2 Correct any errors. One sentence is correct.

1 He had a shave himself and left.
2 I don't feel myself very well today.
3 The children hurt themself in the playground.
4 Jack introduced himself to Clara.
5 Jenny never went to school; in fact, she taught her to read.

For a change,
do an exercise in your
head or orally with a partner.
Check your answers, then
write them in.

each other v. reflexive pronouns

Compare:

Liz and Kate looked at	**themselves**. = Liz looked at herself, Kate looked at herself
	each other. = Liz looked at Kate, Kate looked at Liz
The boys had to look after	**themselves**. = each boy looked after himself
	each other. = each boy looked after the other boy

go to **exercise 3.3**

obligation, necessity, and prohibition

must, have to, have got to

You can use *must*, *have to*, and *have got to* to express obligation. *Have to* is very common in spoken English.

> I'm sorry I can't come out tonight but I really **have to** get some work done.
> We **have to** wear name badges at the sales conference next week.

Must is sometimes preferred for an obligation we feel ourselves.

> I **must** get a lot fitter before I run the marathon. = it's my opinion
> I **must** post this letter before 6 o'clock – it's Sam's birthday tomorrow.
>   = I feel it's important for me to do this

Have to, *have got to*, and *must* are used for external obligation. *Must* is common in written rules.

> Candidates **must** answer all six questions. = a written rule
> The receptionist says I **have to** hand in the key before 12 o'clock. = external obligation
> We'**ve got to** improve our sales figures by the spring. = an order from the boss
> You **have to** wear a seatbelt. = the law says so

natural English *have got to*

Have got to is usually only used in spoken English, or written fiction, and is quite common. It can be used for internal and external obligation.

> I'**ve got to** get out more – I'm going mad here!
> I'**ve got to** post this letter before six o'clock.

Mustn't and *don't have to* / *haven't got to* don't mean the same thing: *mustn't* means that something is wrong, dangerous, or not permitted; *don't have to* and *haven't got to* mean that something isn't necessary.

> You **mustn't** let the dogs run loose in the street. = it's wrong and not permitted
> You **mustn't** drink that water. = it's dangerous
> She **doesn't have to** type her own letters. = it's not necessary
> We **haven't got to** be there until nine o'clock. = it's not necessary

When you talk about a future obligation, *will have to* is normally used if the obligation doesn't begin until a point in the future.

> He'**ll have to** be more responsible when he becomes a parent himself.

You can use *have (got) to* for obligations that refer to the future but are already established.

> I **have to** go back this afternoon and collect my things.
> We'**ve got to** work on Saturday – the manager told us yesterday.

go to **exercises 3.4** *and* **3.5**

3.3 Tick ✓ the sentences which are logical.

1 a They kissed each other on the cheek.
  b They kissed themselves on the cheek.
2 a Can you look after yourselves today?
  b Can you look after each other today?
3 a We disagree with ourselves.
  b We disagree with each other.
4 a Those girls often talk to themselves.
  b Those girls often talk to each other.
5 a We always consult each other.
  b We always consult ourselves.

3.4 Put *have to*, *don't have to*, *will have to*, *must*, or *mustn't* in the gaps.

1 When you're in New York next week, you _____ speak English.
2 Oh, great, it's Sunday. I _____ get up early – I can relax.
3 Listen, it's the law. You _____ pay taxes and that's all there is to it.
4 I've got an exam tomorrow morning. I _____ forget to set my alarm.
5 My hair is a terrible mess. I _____ go and get it cut.

3.5 Circle the correct or most appropriate answer.

1 You mustn't / don't have to put this dish in the microwave – it'll break.
2 I think we have to / will have to paint the living room next year.
3 My mother is expecting me to ring, so I mustn't / haven't got to forget.
4 The guy in the bank says I've got to / must fill in the form and return it with the money.
5 Dogs must / have got to be on a lead.

> Is this the same in your language? If not, make a note of the difference.

should and ought to

You can find details of the different uses of *should* on *p.153*. *Ought* /ˈɔːt/ *to* is very similar and can replace *should* in most cases but it is less common.

> You **should / ought to** ring your mother before you go. = weak obligation
> I think you **should / ought to** leave the washing up until later. = advice
> Those cups **should / ought to** be in the other cupboard. = the correct place in this situation
> He's got a map so he **should / ought to** find the place easily. = you think this will happen

The main difference is that the negative form *ought not to / oughtn't to* is rarely used in place of *shouldn't*, and almost never used in the past in place of *shouldn't have* + past participle.

Should and *ought to* are sometimes interchangeable with *must*, but both are weaker than *must*.

> I **must** ring my mother. v. I **should / ought to** ring my mother.

Must conveys a stronger obligation on the speaker's part.

> You **mustn't** eat your sandwiches in here. = it's wrong / not permitted
> You **shouldn't** eat your sandwiches in here. = it's not really the correct thing to do

Mustn't conveys a stronger sense that something is prohibited.

be allowed to + infinitive

You can use *be allowed to* when you talk about things you can do or are permitted to do.

> You**'re allowed to** take a dictionary into this exam. = you're permitted to do it / you can do it
> We **aren't allowed to** take these books out of the library. = we're not permitted to do it

Be careful!

> You**'re** not **allowed to** walk on the grass. NOT ~~It's not allowed to walk on the grass.~~

go to **exercise 3.6**

time sequencers

You can use these words and phrases to express time <u>before</u> an event.

(shortly) (long)	before	+ noun / -*ing* + clause	prior to (formal) + noun / -*ing*
She found out the truth	**shortly before** **long before**	the wedding. getting married. she got married.	
	prior to	the wedding. getting married.	

You can use these sequencers to express time <u>after</u> an event.

(shortly) (soon) (long)	after	+ noun / -*ing* + clause
since		

3.6 Write in one missing word in each sentence.

1 He can't come – he's to go to the dentist.
2 Don't you think we ought leave soon?
3 When I was young, we weren't to stay up late.
4 You should leave your bag here – someone might steal it.
5 I don't think you allowed to park in front of this entrance.

> Write in pencil, then you can rub out your answers and do the exercise again later.

Joan met Louis	(shortly) (soon) (long)	after	her move to Rome. moving to Rome. she moved to Rome.
She's been home twice		since	

You can use *while* or *when* for two things or situations happening at the same time, usually for two longer actions over a similar period of time, or a shorter action happening during a longer action.

while	+ *-ing* + clause	when	+ clause

While	working	for the bank, I learnt to do spreadsheets.
When / While	I was working	
When / While	Bill was fixing the car, I was tidying the house.	

go to **exercise 3.7**

3.7 Write complete sentences. Use the sequencer in brackets.

1 David / climb / mountain / breakfast (soon after)
2 Helena / prepare / presentation / meet / new boss (prior to)
3 accident / happen / start / rain (shortly before)
4 live / Saudi Arabia / Christine / study / Arabic (while)
5 Cherie / have / baby / lose weight (since)

four

nouns in groups

There are three common ways to group nouns.

noun + noun

These are two or more words which specify a single idea; they are also called compounds.

horror film	film director	bottle opener
railway station	credit card	human resources manager
car park attendant	bus stop	box office

noun's / s' + noun

This structure is often used to show something or someone belongs to, or is associated with, a person / animal, a group or an institution.

my grandmother's house	the dog's tail
the boy's father (one boy)	the government's decision
the boys' father (more than one boy)	the school's policy

go to **exercise 4.1**

noun + preposition + noun

When something belongs to or is associated with an object / thing, we usually use an 'of' structure. Certain words are common with this form (e.g. top, bottom, front, back, side, beginning, start, end, edge).

the back of the cinema	the end of the book	the start of the race
the bottom of the ocean	the beginning of life	the edge of the table

go to **exercise 4.2**

cover & check exercises

4.1 Rephrase the sentences using the noun

's / s' + noun structure.

1 The cat has white paws.
   The _____ are white.
2 The doctors have a clinic in the centre.
   The _____ is in the centre.
3 Mary isn't the mother of those girls.
   Mary isn't _____ .
4 This is a report by the committee.
   This is the _____ .
5 That old car belongs to my parents.
   That's _____ old car.

4.2 Correct the errors.

1 The film's end was very sad.
2 I gave the money to the uncle of Jake.
3 He's been made the manager of sales.
4 Can we sit at the train's front?
5 See you at the station of buses at 10.00.

future continuous

You can use the future continuous to emphasize that something will be in progress at a particular time in the future.

By 2020, almost everyone **will be watching** the news on the Internet.

Certain time phrases are very common with the future continuous.

In five years' **time**, she'll be studying at university. NOT She'll study at university.
By the end of the century, we'll be living much longer. OR ... we'll live much longer
This time next week, I'll be sitting on the beach in the Bahamas. NOT I'll sit ...

You can use it to refer to a future event / activity which is planned or expected to happen in the normal course of events.

I'll be teaching your class next year **whatever happens**.
I'll be passing the letterbox **anyway**, so I'll post that for you.
We'll be meeting her **in any case**, so I'll pass on the message.

natural English *anyway*, *in any case*, *whatever happens*

Anyway, *in any case*, and *whatever happens* are commonly used to emphasize that the situation or event is inevitable.

I'll be phoning Mum tonight **anyway** / **in any case**, so I'll give her the news.
We'll be staying in **whatever happens**, so do come round.

Don't use the future continuous when the meaning of the verb conveys a single action or state.

Knowing John, he **'ll be losing lose** his laptop if he takes it on the trip. (He can only lose it once.)
Everyone **will be having have** a mobile phone in ten years' time. (*have* is a state verb)

go to **exercises 4.3** *and* **4.4**

4.3 Circle the correct tense. Both answers may be correct.
1 This time tomorrow, we'll arrive / be arriving in Lisbon.
2 I'll know / be knowing the date of the meeting by the end of the week.
3 Do you think you'll live / be living here in five years' time?
4 I'll spend / be spending the weekend with my brother, so I can tell him then.
5 Don't ring me this evening – I'll have / be having dinner with Lucy.

4.4 Put *anyway*, *in*, *still*, *this*, or *by* in the gaps.
1 We'll be leaving for Rio _____ a couple of weeks' time.
2 She'll be earning a fortune _____ the end of the year.
3 I'll be going past your house _____, so I can easily give you a lift.
4 If you come and see us ten years from now, we'll _____ be renovating this old house.
5 I can't believe it. _____ time tomorrow, I'll be sitting on a plane on my way to New Zealand.

Is this grammar the same in your language? If not, make a note of the difference.

five

narrative tenses

past continuous

Use the past continuous to talk about something that was in progress at or around a particular past time.

They **were building** those flats when we moved in across the road.
I came out of the cinema and it **was pouring** with rain.

Quite often the event in progress is interrupted by a single action, and so past simple and past continuous are used together.

I **was** just **having** my lunch when he **phoned**.
We **were driving** to Oxford when we **heard** the news about the explosion.

You can use the past continuous to give the background situation in a story or anecdote. It gives the listener / reader the context of the main event.

I **was sitting** in the park the other day, and it **was raining**, so I **was feeling** a bit miserable, when suddenly this stranger came up to me and gave me $100.

cover & check exercises

past perfect simple and continuous

Use the past perfect simple when you're describing a past event or situation and you want to show that another past event/situation happened earlier.

He left.   I phoned.
When I phoned him, **he'd** already **left**. = He left <u>before</u> I phoned him.

I knew **I had met** him somewhere. = I met him <u>before</u> this occasion I'm describing now.

If the sentences include *before* and *after*, the order of events is often clear, so the past perfect is optional.

The accident (**had**) **happened** before we arrived.

go to **exercise 5.1**

You can use the past perfect continuous when an earlier situation or activity lasted for a longer period of time and continued up to the point in the past that you're talking about.

| 5.00 | 6.00 | 7.00 | 8.00 | 9.00 | 10.00 | 11.00 |

I'd been working for four hours ...   when the others arrived.

With the simple form it's the completion of the activity that is emphasized; with the continuous form it's the continuation that's emphasized.

We'd had two drinks when the cabaret started. = We finished the drinks before the cabaret.
We'd been drinking for some time when the cabaret started. = The drinking continued for a period up to the time when the cabaret started.

The simple form often describes <u>how many times</u> something happened, and the continuous form describes <u>how long</u> something happened. Compare:

I'd read three of his novels by the time I went to university.
I'd been reading his books for years by the time I went to university.

See also present perfect simple and continuous, *p.164 and p.165*.

go to **exercise 5.2**

so and *such*

Notice these constructions with *so*.

so + adjective / adverb	*so* + *much* / *many* + noun
I felt **so happy**.	He had **so much money**.
I was terrified – she drove **so quickly**.	She tried to ring him **so many times**.

Notice these constructions with *such*.

such + *a* / *an* + (adjective) + noun (C)	*such* + adjective + noun (U)
such a funny film	such hot weather
such a nightmare	such bad news

such + adjective + plural noun	
such clever boys	such nice children

5.1 Put the verbs in brackets into the past simple or past perfect simple.

1 She _____ (ring) after I _____ (speak) to them.
2 I _____ (already tidy up) when they _____ (get) here.
3 There _____ (be) a concert last Friday but we couldn't go – we _____ (spend) all our money.
4 Sitting on the bus I _____ (remember) that I _____ (forget) to lock the front door.
5 I _____ (be) tired because I _____ (stay) up very late the night before.

5.2 Choose a suitable verb in the past perfect simple or continuous to explain what had happened / had been happening in each situation.

examples

When I went out, the roads were still wet because **it had been raining**.

He couldn't play on Saturday because **he had injured** his foot.

1 Both boys had dirty knees because …
2 He was wearing his suit because …
3 She had to walk all the way home because …
4 He was sweating and out of breath because …
5 She had a cut on her knee because …

For a change, do an exercise quickly in your head.

So and *such* constructions are often followed by *that* clauses.

It was	**such a stressful experience that**	she never went back.
It was	**so stressful that**	

go to **exercise 5.3**

adjectives and adverbs

gradable and ungradable adjectives

Some adjectives are gradable, e.g. something can be *quite* good or *very* good, while others are ungradable and only have one extreme meaning, e.g. *awful*, *enormous*.

extreme				extreme
freezing	cold	warm	hot	boiling

Compare:

gradable adjectives	hot	nice	tired	frightening
ungradable adjectives	boiling	delightful	exhausted	terrifying

intensifying adverbs

We use intensifying adverbs (e.g. *extremely*, *really*, *absolutely*, *totally*) to show that something is true to a large degree. Notice which adverbs are used with gradable and ungradable adjectives.

	gradable adjectives		**ungradable adjectives**
incredibly	cold	**absolutely**	terrifying
extremely	hot	**really**	boiling
really	nice		delightful
very	tired		exhausted

Some intensifying adverbs collocate with certain ungradable adjectives, but not others.

absolutely	ridiculous	**absolutely**	furious
completely		NOT ~~completely~~	
totally		NOT ~~totally~~	

go to **exercise 5.4**

modifying adverbs

You can modify gradable adjectives with certain adverbs:

a small degree		**a large degree**
a bit	quite	very
a little	fairly	really
slightly	rather	extremely
	pretty	incredibly

A bit, *a little*, and *slightly* are often used with adjectives with a negative meaning, or with positive or negative comparative adjectives.

a bit late	a little slow	slightly annoying
a bit happier	a little happier	slightly older

Fairly and *quite* have a similar meaning; *quite* is a little stronger.

5.3 Rewrite the sentences using *so* in place of *such*, and *such* in place of *so*.

1 The work was so hard that I gave up the job.

_____

2 His sister was such a bright woman that she got the top job.

_____

3 We went back the following year because the resort was so beautiful.

_____

4 He had such a bad temper that I left him.

_____

5 The gardens were so lovely that we stayed all afternoon.

_____

5.4 Put G (gradable) or U (ungradable) for each underlined adjective.

1 He has a <u>wonderful</u> garden.
2 We found the city <u>expensive</u>.
3 The house was <u>dirty</u> and <u>freezing</u>.
4 Her children are <u>noisy</u> but <u>charming</u>.
5 It was a <u>dreadful</u> film.

Write *extremely* or *absolutely* before each adjective. Change *a* to *an* where necessary.

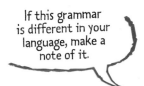

If this grammar is different in your language, make a note of it.

Rather is often used with negative adjectives.

It's **rather cold**.   The talk was **rather boring**. = quite

Rather with positive adjectives often means something was better than expected.

The film was **rather interesting**, actually. = I thought it might be quite boring.

Pretty, *a bit*, and *really* are very common in spoken English.

Quite has two uses. Compare:

quite + gradable adjective
The weather was **quite nice**. = not very good, but reasonable

quite + ungradable adjective
His behaviour was **quite terrifying**. = absolutely terrifying

go to **exercise 5.5**

go to **exercise 5.5**

5.5 Put *quite*, *rather*, or *a bit* in the gaps.

1 The bus was only two minutes late.
   The bus was _____ late.
2 The film made me laugh a few times.
   The film was _____ funny.
3 The talk was half an hour, but twenty minutes would have been better.
   The talk was _____ long.
4 The party was OK, but not great.
   The party was _____ good.
5 The food was better than I expected.
   The food was _____ good, in fact.

six

past simple and present perfect passive

Only transitive verbs (i.e. verbs which take an object) have a passive form.

They **sold** all the supplies. (transitive)   The taxi **arrived** late. (intransitive)
All the supplies **were sold**.

You can use passive forms when talking about an action where you're not interested in saying who did the action, or it's obvious who did it, or it's not necessary to say who did it. The person or thing affected by the action is more important than who did it.

He**'s been given** a new job. (It isn't important who gave him the job.)
The building **was knocked down**. (Who did it isn't important.)
She **was arrested** outside the parliament building. (It was obviously done by the police.)

If you want to emphasize <u>who</u> did the action, because it's important, you can use *by* + agent.

A I thought that was a Tarantino film.
B No, it **was directed by** Guy Ritchie.

Passive forms are common in academic and scientific English.

Several factors contributing to the patient's condition **were identified**.
The results **have been analysed** and it **has been discovered** that the process is unreliable.

go to **exercise 6.1**

go to **exercise 6.1**

In news stories, present perfect and past simple passive forms are common. When you give news, you're often more interested in what's happened to someone or something than who did it.

Two people **have been arrested** in connection with the robbery.
A ten-year-old boy **has been found** alive in a cave after disappearing three days ago.

cover & check exercises

6.1 Make these sentences passive. Use *by* + agent only where necessary.

1 Someone stole my bicycle last night.
   _____
2 Several people have told me that it's a great restaurant.
   _____
3 Sir John Mackintosh will make the final decision tomorrow.
   _____
4 The Chinese invented fireworks.
   _____
5 They don't serve children under 16 in this bar.
   _____

When more detailed information is then given, the tense used is often the past simple.

> Two people **have been arrested** in connection with the robbery. They **were taken** to Bow Street police station and ...

Certain verbs frequently used in news stories are common in the passive form.

hurt	injure	wound	capture	attack	kill
assassinate	murder	damage	destroy	hijack	kidnap
threaten	evacuate	accuse	arrest	charge	sentence

go to **exercise 6.2**

In news reporting, certain reporting verbs are common in passive constructions.

> The man **is believed / said to be** armed and dangerous.
> He **is known to have visited** the area in previous days. (past infinitive)
> It **is thought / believed that** all the children escaped safely.

go to **exercise 6.3**

indirect questions

With *wh-* questions, the main verb usually comes after the subject (i.e. positive word order), and the auxiliary *do / does / did* isn't used. Look at these examples.

direct questions	indirect questions
Where**'s the station**?	Do you know where **the station is**?
What time **does it leave**?	Could you tell me what time **it leaves**?
How **do you feel** about it?	Could I ask you how **you feel** about it?

With *yes / no* questions, we need *if* or *whether* followed by positive word order.

direct questions	indirect questions
Are you planning to leave?	I'd like to know **if you're planning** to leave.
Do you need it?	I was wondering **whether you needed** it.
Does she want to go?	I'm not sure **if she wants** to go.

You use indirect questions in reporting (see **unit twelve**), but in the examples above, indirect questions are used as a softer or more polite way of asking for information. These expressions are often used to introduce indirect questions:

Could you tell me ...?	Do you know ...?	I was wondering / I wondered ...
Have you any idea ...?	I'd like to know ...	I'd be interested to know ...

go to **exercise 6.4**

For information on **reported questions**, go to *p.174*.

6.2 Circle the correct form.

1 'Good evening. Here is the seven o'clock news. Three people were / have been arrested in connection with the terrorist attack on the town hall.'
2 The factory was / has been redeveloped in 1980, and since then it was / has been used as a sports centre.
3 Penicillin was / has been discovered in the early twentieth century.
4 It was just / has just been announced that 2000 jobs were / have been lost at National Chemicals.
5 This photo of Dad was / has been taken by my brother.

6.3 Transform these sentences. Use the verbs in brackets.

1 People say he is a millionaire. (believe)
   He _____ .
2 People believe that Pedro Gonzales will win the election. (think)
   It _____ .
3 We all think the new manager is very efficient. (know)
   The _____ .
4 They say he's lost a fortune. (say)
   He _____ .
5 People think the man's identity will never be established. (believe)
   It _____ .

For a change, do an exercise orally with a partner. Check your answers, then write them in.

6.4 Change these questions into indirect questions. Use a different introductory expression for each question.

1 What time does it start?
2 Why doesn't this door open?
3 What do you think about it?
4 Are you busy tonight?
5 Did he find the hotel?

seven

be supposed to / be expected to

You can use *be supposed to* (*do*) to talk about what someone should or shouldn't do because of rules or other people's authority. We often use it when suggesting that perhaps the rules may be broken in some way.

> We**'re not supposed to** be here – it's for first class passengers only.
>   = according to the authorities; but the speaker is there.
> At school, we **were supposed to** do two hours' homework a night.
>   = the teachers said so; perhaps they didn't always obey.

Be expected to (*do*) is used when someone has an obligation or duty to do something. It doesn't suggest whether it was carried out or not.

> You **aren't expected to** pay tax on that bill. = There's no obligation to pay tax.
> At school we **were expected to** stand up when the teacher arrived.

Compare:

> We **were supposed to** do homework every night. = The teachers told us to do it, but we didn't necessarily always do it.
> We **were expected to** do homework every night. = The teachers told us to do it.

go to **exercise 7.1**

present perfect simple

You can use the present perfect to talk about events that have or haven't happened in a period up to now. It isn't important exactly <u>when</u> the things happened.

| before now | Rome | Rome Rome | now |

> I**'ve been** to Rome several times. (i.e. in my life; it isn't important when I went there)
> She**'s** never **done** that in her life. (i.e. at any time before now)

You can often use the adverbs *ever*, *never*, *always*, and *before* with the present perfect.

> Have you **ever** had an operation? (i.e. in your life)
> Have you met him **before**? (i.e. before this occasion)
> I've **never** read *War and Peace*.
> I've **always** wanted to try rowing.

If a finished time expression is used, e.g. *last week* / *in 1999* / *two weeks ago*, you normally use the past simple.

> I met him last week. NOT ~~I've met him last week.~~
> Julie e-mailed me a couple of days ago. NOT ~~Julie's e-mailed me a couple of days ago.~~

go to **exercise 7.2**

cover & check exercises

7.1 Put the correct form of *be supposed to* / *be expected to*.

1 It's a very small airport, so we _____ carry our luggage onto the plane.
2 I _____ (not) touch my grandmother's ornaments when I was very young, but I did.
3 In my last job, I _____ (not) use a computer, so I'm not very good with them.
4 I'm sorry, you _____ (not) smoke in here.
5 If you go for that job interview, you _____ to speak English for ten minutes at the end.

7.2 Circle the correct tense.

1 Have you always liked / Did you always like jazz?
2 I posted / have posted the letter yesterday.
3 We spent / have spent our holidays there when I was a child.
4 Has she ever had / Did she ever have cosmetic surgery? She looks so young.
5 Jo ran / has run the marathon several times, so he's very fit.

> Make a note of any differences between this grammar and your language.

You can use the present perfect to describe something that started in the past and continues up to now (or didn't happen in the period of time up to now). *For* and *since* are common with this meaning.

> She**'s lived** in that flat **for** years. (i.e. She still lives there now.)
> I**'ve been** a doctor **since** 1990. (i.e. I am still a doctor now.)
> How long **have** you **had** that car? (i.e. I know you still have it.)
> I **haven't seen** her **since** last Thursday. (i.e. the last time I saw her was Thursday.)

If something started and finished in the past, you use the past simple. Compare:

> She**'s worked** in the same office for ten years. (i.e. She *still works* there.)
> She **worked** in the same office for ten years. (i.e. She *doesn't work* there now.)

You use the present perfect to talk about things that happened in the recent past and are important now, often with *just*, *already*, and (*not*) *yet*.

> **A** Have a biscuit.
> **B** No, thanks, I've **just** had lunch. (i.e. a short time ago, so I'm not hungry)

> She's finished the exercise **already**. (i.e. more quickly than expected)
> Haven**'t** you finished your supper **yet**? (i.e. I can see you're still eating it)

Recently and *lately* can be used to mean 'in the last few days / weeks', but *recently* can be used with the past simple too.

> I haven't seen Mr Barrett **recently / lately**.
> She went to France on holiday **recently / ~~lately~~**.

Don't use *recently* with an expression of time:

> I got a pay rise recently. NOT ~~I got a pay rise recently last Monday.~~

go to **exercises 7.3** *and* **7.4**

present perfect continuous

You can use the present perfect continuous to talk about situations or actions happening in a period up to now.

> the accident   now

> She**'s been living** with her sister since the accident. = after the accident she moved in with her sister; she's still there

In some cases, these actions may have stopped recently but have present results.

> started jogging   stopped jogging   now

> **A** You look terrible!
> **B** Yes, I**'ve been jogging**. = I was jogging recently but stopped; I still feel hot and tired.

> Look at the street – It**'s been raining**. = it was raining and stopped recently

If you want to emphasize the fact that the activity is continuous, use the present perfect continuous. To emphasize the activity is completed, use the present perfect simple. Compare:

> I**'ve been decorating** the living room. = a recent activity; the decorating is not necessarily finished.
> I**'ve decorated** the living room. = a recent activity; the decorating is definitely finished

7.3 Complete the sentences with an appropriate adverb.

1 A Do you know where Chris is?
   B Yes, I've _____ seen him in the canteen. He'll be back here soon.
2 A Have you had dinner _____?
   B No, I've only been home _____ seven thirty.
3 I'm off to Canada next month. I've never been there _____ so I'm looking forward to it.
4 I've _____ hated fish – I just don't like the texture.
5 Has Lucy _____ told you why she married Tom?

7.4 Complete the sentences using the present perfect simple or past simple.

1 My two brothers are meeting tomorrow. They _____ (not see) each other since they were children.
2 I can't give you a lift because I _____ (not get) the car back from the garage yet.
3 Helena _____ (work) in Italy for ten years, then she moved to Poland. She _____ (live) there ever since.
4 Have you got a plaster? I _____ (cut) my finger.
5 My aunt _____ (live) in the same house for thirty years. She'll never move.

> Write in pencil, then you can rub out your answers and do the exercise again later.

The simple form describes how many times something happened, and the continuous form is used to emphasize how long something happened. (*How long ...* + present perfect is also common, however.)

I've been playing football a lot recently.
~~I've been playing football several times this week.~~
I've played football several times this week.

I've been sending e-mails all day.
~~I've been sending twenty e-mails today.~~
I've sent twenty e-mails today.

go to **exercise 7.5**

uncountable nouns

Uncountable nouns:

– don't usually have a plural form, e.g. advice NOT ~~advices~~
– aren't usually used with *a / an*, e.g. the / some advice NOT ~~an advice~~
– are used with a singular verb, e.g. the advice is ... NOT ~~the advice are~~ ...

Some uncountable nouns in English are countable in other languages and this often causes difficulty for learners. These are some of the most common:

information	luggage	machinery	furniture	traffic
advice	travel	equipment	research	luck
spaghetti	news	knowledge	grass	work

go to **exercise 7.6**

You can often change uncountable nouns into countable expressions by adding a noun phrase (often *a piece of*) to the beginning.

a piece of information	a bit of advice	a piece of research
a piece / slice of bread	an item / a piece of news	a blade of grass

natural English *a bit of*

In spoken English, you can use *a bit of* with a very wide range of uncountable nouns to make them countable.

There was **a bit of traffic** earlier.	I can probably get **a bit of work**.
We'll get there with **a bit of luck**.	It's a useful **bit of equipment**.

go to **exercise 7.7**

Many nouns have uncountable (U) and countable (C) uses with different meanings.

Have you got any **coffee** (U)? = the product
Could we have **two coffees** (C)? = two cups of coffee

I need some more **paper** (U).
I'll get **a paper** (C). = a newspaper

I haven't got enough **experience** (U) for the job. = knowledge and time in the job
My trip to India was **a wonderful experience** (C). = something that happened which influenced me

7.5 Tick ✓ the correct sentences.

1 a ☐ Tessa's been working in the garden all day.
   b ☐ Tessa's worked in the garden all day.
2 a ☐ The doctor has been visiting me three times recently.
   b ☐ The doctor has visited me three times recently.
3 a ☐ He's been borrowing $2,000 but he'll pay it back at the weekend.
   b ☐ He's borrowed $2,000 but he'll pay it back at the weekend.

7.6 Cover the list on the left. Are these nouns countable (C) or uncountable (U)?

1   machinery
2   fact
3   news
4   research
5   journey
6   spaghetti
7   grape
8   luck
9   traffic
10 equipment

7.7 Cover the list on the left. Make these uncountable nouns into countable expressions. Use a different noun at the beginning each time.

1 advice
2 information
3 news
4 bread
5 grass

plural nouns

Plural nouns:

– usually end in -s, e.g. clothes, stairs
– aren't used with *a / an*, e.g. the / some trousers NOT ~~a trousers~~
– need a plural verb, e.g. The stairs are dangerous. NOT ~~The stairs is dangerous.~~

Other common nouns that are usually plural in English include:

jeans	pants	scales	congratulations	regards
trousers	tights	expenses	contents	savings
shorts	scissors	funds	facilities	customs (at a frontier)

go to **exercise 7.8**

You can make some plural nouns (especially clothes) singular by adding *a pair of* at the beginning, e.g. a pair of jeans, two pairs of trousers, a pair of scissors.

fact and non-fact: *do, will, would*

Imagine someone is talking to a landlord about a flat.

Do I have to pay the rent in advance?
(This probably means the person has already decided to take the flat.)
Will I have to pay the rent in advance?
(This probably means they haven't decided to take the flat, but it's a possibility.)
Would I have to pay the rent in advance?
(This probably means the person hasn't decided to take the flat. It's less definite or likely than *will* above.)

You've met these choices before in conditional sentences:

If I **take / took** the flat, **will / would** I have to pay the rent in advance?

The *if* clause is often understood but not always needed in spoken English.

go to **exercise 7.9**

7.8 Cover the list on the left. Are these nouns plural (P) or uncountable (U)? Are they followed by a singular or plural verb?

1 jeans
2 scissors
3 news
4 mathematics
5 expenses

7.9 Write *do / does, will*, or *would*. If two answers are correct, write both.

1 This house you've just bought – _____ you have to do much decorating?
2 I'm not going to Alaska for my holiday after all – it _____ be too cold for me.
3 I think I should definitely accept this job – it _____ give me the chance to travel.
4 When he starts the course, _____ he have to go to lectures every day?
5 I'm not going to get a dog after all – I just _____ not be able to look after it in a small flat.

eight

verb patterns

Notice that some verbs can be followed by more than one construction.

verb + (*not*) + infinitive	verb + (*that*)	verb + -*ing*
promise to do	promise (that)	suggest
offer	suggest	deny
pretend	pretend	admit
agree	agree	resent
attempt	admit	
threaten	suspect	
claim	claim	
	deny	

go to **exercise 8.1**

cover & check exercises

8.1 Rewrite these sentences.

1 I'll help you.
He promised _____.
2 Why don't we go out?
She suggested _____.
3 I didn't do it.
He denied _____.
4 OK, it's true – I stole the money.
She admitted _____.
5 I'll tell your parents.
He threatened _____.

Here are some more verb patterns which include an object.

verb	+ object	+ that		verb	+ object	+ (not) infinitive
tell	her	that		tell	him	to
promise				ask		
warn				warn		
persuade				persuade		
convince				allow		

His mother **warned him not to climb** the tree.

go to **exercise 8.2**

Some verbs are commonly followed by a particular preposition.

verb	+ preposition		verb	+ object	+ preposition
insist	**on** sth		accuse	sb	**of** (doing) sth
rely	**on** sb / sth		blame	sb	**for** sth
consist	**of** sth		prevent	sb	**from** (doing) sth
suffer	**from** sth		congratulate	sb	**on** sth
concentrate	**on** sth		remind	sb	**of** sth

Both the children have **suffered from** colds this year.

go to **exercise 8.3**

link words – contrast and concession

You can contrast two ideas in <u>one</u> sentence with these link words. The second idea is usually either surprising or unexpected after the first.

Although we left early, we had a lot of traffic problems.
The children didn't seem tired, **although** it was getting late.
I managed to get to sleep **despite** the noise.
In spite of wearing two pairs of gloves, his hands were still cold.
We got lost **despite** the fact that they gave us very clear instructions.

Despite and *in spite of* can be followed by a noun, an *-ing* form or *the fact that* + clause. *Although* can only be followed by a clause. These link words are more common in written English.

You can contrast two ideas in two sentences using these link words.

It's not one of the best areas in the city. **However**, it's better than it used to be.
It won't be easy to get a hotel now. **Nevertheless**, I'm sure we'll find something.
I really enjoyed staying there. The people, **however**, weren't very friendly.

Both words can begin a sentence or come after the subject, and both are used with commas, as in the examples. Of the two link words, *however* is much more common, and both are used more frequently in written English.

natural English *mind you, still, though*

In spoken English, we can also express contrasts with *still, mind you*, and *though* (which comes at the end of the clause).

I wasn't very keen on the gallery. **Still / Mind you**, we didn't have to pay to get in.
We were hoping to go to the concert. I couldn't get any tickets, **though**.

go to **exercises 8.4** *and* **8.5**

8.2 Match the sentence halves.

1 Steve promised me
2 The teacher allowed us
3 The accused man convinced us
4 The cleaner warned me
5 Colin persuaded me

a that he was innocent.
b not to buy the car.
c that he would be home by ten.
d to use a dictionary in the exam.
e that the floor was slippery.

8.3 Fill the gaps with the correct preposition.

1 We tried to prevent her _____ making a fool of herself.
2 They blamed me _____ the mistakes.
3 That girl reminds me _____ my sister.
4 I often suffer _____ hay fever in the summer.
5 The mixture just consists _____ flour and water.

8.4 Circle the correct word.

1 We got a seat, despite / although it was quite full.
2 In spite / Despite the bad weather, we still went ahead with the game.
3 He won the race in spite of / although feeling ill.
4 They said it was adults only. Most of them, however / although, were under 18.
5 I go there quite often, although / however I find the people a bit unfriendly.

8.5 Complete the sentences with a suitable link word or phrase.

1 The boys enjoyed it _____ the rain.
2 We decided to stop for something to eat, _____ we weren't very hungry.
3 The headteacher had lived and worked at the school for years. _____, local people didn't trust him.
4 Sarah went to the party _____ the fact that she'd been ill all day.
5 A What was the disco like?
   B Not very good. _____, it was better than last week.

nine

making comparisons

as + adjective / adverb + *as*

We use *as ... as* to say two things or situations are equal or unequal.

> Is Joe **as** good-looking **as** Tom?
> You're **as** young **as** you feel.
> My brain doesn't work **as** well **as** it used to!
> In the test, Chris didn't do **as** badly **as** Mike. = Mike did very badly; Chris did quite badly.

You can modify these comparative structures with certain adverbs.

> Iceland is **just** as cold as Alaska. = emphasizing that they are the same
> My flat is **twice** as big as my neighbour's. = My flat is double the size of my neighbour's.
> Carole is **nearly** as tall as Anna. = Anna is a little bit taller.
> Carole **isn't nearly** as tall as Diane. = There is a big difference; Diane is a lot taller.

go to **exercise 9.1**

the + comparative, *the* + comparative

This means that when one thing changes, another changes with it.

> **The younger** you are, **the easier** it is to learn.
> **The more** you spend, **the more** you need.
> **The faster** the car, **the more dangerous** it is.
> **The sooner** we sell this car, **the better**.

go to **exercise 9.2**

superlatives

Superlatives can be followed by certain prepositions including *in* (for places or groups) and *of* (for time or before plurals).

> The Sahara is the biggest desert **in** the world. NOT ~~of the world~~
> The youngest student **in** the class was also the most intelligent.
> February is the shortest month **of** the year.
> He was the greatest athlete **of** them all.

The superlative can be followed by a clause, often with *ever* + present perfect.

> That's the best meal **I've ever eaten**.
> He's the most irritating man **I've ever met / you can imagine**.
> What's the funniest thing that **has ever happened to you**?

go to **exercise 9.3**

link words

You can use *as* to introduce the reason for something. It's similar in meaning to *because*, but is less frequent. It is also commonly used at the start of the sentence.

> **As** no one was there, I left a message. = I left a message because no one was there.
> **As** it was getting dark, we decided to go home. = We decided to go home because it was getting dark.

cover & check exercises

9.1 What do these sentences mean?

1 Jackie did just as well as Molly in the test. = Molly did better in the test.
yes ☐ no ☐

2 The film wasn't nearly as good as the book. = The book was a lot better.
yes ☐ no ☐

3 Jill doesn't go out as much as she used to. = She goes out less now.
yes ☐ no ☐

9.2 Complete the sentences with a suitable comparative.

1 The older the machine, the _____ it goes wrong.
2 The sooner we leave, the _____ .
3 The more you eat, the _____ you get.
4 The harder you work, the _____ you earn.
5 The bigger the diamonds, the _____ they are.

9.3 Complete the sentences with either preposition + phrase or *ever* + present perfect.

1 We bought the most expensive watch

_____ .

2 It was the longest day _____

_____ .

3 What's the funniest film _____

_____ ?

4 My neighbour is the kindest person

_____ .

5 The Nile is the longest river _____

_____

natural English *so*

In spoken English it's much more common to use *so* to explain the result.

> No one was there, **so** I left a message.
> It was getting dark, **so** we decided to go home.

You can use *so* (*that*) and (*in order*) *to* when you express an intention or reason for doing something.

> My dad came home early **so** (**that**) he could watch the match on TV.
> They had to go (**in order**) **to** get the last bus.
> I posted the letter today **so** (**that**) it would arrive in the morning.

In spoken English we often use *so* without *that*, and *to* without *in order*. After *so* (*that*), modal verbs such as *can*, *could*, or *would* are very common.

In case means 'because of the possibility that …'

> Take an umbrella **in case** it rains. = because of the possibility it may rain

Notice that *in case* is followed by a present tense, and not *will*.

> Let's take the camera **in case we want to** take photos.
>   NOT Let's take the camera in case we ~~will~~ want to take photos.

Otherwise can be used to say what the result would be if something didn't happen. It can be paraphrased as 'if not'.

> We'd better go now, **otherwise** we'll be late. = If we don't go now, we'll be late.
> I'm going to the bank, **otherwise** I won't have enough money. = If I don't go to the bank …

go to **exercises 9.4** *and* **9.5**

9.4 Combine the sentence halves using the correct link word / phrase.

1 Take some sandwiches
2 I went into town
3 I had to stay in bed
4 Take that overcoat,
5 I went to the library

so that	as	in case
otherwise	in order to	

a you'll be cold.
b I could work in peace.
c buy some books.
d you get hungry.
e I had a migraine.

9.5 Complete the sentences with a suitable link word / phrase.

1 Remind John about the party, _____ he'll forget.
2 Daisy went on the course _____ she could get a better job.
3 Buy an extra ticket _____ Sarah decides to come with us.
4 _____ it was raining, we decide to stay in.
5 We need to know your date of birth _____ issue you with a licence.

ten

articles

definite or zero article

Don't use an article with plural nouns or uncountable nouns when you're talking about things in general:

> **Computers** are getting much cheaper nowadays. = computers in general
> **Exercise** is great for **children**. = exercise in general and children in general

You can use the definite article with plural and uncountable nouns when you're describing particular things:

> I didn't like **the pets** in that shop – they didn't look very healthy.
> The problem is only with **the computers** in the sales department.

You can sometimes talk about things in general using the definite article with a singular countable noun.

> Where would we be without **the telephone**? = telephones in general
> **The human brain** is extraordinarily complex. = human brains in general

go to **exercise 10.1**

cover & check exercises

10.1 Cross out any incorrect uses of the definite article in these sentences.

1 Where are the children?
2 Is the love the most important thing?
3 Have you seen the glasses that were here?
4 People say that the exercising is the best way to lose weight.
5 The computer has changed our lives.

> Cover the grammar, then try the exercise. Look at the grammar again if you're unsure.

You can also use the definite article with a limited range of adjectives to describe a group of people who share a particular quality:

> She collects money for **the blind**.
> They took **the injured** to hospital.

Other adjectives used in this way are: *the deaf*, *the sick*, *the rich*, *the poor*, *the unemployed*, *the homeless*, and *the elderly*.

go to **exercise 10.2**

definite article (*the*) or indefinite article (*a / an*)

Use *a / an* to refer to a person or thing. The listener / reader may not know which person or thing you're talking about, or it may not be important to know which specific one is being described.

> We saw **a rabbit** in the garden eating our lettuces.
> They live in **a farmhouse**.
> I know **a good lawyer**.

Use the definite article *the* if:

– the person or thing has been mentioned before

> We saw **a rabbit** in the garden eating our lettuces. Of course, when **the rabbit** saw us, it soon disappeared into the bushes.
> They live in **a farmhouse**. It's in a remote area and I think **the house** was built over 200 years ago.

– the person or thing is clearly identified in the context

> Have you got **the book** I lent you?
> I answered **the question** about the civil war.

– it's obvious which one is meant. Sometimes this is because it's 'the only one'.

> I'm just going to feed **the dog**. = it's obvious which dog
> I think they're in **the garden**. = it's obvious which garden
> I was clearing up and I put it in **the fridge**. = there's only one fridge
> It's the biggest in **the world**. = there's only one world

go to **exercise 10.3** *and* **10.4**

relative clauses

Defining relative clauses explain which person or thing you're talking about.

> He's the man **who lives opposite me**. (This tells us which man the speaker means.)
> I spoke to the woman (**who**) **you pointed out to me earlier**.

Non-defining relative clauses give additional information about someone or something which has already been identified or is known.

> The Eiffel Tower, **which was built in the late nineteenth century**, dominates the Paris skyline. (This gives extra information about the Tower.)
> The Irish boy band, **who arrived in a white Cadillac**, were immediately rushed into the hotel.
> She bought a bicycle, **which turned out to be very useful**.

go to **exercise 10.5**

10.2 Cover the list of adjectives on the left. Now complete these sentences.

1 There's little hope of work for the _____ here.
2 They've built a new retirement home for the _____ .
3 Obviously the _____ have to pay higher taxes.
4 It's a place for the _____ to sleep.
5 Ambulances came and took away the _____ .

10.3 Fill the gaps with *a / an* or *the*.

1 A There was _____ piece of paper here just now.
   B Oh! Do you mean _____ piece of paper with telephone numbers on?
   A Yes.
   B Oh dear. I threw it in _____ bin.
2 What happened to _____ chair that used to be here?
3 A I met them in _____ restaurant.
   B Yeah. Which one?
   A _____ one next to _____ cinema in Clarence Street.
4 It was _____ very big dog, so I ran.
5 You shouldn't sit in _____ sun too long.

10.4 Look at your answers in **10.3** again. Where the definite article is used, is it because:

a the person or thing has been mentioned before?
b the person or thing is defined in the context?
c the person or thing is obvious or the only one?

10.5 Underline the relative clauses. Write D for defining relative clauses or ND for non-defining relative clauses.

1 She lives opposite the man who committed the crimes.
2 My brother Joe, who has never been involved in any accidents, must be the world's safest driver.
3 The photos I showed you were all taken by a professional photographer.
4 Henry, who is becoming more and more eccentric, often comes to dinner with us.
5 That was the book I was telling you about.

defining relative clauses

In defining relative clauses, you use the pronouns *who*, *which*, *that*, and *whose*.

She's the woman	who	gave me the money.
	that	
NOT She's the woman who ~~she~~ gave me the money.		

He lived in the building	which	got burned down.
	that	
NOT He lived in the building which ~~it~~ got burned down.		

In these examples, *who*, *which*, and *that* are the subject of the relative clause. In this case, you cannot omit the relative pronouns.

In defining relative clauses, the pronouns *who*, *which*, *that*, and *whose* can be the object of the relative clause i.e. the relative clause has its own subject pronoun / noun.

	object	subject	
That's the woman	(who)	I	was telling you about.
	(that)	Mary	saw outside her house.
I bought the table	(which)	I	had seen in the window.
	(that)		

In these examples, it's very common in spoken English to omit the relative pronouns.

Whose means 'belonging to'. You cannot omit *whose*.

| I didn't know **whose coat** it was. |
| That's the boy **whose mother** was rude to me. |

go to **exercise 10.6**

non-defining relative clauses

You use the pronouns *who*, *which*, and *whose* in non-defining relative clauses. This type of relative clause is more common in written than spoken English. Notice that the relative clause is separated from the main clause by commas.

| The President, **who was accompanied by his wife**, spoke to staff and patients during the visit. |
| My cousin Phil, **who the police had interviewed earlier**, arrived at my house in a panic. |
| The demonstrations, **which were attended by half a million people**, were largely peaceful. |
| I lost my cheque book last week, **which was a nuisance**. |
| Mrs Johnson, **whose four sons are all vets**, presented the prizes. |

go to **exercise 10.7**

10.6 Combine the sentences using an appropriate relative pronoun.

1 The dustman has won the lottery. He empties our rubbish.
2 A car contained secret government documents. It was stolen last night.
3 A private detective has been accused of robbery. He works for the princess.
4 I found a credit card. I lost it several days ago.
5 A woman has paid the rescuer £1,000. Her cat was rescued from a tree.

10.7 Add *who, which*, or *whose*. Put commas round the non-defining clauses in each sentence.

1 The volcano local people had been worrying about for years suddenly erupted on Saturday.
2 Two Olympic athletes were accused of taking drugs have received a formal apology.
3 The gallery had only been open for six months had to close owing to lack of support.
4 Alison Mansell parents were at the performance sang the solo with great skill.
5 The money was stolen from my bank account was very upsetting.

eleven

conditional clauses

past conditionals

To form the past conditional (also called the 'third conditional'), use *if* + *had* + past participle, *would have* + past participle.

> If **I'd (had) gone** abroad, **I'd (would) have earned** more money.
> What **would have happened** if she**'d disappeared**?
> If he**'d spent** the money, I'm sure he**'d have told** us.
> He **wouldn't have missed** the train if he**'d left** a bit earlier.

Contracted forms of *had* and *would* are particularly common in spoken English. Notice also that in written English you need a comma at the end of the *if* clause in the middle of the sentence.

We use the past conditional to talk about imaginary past events.

> If **I'd seen** him, **I'd have given** him your message.
>   = I didn't see him, so I didn't/couldn't give him the message.
> If they **hadn't lost** the map, **they would have found** the place easily.
>   = They lost the map, so they didn't find the place easily.

The main clause often has *would have*, but we can also use *could have* (= would have been able) or *might have* (= would possibly):

> If we'd known Chris was coming, we **could have given** him a lift.
> It **might have been** easier if we'd all travelled together.

go to **exercises 11.1** *and* **11.2**

mixed conditionals

It's possible to mix conditional sentences and talk about the present consequence of something you did or didn't do in the past.

past condition	present consequence
If I'd gone to university,	I **wouldn't be** in this job now.
If we **hadn't taken** the wrong road,	we **could be** there by now.

We can also describe how a past event affects a present or future situation.

> If I **didn't have to write** this essay today, I **could have gone** to the wedding.
>   = I already had an essay to write so I couldn't/can't go to the wedding.
> If she really **liked** him, she **wouldn't have said** such horrible things to him.
>   = I believe she didn't like him and doesn't like him now. That's why she said those things.

go to **exercise 11.3**

cover & check exercises

11.1 **What do these sentences mean?**
Tick ✓ the correct answers.

1 If she'd locked the front door, the burglar couldn't have got in.
   a ☐ The burglar entered the house.
   b ☐ She locked the door.
2 You might have seen Jackson if you'd got there earlier.
   a ☐ It's certain you'd have seen him.
   b ☐ You got there too late to see him.
3 Everyone would have been upset if Lily hadn't gone to the wedding.
   a ☐ Lily didn't go to the wedding.
   b ☐ Lily did go to the wedding.

11.2 **Add one missing word in each sentence.**

1 I wouldn't phoned your mother if I'd known where you were.
2 If he told me earlier, I would have changed the arrangements.
3 We would have got here on time if we had missed the train.
4 What would have happened she'd lost the documents?
5 Dina would cut herself if her mother hadn't taken the scissors away.

11.3 **Tick ✓ the possible sentence endings.**
Both endings may be possible.

1 If I'd been given the job,
   a ☐ I would be the boss by now.
   b ☐ I would have been delighted.
2 If she'd inherited some money,
   a ☐ she wouldn't be doing that job.
   b ☐ she would spend it all.
3 If you'd listened to my advice,
   a ☐ you'd work from home.
   b ☐ you'd be rich and famous now.
4 If he really were so clever,
   a ☐ he wouldn't have failed his degree course.
   b ☐ he would be in a great job now.
5 If Shakespeare were alive today,
   a ☐ he would have been famous.
   b ☐ he would be publishing plays on the Internet.

reporting what people say

When you report what people say, you use a reporting verb (usually in the past tense) and you can make further changes to the tense, pronouns, and other words used in the direct speech. These are the main tense changes:

direct speech	reported speech
I'm very busy	He said (that) **he was** very busy.
I'm leaving soon	She said (that) **she was leaving** soon.
I **lost** it.	He said **he'd lost** it.
I **haven't seen** him.	She said **she hadn't seen** him.
I'll take them.	He said **he would** take them.
I **can** send it later.	She said she **could** send it later.

natural English *reporting*

In spoken English, *that* is usually omitted, and we often don't make all the tense changes, even with the reporting verb. These are all possible:

He said **he's** very busy.   He **was saying he's** very busy.   He **says he's** busy.

go to **exercise 11.4**

As reported speech often occurs later than the direct speech it's reporting, a number of time and place words also change. These are typical:

direct speech	reported speech
here, now	there, then
today, tonight, this week	that day, that night, that week
yesterday	the previous day / the day before
tomorrow	the following day / the next day

Say and *tell* (sb) are the most common reporting verbs, but these verbs are commonly used as well: *explain, mention, promise, suggest, advise* sb, *warn* sb, *answer*.

She **promised** (that) she would help us.
He **explained** that the office closed early on Wednesdays.

go to **exercise 11.5**

For more information on **verb patterns**, go to *p.151*.

11.4 Change these spoken reported statements into more correct written reported statements.

1 She says she'll finish it later.
2 He was saying it's no good.
3 She said she can't come.
4 He says they've broken the front window.
5 They say he was sent to prison.

Write in pencil, then you can rub out your answers and do the exercise again later.

11.5 Report these statements. Use *mention, warn, promise, explain,* or *suggest.*

1 'The road was blocked yesterday because of the snow.'
   Anita _____
2 'I won't forget to bring the money – really.'
   Dave _____ .
3 'By the way, I'll be late tonight.'
   Sue _____ .
4 'Why don't we invite Patsy to the party?'
   Liam _____ .
5 'You know, your journey will be quite dangerous.'
   The policeman _____ .

---

twelve

reported questions

cover & check exercises

Reported questions are similar to indirect questions. With *wh-* questions, the auxiliary verb is omitted and the word order is positive. In written English particularly, there will be tense changes as with reported statements.

direct question	reported question
Why **do you need** it?	I asked him why **he needed** it.
What time **is it**?	Sheila wanted to know what time **it was**.
When **did he go**?	She asked me when **he had gone**.
How long **have you been** here?	Andy was wondering how long **you'd been** there.

With *yes/no* questions, we need *if* or *whether* followed by positive word order.

direct question	reported question
Does she work in this office?	He asked me **if she worked** in this office.
Are you married?	Rita wanted to know **whether you were** married.

> **natural English** *whether/if ... or not*
>
> We often use *whether* (and occasionally *if*) + *or not*.
>
> > He asked me **whether/if** I was going **or not**. = whether I was going or I wasn't going.
> > He asked me **whether or not** I was going. BUT NOT ~~He asked me if or not I was going.~~

Common reporting verbs in questions are *ask*, *want to know*, and *wonder*.

go to **exercises 12.1** *and* **12.2**

as, like, such as

as + noun

You can use *as* + noun to say someone or something has a particular job, role or function. Here, *as* is a preposition.

> My sister worked **as a waitress** last year. You could use this piece of wood **as a ruler**.

as + clause

You can use *as* + clause to say that things happen in a similar way. Here, *as* is a conjunction.

> Joe got up at 7.00, **as he always does**. = in the same way as usual
> We had cheese after the main course, **as the French do**.

These are commonly used phrases with *as* which you can learn.

> **As I said before, ...   As we discussed, ...   As you know, ...   As we agreed earlier, ...**

> **natural English** *like/as*
>
> In informal English, people often use *like* as a conjunction instead of *as*.
>
> > Jack got up late **as/like** he always did.
> > Ana forgot to ring, **as/like** she did last time.

like + noun/pronoun

You can use *like* + noun/pronoun to say that people or things are similar. *Like* is a preposition here.

> He looks **like a bank manager**.   NOT He looks ~~as a bank manager~~.
> This painting is **like a photo**.

like + noun, such as + noun

You can use *like/such as* to list examples. Here, *like* is a preposition.

In cities	like such as	Rome and Milan, traffic is a terrible problem.
I'm not very keen on vegetables	like such as	cabbage and cauliflower.

go to **exercise 12.3**

12.1 Write in one missing word.
1 He wanted to know his job was safe or not.
2 Sue wondering why the delivery had been delayed.
3 The receptionist asked me whether I stayed there before.

12.2 Change into reported questions. Use at least three different reporting verbs.
1 What's her name?
2 Why did Pam leave so early?
3 Can you park in such a tiny space?
4 Where has Colin taken the kids?
5 Do you know them?

> For a change, try doing an exercise orally with a partner.

12.3 Put *like*, *as*, or *such as*. More than one answer may be possible.
1 I've been to the beach _____ I always do on Saturdays.
2 I've got a job _____ a hotel receptionist this summer.
3 He loves female solo artists _____ Celine Dion and Shania Twain.
4 My sister looks a bit _____ me.
5 I had to use that glass _____ a vase to put the flowers in.

OXFORD
UNIVERSITY PRESS

Great Clarendon Street, Oxford OX2 6DP

Oxford University Press is a department of the
University of Oxford. It furthers the University's
objective of excellence in research, scholarship,
and education by publishing worldwide in

Oxford New York

Auckland Bangkok Buenos Aires Cape Town
Chennai Dar es Salaam Delhi Hong Kong Istanbul
Karachi Kolkata Kuala Lumpur Madrid Melbourne
Mexico City Mumbai Nairobi São Paulo Shanghai
Taipei Tokyo Toronto

Oxford and Oxford English are registered trade marks
of Oxford University Press in the UK and in certain
other countries

ISBN 0 19 437331 2

Printed in China

Acknowledgements

The Publisher and Authors are grateful to those who
have given permission to reproduce the following
extracts and adaptations of copyright material:

pp.10 / 11 Extract from Fitness & Health, 5th edition by
B. J. Sharkey, 2002 (Champaign, IL: Human Kinetics).
Appeared in The Sunday Times Brainpower, Week 6,
reproduced by permission of Human Kinetics Publishers;
p.16 'Six ways to have a successful conversation' from
The Confidence Course: Seven Steps to Self-Fulfillment
© 1997 Walter Anderson. Reproduced by permission
of HarperCollins Publishers Inc; p.26 'Words fail me' by
Justine Picardie © Telegraph Group Limited 1999.
Reprinted in Cover Magazine May 1999. Reproduced by
permission of Telegraph Syndication; pp.37 / 38
Information about Eden. Reproduced by permission of
Channel 4 and The RDF Media Group; p.47 'The van
that drove through Braveheart' by Tim Reid © Times
Newspapers Limited 31 July 1999. Reproduced by
permission; pp.62 / 63 'Best of times, worst of times:
Interview with Dava Sobel' © Danny Danziger Sunday
Times Magazine 28 November 1999. Reproduced by
permission of Danny Danziger; pp.70 / 71 'On top of the
world' by William Greaves Radio Times 14-20 August 1999.
Reproduced by permission of Radio Times; p.79 'Tricks
of the trade: How to Read the News' by Fiona Sturges
Independent on Sunday 21 September 1997. Reproduced
by permission of Independent Newspapers (UK) Limited;
p.83 'Pneumonia draws caring students to prof' by
Elizabeth Inman China Daily 7 March 1995. Reproduced
by permission of China Daily; p.95 'Single white female'
© Sue Reid / Times Newspapers Limited 25 June 2000.
Reproduced by permission of Times Newspapers Limited;
p.107 'Let's make matrimony more attractive to men' by

Mark Hughes-Morgan The Evening Standard 16 June 1999.
Reproduced by permission of Atlantic Syndication
Partners; p.115 'My day-long ordeal as a 75-year-old'
by Jack O'Sullivan The Independent 12 December 1998.
Reproduced by permission of Independent Newspapers
(UK) Limited; pp.128 / 129 'A time to forgive' © The
Guardian 3 January 1998. Reproduced by permission
of Guardian Newspapers Limited; p.139 'How it feels to
face Chris Tarrant' by Jane Slade and Annie Davies
Daily Mail Weekend Magazine 8 April 2000. Reproduced
by permission of Atlantic Syndication Partners;
Phonemic chart reproduced with the kind permission
of Adrian Underhill and available from Macmillan ELT.

Although every effort has been made to trace and contact
copyright holders before publication, this has not been
possible in some cases. We apologize for any apparent
infringement of copyright and if notified, the publisher
will be pleased to rectify any errors or omissions at the
earliest opportunity.

Recordings directed by Martin Williamson, Prolingua
Productions. Technical presentation by Leon Chambers,
recorded at The Soundhouse Ltd.

Illustrations by Claire Bretécher
pp.2 (Agrippine with pushchair, Agrippine with friend),
3 (Agrippine's teacher), 4 (Agrippine alone, Agrippine in
bookshop), 5 (Agrippine's mum), 7, 8 / 9, 32 / 33, 56 / 57,
80 / 81, 102 / 103, 124 / 125 and cover illustrations
copyright © Claire Bretécher 2003.
Combined work (text and illustrations) copyright ©
Oxford University Press 2003.

Other illustrations commissioned by Geri May.
Stefan Chabluk pp.96 / 97; Paul Collicutt pp.100, 111;
Bob Dewar pp.136, 137; Mark Draisey pp.20, 21;
Phil Healey pp.40, 47, 86, 116; Sarah Kelly pp.63, 94,
106, 140; Kveta p.92; Belle Mellor pp.15, 65, 141;
Michael Munday p.29; Paul Oakley pp.25, 143; Jacqui
Paull pp.58 / 59; Roger Penwill pp. 112, 113; Gavin
Reece pp.39, 60, 64; Marco Schaaf p.64; Harry Venning
pp.44, 45; Kath Walker pp.68, 69; Geoff Waterhouse
pp.90, 91; Lee Woodgate pp.23, 84, 126, 138.

Photographs researched by Suzanne Williams.
The Publisher and Authors would also like to thank the
following for permission to reproduce photographs:

Allsport pp.7 (N. Wilson / dinghy sailors), 10 (S. Botterill),
11 (R. Kinnard / football training), 144 (J. Gichigi / chess),
144 (P. Rondeau / boules); BBC Picture Archives pp.71
(both), 72; BBC Picture Archives / Question Time p.117;
BBC Radio Times pp.70 / 71; Courtesy of Lynne Brackley
p.23 (Lynne); The Bridgeman Art Library p.142 (Auguste
Rodin (1840-1917), The Thinker, bronze, Museo d'Arte
Moderno di Ca Pesaro, Venice, Italy); Bubbles Photo
Library pp.66 (Frans-Rombout), 66 (D. Hager); Courtesy
of Andre Buurman / The Independent p.115; Courtesy
of Carlton Television Ltd / Mr & Mrs with Julian Clary p.146;
Channel 4 p.40 (Eden Show); Corbis pp.6 (G. Dagli Orti /
stone relief), 23 (R. Pickett / hamster), 42 (S. Kushner /
Ryan), 48 (P. Giardino / driving), (J. Choo / Asian woman),
97 (T. Thompson), 99 (S. Ginott / hotel), 114 (D. Modricker /
bowling), 131 (T. Vine / Darren), 144 (D. Modricker /
woman and cards); Courtesy of Ralph van Dijk / Hobson's
p.23 (Ralph); © Dorling Kindersley p.109; Courtesy of
Michael Fenton Stevens / The Richard Stone Partnership
p.23 (Michael); Courtesy of Julia Ford / Conway Van
Gelder p.14 (Julia); Getty Images cover (Whit Preston /
blue sky), cover and throughout (Uwe Krejci / 2 people),
7 and throughout (Rutz Manfred / ear), 10 and throughout
(Alexander Walker / reading newspaper), 17 and
throughout (Photodisc / finger on map), 18 and throughout
(Stephen Simpson / speaking woman), pp.7 (Chabruken /
black man smiling), 14 (Brooklyn Productions / driving
lesson), 14 (D. Paul Production / school), 14 (N. Dolding /
dancing), 14 (Surgi Stock / yoga), 17 (W. Krysl), 18 (D. Paul
Production), 22 / 23 (C. Tomaidis / airport), 24 (C. Serrao /
airport security), 26 (Davies & Starr / cauliflower),
(T. Schierlitz / tap), (L. Dutton / book), 30 (C. McPherson),
31 (B. Ayres), 34 (R. Wright / father with child), 34 (D.
Boissavy / in car), 34 (B. Torrez / group), 36 (J. Hernandez),
37 (T. Mead), 38 (T. Rakke), 40 (E.P. O'Brien), 41
(M. Barraud / Jonny), 42 (J. McBride / Tarsha), 42
(P.L. Harvey / Alison), 42 (Yellow Dog Productions / Justin),
42 (P.L. Harvey / Sachi), 42 (Photomondo / Polly), 48 (M.
Krasowitz / car breakdown), 53 (W. Ashton / Lars), 54
(Sparky), 58 (D. Johnston / sports car), 65 (R. Mackechnie /

Lucy), 65 (A. Weinbrecht / David), 66 (P. Cutler), 74
(K. Weingart), 77 (D. Kenyon / prisoner), 77 (B. Hippisley /
goal save), 86 (White, Packert), 99 (S. Simpson / departure
lounge), 100 (A. Powdrill / Carter), 101 (J. Silva / couple
& motorbike), 101 (Photomondo / man on bed watching
tv), 101 (S. Cohen / children playing), 101 (G. Ceo / indoor
golf), 101 (D. Fourie / mother & kids), 114 (R. Daly /
surfing), 114 (T. Macpherson / games arcade), 118 (S.
Sanchez / hospital), 118 (A. Shah), 119 (V. Besnault),
120 (D. Bosler / woman), 120 (A. Pollok / man), 120
(A. Sacks / teenage girl), 123 (J. Kopec / whales), 127
(N. Daly), 128 (D. Lees), 128 (A. Errington), 131
(J. Tisne / Nicola), 134 (A. Mo), 144 (children and
game); Courtesy of Grey Worldwide p.107; Guy Jordan
p.95; John Birdsall Photography pp.88, 124; By kind
permission of Kawasaki Motors UK 137; The Kobal
Collection p.46, 96; Masterfile p.6 (woman & man shake
hands), 12 (four students), 34 (mother and baby), 58
(cyclist), 82, 104; Courtesy of Eric Meyers p.14 (Eric);
PA Photos / Press Association pp.48 (T. Ockenden / group
of teenagers), 51 (EPA), 66 (B. Curtis), 77 (B. Batchelor /
fire service), 78 (M. Walter), 118 (Canadian Press / fashion),
123 (R. Vieira / dog show), 130 (J. Giles); Courtesy of
RDF Media / Coda TV / www.coda.tv and Channel 4 pp.38
(having supper, dressing up, sitting in semi-circle), 40
(dining area, tropical pool); Royalty Free pp.118 (EyeWire /
bear), (Ingram Publishing / elephant, crocodile, panda,
zebra , scorpion), 26 (Photodisc / broccoli, loo, syringe),
87, 100 (Photodisc / couple), 101 (Photodisc / woman
with animals), 118 (Photodisc / snake, owl); Science Photo
Library p.118 (Novosti / rabbits); By kind permission of
Richard Sutcliffe / www.whirl-y-gig.org.uk, photography
by Peter Galbavy p.35; Courtesy of Gertrude Thomas p.14
(Trude); Courtesy of Youareable.com and Joe Rajko p.105
(C. Rich); John Walmsley pp.14 (chefs), 18 (basketball),
19 (reading), (rugby), 28, 42 (Isabel), 42 (Tango), 48
(classroom), 53 (Caroline), 114 (woman with dog);
Courtesy of William Ward p.73.

Commissioned photographs
Studio and location photography by Steve Betts pp.11,
12, 27, 39, 50, 62, 72, 85, 91, 92, 97, 113, 117, 129, 140
(test your partner), 75 (reporter and two men), 93
(reporter and woman), 121 (man and woman in office),
132 (woman with present), back cover pocket (authors).
Mark Mason Studios pp.26 / 27 (Point It, by kind
permission of Dieter Graf / Graf Editions).
With additional thanks to Café 206, London.

The Publisher and Authors would like to thank the
following readers and teachers for their invaluable
help with the development of the student's book,
listening booklet, and teacher's book material:

Maggie Baigent, Jan Borsbey, Brian Brennan, Jo Cooke,
Olivia Date, Richard Frost, Jane Hudson, Amanda Jeffries,
Marcel Sanchez, Jo Savage, Mike Sayer, Scott Thornbury,
Simon Wilkinson, Louise Williams.

The Authors would particularly like to thank the following
people for their help with the initial research and piloting:

Alastair Banton, Tom Bradbury, Philip Curren, Francis
Duncan, Heather Miletto, Louise Porter-Taylor, Lyn and
David Scott. Also the teachers at Edwards School of
English, The London School of English, International House,
London, and Golders Green College of English.

The Publisher and Authors would also like to thank:

Kenna Bourke for reading and editing the language
reference section, Theresa Clementson for reading and
editing the teacher's book, Catherine Ridley and William
Ward for their contributions to the listening material,
Martin Williamson for his enormous contribution to
the shaping of the listening material, and to (all the)
the following actors whose own ideas, anecdotes, and
humour are such an important part of the recordings:

Gareth Armstrong, Deborah Berlin, Carolyn Bonnyman,
Carole Boyd, Lynne Brackley, Jenny Bryce, Tyler
Butterworth, Lolita Chacrabati, Jane Collingwood,
DeNica Fairman, Elly Fairman, Michael Fenton-Stevens,
Julia Ford, James Goode, Nigel Greaves, Joanna Hall,
Jeff Harding, John Hasler, Federay Holmes, Jenny Howe,
Frances Jeeter, Jonathan Keeble, Lorelei King, Nick
Mercer, Eric Meyers, Richard Mitchley, David Monteith,
Cecilia Noble, Paul Panting, Alison Pettitt, Juliet Prague,
Marcella Riordan, David Shaw-Parker, Gertrude Thomas,
Patience Tomlinson, Ralph van Dijk , Larrington Walker,
Clare Wille, James Wilson.